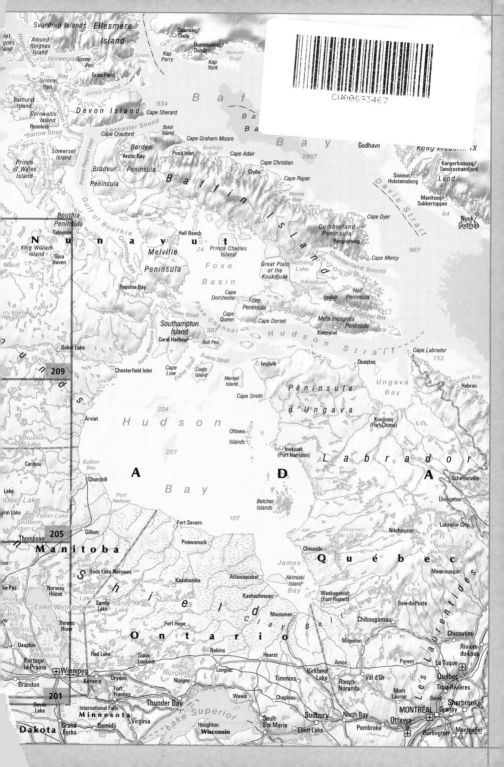

WESTERN CANADA

Situated on the Pacific coast, against the magnificent backdrop of the Coast Mountains, Vancouver is one of the most beautiful cities in the world. The futuristic skyline of its downtown area contrasts with the beautifully restored old town.

Photo Guide

WESTERN CANADA

A visit to Banff National Park with its spectacular scenery is a truly unforgettable experience. Many of the park's mountains are over 3,000 metres (9,843 feet) in height, often overlooking glorious lakes, such as Herbert Lake, shown here.

SMART START

PROFILE

Scenery and
the natural world 8
The tide of history 10
Art and culture 12
The country and
its people 14

Major cities **16**

Vancouver 18
Calgary 20
Victoria 22

Road trips **24**

Route 1:
From the coast to the
Rocky Mountains 26
Route 2:
Exploring Vancouver
Island 28
Route 3:
The Trans-Canada
Highway 30

THE HIGHLIGHTS

**British Columbia:
Vancouver
and surroundings** **32**

Area map 34
Downtown 36
Gastown 38
Chinatown 40
False Creek 42
Granville Island 44
English Bay 48
Stanley Park 50
Fort Langley 52
Garibaldi Provincial Park 54
Best addresses 56

**British Columbia:
Vancouver Coast,
Vancouver Island** **60**

Area map 62
Johnstone Strait,
Queen Charlotte Strait,
God's Pocket Marine
Provincial Park 64
Victoria: Inner Harbour,
Parliament Buildings 68
Victoria: Royal British
Columbia Museum,
Thunderbird Park 70

Victoria: Butchart
Gardens 72
Goldstream Provincial
Park, Cowichan Valley,
Strathcona Provincial Park 74
Pacific Rim National Park 76
Tofino, Nootka Sound 78
Tweedsmuir
Provincial Park 82
Best addresses 84

**British Columbia:
Queen Charlotte
Islands/Haida Gwaii** **86**

Area map 88
Graham Island,
Moresby Island 90
SGang Gwaay
(Anthony Island) 94
Best addresses 96

**British Columbia:
Thompson Okanagan,
Cariboo** **98**

Area map 100
Fraser River Valley,
Chilliwack River Valley 102

Okanagan Valley,
Shuswap Lake Area 106
Mount Revelstoke
National Park 108
Glacier National Park 110
Wells Gray
Provincial Park 112
Mount Robson
Provincial Park 114
Barkerville,
Quesnel Museum 116
Best addresses 118

**British Columbia:
Kootenay Rockies** **120**

Area map 122
Yoho National Park 124
Kootenay National Park 126
Mount Assiniboine
Provincial Park 128
Best addresses 130

**British Columbia:
Northern Districts** **132**

Area map 134
Tatshenshini-Alsek
Provincial Park 136

CONTENTS

The *Photo Guide* series is as informative and practical as a travel guide, but as lavishly illustrated as a coffee-table book. Each guide is packed with all the important information you need to make your visit a success and is complemented by an atlas section to help you find your way around. Expert writers provide an insight into the history and culture of each region, highlight the top sights and excursions, and recommend local hotels and restaurants. Special features on the most beautiful cities and the best excursions combined with detailed and accurate maps make sure you get the most out of your trip.

IN FOCUS

ATLAS

Atlin Provincial Park
and Recreation Area   140
Stikine River Provincial
Park, Mount Edziza
Provincial Park   142
Stewart-Cassiar Highway
(Highway 37)   144
Stewart, Salmon Glacier 146
Kitwancool, 'Ksan
Historical Village
and Museum   148
Muncho Lake
Provincial Park   150
Best addresses   152

Alberta   **154**

Area map   156
Calgary   158
Dinosaur Provincial Park 162
Head-Smashed-In
Buffalo Jump   164
Waterton Lakes
National Park   166
Banff National Park:
Vermilion Lakes, Mount
Rundle, Ha Ling Peak   168

Banff National Park:
Johnston Canyon,
Castle Mountain   170
Banff National Park:
Valley of the Ten Peaks,
Moraine Lake,
Lake Louise   172
Jasper National Park:
Athabasca River,
Sunwapta River   176
Jasper National Park:
Maligne Canyon,
Medicine Lake,
Maligne Lake   178
Jasper National Park:
Pyramid Lake,
Patricia Lake,
Beauvert Lake   180
Edmonton   182
Elk Island National Park,
Ukrainian Cultural
Heritage Village   184
Wood Buffalo
National Park   188
Best addresses   190

Festival Calendar   **194**

Features

The museums of
Vancouver   46
The Inside Passage   66
Wildlife on the
Canadian Pacific coast   80
The Haida Nation   92
Commercial salmon
fishing   104
Bears: black, brown,
and white   138
The Calgary Stampede   160
The Icefields Parkway   174
The First Nations:
the first Americans   186

Key   **196**
South British Columbia
South-West Alberta   198

South-East Alberta
South Saskatchewan
South-West Manitoba   200

North British Columbia
North-West Alberta   202

North-East Alberta
North Saskatchewan
North Manitoba   204

Yukon Territory
Northwest
Territories West   206

Northwest
Territories East
Nunavut   208

Beaufort Sea   210

Places index   **212**

General index   **218**

WESTERN CANADA PROFILE

Canada, the Beautiful – or, to be more precise, Western Canada – is still a wilderness of untouched natural beauty, an almost inconceivably vast land of majestic mountains, endless forests, tranquil lakes, and rushing rivers. Often there is not a soul in sight on its long cross-country highways or the tracks and trails that wend their way through its woodland – that is, other than animals such as bear, elk, and caribou. Endless tundra stretches across the wide expanse of the Yukon Territory, thick forest covers more than half of British Columbia, and flat grasslands characterize Alberta. It is the perfect place for anyone seeking solitude while still being within reach of civilization, with bustling cities like Vancouver and Victoria.

WESTERN CANADA PROFILE: THE LAND OF THE MAPLE

On the road again: the Trans-Canada Highway runs right across Canada, from St John's on Newfoundland in the east, all the way to the country's westernmost point at Victoria on Vancouver Island. Linking the ten Canadian provinces, the entire route is over 7,000 km (4,350 miles) long. It is Canada's only transcontinental road, and one of the longest highways in the world.

Yukon Territory

The tundra of the Yukon Territory is characterized by permafrost and sparse vegetation, where just a few plants survive the Arctic winters thanks to the thick blanket of snow that protects them from the harsh climate. The snow along the Arctic coast begins to melt in May and June. Having been cocooned beneath their white covering, the plants have already started

The Northern Lights play above Yukon Territory.

to develop buds and leaves, and the temperature need only reach 0°C (32°F) for the vegetation to burst into life once more. It is not long before they are in full bloom. Peat moss dominates the wetlands, while lichen and low-growing shrubs, which bear berries in the autumn, grow in the drier areas. The rocky southern slopes are bathed in the low sun, whose warm rays transform them into veritable flower gardens. In summer, the Arctic Circle becomes a breeding ground for over a hundred bird species, although most return south by the time autumn comes.

Forests and lakes

Western Canada comprises the three provinces of British Columbia, Alberta, and the Yukon Territory. British Columbia covers an area of 948,600 sq km (365,928 sq miles), with half of its 3.4-million population concentrated in and around Vancouver. The capital city is Victoria, on Vancouver Island. The jagged British Columbia coastline is some 7,000 km (4,350 miles) long, not including the various island coastlines, such as Vancouver Island and the Queen Charlotte Islands. Fjords and coastal cliffs typify the West Coast, lending it its unique character. The Coast Mountains run from north to south, with Mount Wadding-ton – at 4,016 m (13,176 feet) – the highest summit. The plateau that dominates central British Columbia encompasses numerous lakes and smaller mountain ranges, like the Columbia, Cariboo, and Skeena Mountains. The Rocky Mountains lie to the east, with Mount Robson, the highest summit in the Canadian Rockies, reaching a height of 3,954 m (12,972 feet). The Rockies' mountain crests mark the watershed of two river systems, with the rivers of British Columbia flowing not into the Arctic but into the Pacific Ocean. Two of the longest rivers in the province are the Fraser and Columbia. For European visitors, the never-ending cedar and spruce forests are particularly amazing. This is nature untamed, untouched, and in the raw, especially in the north, where the vegetation decreases in height as the tundra and Arctic regions begin. In southern

British Columbia, there are some very dry, sunny areas like Okanagan Valley, which is well suited to vineyards and fruit plantations.
Alberta covers an area of 661,200 sq km (255,223 sq miles). It has a population of 2.8 million, with Edmonton its capital city. Alberta's western border with British Columbia is marked by the Rocky Mountains. Northern Alberta is characterized by its lakes and coniferous forests, while the topography of the eastern and southern parts of the province – traversed by the plains of the High Prairie – is closely related to that of bordering Montana. This is cowboy country, and it is here that the country's biggest ranches are located. The focal point of the livestock industry is Calgary, but the city is also sustained by the profits of the oil business. Oil has made Alberta the richest of all Canada's provinces, and Edmonton – the continent's northernmost major city – also owes its existence to the discovery of its local oilfields. Situated on the North Saskatchewan River, the city covers a larger area than Chicago, yet has one of the lowest urban population densities in North America, barely 10 percent of that of New York.

Endless forests, vast prairie, and lonely tundra

Western Canada's plant life is as diverse as the region itself. It ranges from the treeless tundra of the Arctic north to the fertile grassy prairies, from the dark woodlands to the damp marshlands and desert-like grasslands, and from the temperate coastal rainforests to

the alpine landscape of the Rocky Mountains. Approximately 60 percent of British Columbia is covered by forest, with temperate rainforest spanning the west coast of Vancouver Island and the Queen Charlotte Islands. While tropical rainforest reveals its full glory after heavy rainfall, the temperate or northern rainforest is dependent upon frequent showers and the coastal mist, as well as temperate summers and mild winters. The majestic red cedars, Douglas fir, and Sitka spruce trees that flourish in this climate are covered in moss and lichen, and fern grows between the tree trunks. The cool, temperate areas are covered by woodland, especially in British Columbia. Both white and black spruces thrive in this climate, with splendid forest lilies and rare orchids standing out from the greenery. Spruce, fir, and pine trees all grow in the mountains and foothills. Hemlock fir and red cedar trees are found along the banks of the Kootenay, Fraser, and Thompson rivers. The mighty Sitka spruces and numerous other conifers are the most striking trees along the coast, with maple, oak, poplar, and alder the most notable deciduous species. Grasslands cover the southern Alberta prairie, and cottonwood and willow trees are found only along the banks of its rivers. The warm climate here even sustains cacti. The north, meanwhile, is characterized by Douglas fir, white spruce, and other coniferous species, with a broad aspen belt marking the transition between the two areas. There are no trees at all in the Arctic tundra, where permafrost impedes the growth of any significant vegetation beyond moss and lichen. Only in the brief summer do wild flowers bloom in the meadows.

Bear, elk, and beaver

Western Canada is an animal lover's paradise, and it is not unusual to see bear and elk at the roadside. There are thought to be over 150,000 black bears and 10,000 grizzly bears in British Columbia alone. The two can be difficult to tell apart, despite the telltale hump in the grizzly's neck and the fact that – weighing in at 500 kg (1,102 lb) – it is significantly heavier than the 250-kg (551-lb) black bear, which is the real-life inspiration for many a cuddly soft toy and children's characters such as Winnie the Pooh. Though essentially shy, the bears can soon become a danger to humans if they feel threatened, particularly if cubs are present. Feeding on aquatic and bog plants, elk, one of the largest of the deer species, can grow to heights of over 2 m (7 feet). The male animals have powerful antlers. Early morning and late evening is the best time to see elk. They are only found in the quietest parts of the forest. The inland coniferous forests are also home to the much smaller red deer (known locally as the wapiti), the even smaller mule deer, and a number of animals prized for their fur, including beaver, marten, badger, fox, and muskrat. Once hunted by the ruthless trappers of the Hudson's Bay Company, their populations have now reached healthy numbers again. The beaver, the world's biggest rodent, can grow to over 1 m (3 feet) long. They build their homes in the pools they create by damming streams and rivers.

Wildlife

Clambering across the slopes of the Rocky Mountains are bighorn sheep and mountain goats. The former are much more easily recognizable due to the fact that they do not shed their distinctive horns. The mountain goats, with their white coats, are far rarer. Catching sight of a wolf, coyote, or fox is equally unusual. Eagles and falcons circle in the skies above the mountain peaks. Below, chipmunks come right up on to the terraces of the hotels and holiday homes. The marmot, meanwhile, announces its presence with its whistle – a noise with which holidaymakers quickly become familiar. The lynx and mountain lion, by contrast, are much rarer sightings.

The wildlife of the southern Alberta prairie has changed dramatically over the course of history. The bison almost became extinct, its population only recovering in recent years on the ranches and in the national parks. There were some 60 million bison around 1900, but at its lowest point the population had fallen to around just 1,000 animals. A larger animal than the bison, the wild buffalo roams the Wood Buffalo National Park in large herds. The most common examples of the prairie's animal life, however, are the antelope and prairie dog. There are also rattlesnakes and – around the ponds – numerous bird species. Huge caribou herds cross the tundra. These North American wild reindeer grow to over 1 m (3 feet) long. Both the male and female animals have antlers, and their meat is still a staple of the diet of the First Nation population. The shaggy muskox, meanwhile, is protected by a hunting ban. It feeds on the sparse tundra vegetation.

Off the Pacific coast, gray and killer whales prowl the waters. The former grows to around 15 m (49 feet) long, while the latter, despite its name, is not considered a great threat to humans. Both are protected by the whale-hunting ban that has been in force since 1982. Around the islands, you can also see seals.

The region's best-known fish has to be the salmon, which can grow to over 1 m (3 feet) long. It is highly prized, and stocks of wild Pacific salmon are now low enough to make it an endangered species. The adult fish leave the sea to swim upriver to spawning grounds, where their eggs are laid and fertilized in the gravel riverbed. The salmon young begin their lives in the fresh water, before eventually finding their way to the sea. The dams and locks on the rivers along which the salmon swim would block their path were it not for the so-called salmon leaps built by the Canadian authorities to facilitate the salmon's movement. Canada geese and other aquatic birds live on the banks of the northern lakes.

An encounter with an elk cow is unusual, but not totally unlikely.

When the days get warmer polar bears revel in the joys of spring.

WESTERN CANADA PROFILE: THE LAND OF THE MAPLE

In 1755, the colonial powers of England and France were locked in battle for North America. In July, General Edward Braddock and his soldiers encountered Native North American and French forces in French-occupied territory. Braddock's troops were taken completely by surprise, and became trapped in a narrow valley. Heavily wounded, Braddock was carried off the battlefield alive, but died soon afterwards (illustration, 1855).

The Royal Canadian Mounted Police

Canada's first prime minister, Sir John A. MacDonald, founded the North West Mounted Police in 1873, with the aim of stopping the illegal whisky trade between the white settlers and the Native North Americans. With their red uniforms and splendid horses, the "Mounties" cut an imposing figure, and their endurance and

It's showtime: on parade at the Calgary Stampede.

sense of justice were legendary. By around 1870, the force numbered over a thousand officers. They acted as intermediaries between white Canadians and the Native North Americans, hunted down criminals, and kept the peace in the distant Yukon Territory. In 1904, England's King Edward VII recognized the force as the Royal Canadian Mounted Police (RCMP). In 1920, the RCMP headquarters moved from Regina to Ottawa. Today the RCMP force employs more than 16,000 officers and 5,000 civilian staff.

Prehistoric settlement

The history of Western Canada begins over 30,000 years ago, when the aboriginal people first crossed from Siberia to the American continent via a land bridge, now covered by the Bering Strait. They settled the forests and steppes of modern British Columbia and Alberta, living as hunter-gatherers, farmers, and fishermen. The ancestors of the Inuit adapted well to the infertile, Arctic landscape of the future Yukon Territory.

Explorers and settlers

Long before Columbus discovered the American continent, Native North Americans along the east coast had already encountered both Vikings and, it is believed, Irish monks. The navigator and explorer John Cabot crossed the Atlantic from Bristol in the west of England in 1497, to land at what is now Newfoundland; the French explorer Jacques Cartier followed him in 1534, landing at both Newfoundland and Labrador. The French navigator and cartographer Samuel de Champlain founded Quebec in the early 17th century; it was the first significant settlement in North America, paving the way for what would become French Canada.
The British entered Canada via Newfoundland and Labrador. During the 18th century, they were embroiled in ongoing conflict with France over the North American territories. Britain eventually emerged victorious from the deciding battles of the Seven Years' War (the conflict that took place in

America was known as the French and Indian War), and went on to occupy French Canada. In 1763, the Treaty of Paris ended the desperate struggle for control of Canada, the French ceding their Canadian territories to the British. The first Europeans to explore Western Canada did so in the 17th century. Trappers working for the English Hudson's Bay Company, founded in 1679, got as far as the future British Columbia. The first white man to reach the Rocky Mountains was Anthony Henday in 1754; meanwhile, Spanish navigators sailed along the coast of British Columbia. Samuel Hearne – another Hudson's Bay Company agent – arrived in Western Canada in 1772, and in 1778 James Cook dropped anchor off Vancouver Island; George Vancouver landed on the west coast in 1792. In 1791, Alexander Mackenzie became the first white man to complete the transcontinental crossing of North America. Two of British Columbia's rivers are named after David Thompson and Simon Fraser, who also ventured inland. In 1821, the Hudson's Bay Company joined forces with its former rival, the North West Company, to form the world's most powerful trading company. By 1850, large numbers of Europeans – mostly from Ireland, Scotland, and Germany – had emigrated to Canada. Many more followed, drawn by the 1858 gold rush along the Fraser River. Throughout the 1860s, gold prospectors set off along the Cariboo Wagon Road to Barkerville, which became the prospectors' main town. Thriving during the gold rush, Barkerville eventually went into decline and became a ghost town.

The founding and opening up of Canada

The Canadian nation was born on 1 July 1867. The British North America Act created the provinces of Quebec and Ontario, which joined with Nova Scotia (New Scotland) and New Brunswick (named after Braunschweig,

Future US president George Washington fought alongside the British colonists against France in the French and Indian War (painting by Charles Willson Peale).

Germany) to form the Dominion of Canada, whose new government was based on the British system. Manitoba joined the Dominion three years later, after the British had suppressed an uprising by the Métis people (descendents of French trappers and Native North Americans). British Columbia joined in 1871; Saskatchewan became a province in 1905. The construction of the transcontinental railway was a crucial factor in the settlement of Western Canada, and many lives were lost building the section across the Rocky Mountains. Once completed, the Canadian Pacific Railway drove forward the settlement of the western areas, which led to an economic boom – although it was 1886 before the first train to Vancouver left from Montreal.

The gold rush and its aftermath

The Yukon Territory was established in the far north of Canada in 1898, born of the need to gain control over the thousands who flocked to the region in the hope of profiting from the gold rush along the Klondike River. What had been one of the most remote places in North America suddenly started to exert an almost magical attraction. There were two main routes to the Yukon goldfields. The White Pass Trail wove its way through the rocky ravines from Skagway, while a narrow path from Dyea led up to the Chilkoot Pass. Boats and rafts carried the prospectors up the Yukon River to Dawson City, a hastily constructed shantytown of wooden shacks that was, at its height, home to several thousand inhabitants. But the gold rush was short lived, and within a few years this former boomtown went into decline. The tributaries of the Klondike River had yielded over ten million dollars worth of gold, but only a lucky few got rich.
Gastown – the town that would later grow into the city of Vancouver – was established in the 1860s. The original settlement was founded by

"Gassy" Jack Deighton, who arrived here with a canoe-load of whisky barrels in autumn 1867 and opened a saloon on what is now Maple Tree Square. The town soon became an important trading hub for trappers, gold prospectors, and lumberjacks. By spring 1886, Gastown could claim a population of some 4,000 people, excluding – as was customary at the time – women, Native North Americans, and foreigners. The incorporation of the city of Vancouver, and its naming after the British explorer George Vancouver, followed later that year. It would turn out to be a fateful 12 months, since the entire city was all but destroyed by fire shortly afterwards. With only a few of the old stone buildings surviving, Vancouver's citizens quickly set about rebuilding, and within a year the reconstruction was complete. No sooner had the last nail been hammered into place than the whistle of a locomotive announced the arrival of the first transcontinental train at Vancouver station. The city was now the terminus of the Canadian Pacific Railway, and it reaped the rewards of the economic growth that the railway brought.

Canada's economic power

In the 20th century, Canada established itself as an important economic partner and a reliable member of the Allied forces in the two world wars. The discovery of its oilfields spawned a new economic boom. Canada joined NATO in 1949, and in 1962 the Trans-Canada Highway became the first and only transcontinental

road to link the country's east and west coasts. The British America Act was replaced in 1982 by a new constitution that made Canada a sovereign power, reducing the role of the British monarch as head of state to an essentially representative function. In 1999, the Inuit were also given greater political independence with

the creation of Nunavut Province, which was split off from the Northwest Territories. The aim was to help Native North Americans to preserve their own identity, moving towards a future autonomous government. Nunavut is the only part of Canada in which Inuktitut is recognized as an official language.

The Canadian Pacific Railroad provided the first transport link between Canada's east and west coasts.

On Highway 2, this old roadhouse between Dawson and Whitehorse is a reminder of the days of the gold-diggers.

WESTERN CANADA PROFILE: THE LAND OF THE MAPLE

Canadian singers and musicians who have enjoyed global success include the multi-award-winning pop diva Celine Dion (born 1968); singer-songwriter Alanis Morissette (born 1974), also in demand for her skills as an actress; legendary writer, composer, and singer Leonard Cohen (born 1934); rock star Bryan Adams (born 1959), who has had a string of number one hits all over the world since the 1980s; Buffalo Springfield founder member and Grammy Award winner Neil Young (born 1945); and Avril Lavigne (born 1984) who is now continuing the musical tradition.

Totem poles

Despite what you might have been led to believe from many a Hollywood film, totem poles were only ever used by the First Nation peoples of the Pacific northwest coast, and were never part of Sioux or Apache culture. The word "totem" roughly translates as "kinship" or "family insignia". The figures and symbols carved into the pole, usually of cedar

A totem pole in Stanley Park, Vancouver.

wood, represent guardian spirits and relate episodes from a family's history. The animals and birds habitually featured included eagles, bears, and beavers. The poles could be up to 20 m (66 feet) high, and were usually erected outside Firts Nations dwellings to protect the families inside. The Haida Indians of the Queen Charlotte Islands are believed to have been the first to erect these poles – those at the Haida village site of Ninstints have been designated a UNESCO World Heritage Site. Modern totem poles, meanwhile, are mostly found along the west coast of Vancouver Island.

Crafts

By the prehistoric era, the early Inuit and the Native North Americans were already active and highly skilled craftsmen. They used natural materials like caribou antlers, walrus ivory, and the soapstone found in the deep northern regions to make figurines and sculptures. These were mostly religious items, depicting good and evil spirits, monsters, and other legendary creatures. Rattles made from whalebone and dyed feathers or drums made from tanned animal hides and decorated with feathers were both essentially ceremonial items. Today, practical items like harpoon points also have artistic merit, not unlike arrowheads in the USA. The Inuit and First Nations peoples also decorated their clothes with bright stones and wooden figurines made from bone or ivory. Vibrant beads started to be worn after the arrival of the first white explorers and settlers. Clothes were made from animal skins sewn together using needles made from bone and thread made from sinew. The anorak is a heavy jacket with a hood that protects the wearer from wind and snow.

The churches constructed by Christian settlers brought the European style of sculpture to Canada, mostly in the form of altar carvings and statues of the saints. One of the most important local artists was Louis Quévillon (1749–1832), whose work can still be seen today in numerous churches in Montreal. The first secular sculptures were not created until the 20th century. However, borrowing heavily from

European art, they do not reflect a uniquely Canadian style.

An original artistic style

Artists who were not First Nation people only began integrating Native American symbols in their work around 1960, so a true Canadian modern art style can really only be said to date from the late 20th century. The earliest paintings and sketches were purely for information purposes, and it is therefore no surprise to find

Cornelius Krieghoff's wintry country scenes (painted around 1855) show Canadian country life as we like to imagine it.

that most history books credit the visionary adventurer and explorer Samuel de Champlain as the first Canadian painter. His sketches of the Huron depicted their lives and customs for those unfamiliar with this Native North American people. The Huron joined forces with the French to fight the British, who had formed an alliance with the Iroquois. In the second half of the 18th century, numerous other explorers followed de Champlain in their use of sketches and quick paintings to illustrate their written accounts

and reports, many of which were made for the military or the government.

One of the most important landscape painters of the 19th century was Cornelius Krieghoff (1815–72). He is best known for his winter scenes and for his depictions of the difficult living conditions on the frontier. Paul Kane (1810–71) journeyed the length and breadth of Canada visiting numerous First Nation settlements, and his legacy of paintings and sketches provide an accurate depiction of the

lives of the Native North American tribes.

Most Canadian painters were trained thousands of miles away in France, and the Royal Academy of Arts was not founded until 1867 – after the establishment of the Canadian state. In the 1920s, the Toronto artists known as the Group of Seven made an important contribution to the development of an independent Canadian art style in the search for a uniquely Canadian identity. An important influence for the group was Tom Thomson (1877–1917), who painted

ART AND CULTURE

spectacular landscapes. The painter and writer Emily Carr (1871–1945) was equally well known, her paintings and prose both heavily influenced by the myths and legends of the First Nations Salish people. In Canada as elsewhere, the end of World War II marked the beginning of modernism. Art became more abstract, and artists started to experiment with new techniques and materials. Today, the art created by the Inuit and First Nation peoples continues to command high prices, espe-

and unfiltered account of life in the wilds of untamed Canada. Rather more emotive depictions are provided by two female immigrants and writers who experienced the harsh reality of life in the far west and north at first hand – Mrs Moodie spent years living in the Canadian bush, while Susan Allison was the first white woman to cross the Hope Mountains on horseback. Unlike the sober reports of the early settlers, the accounts left by these two women offer a somewhat

Robert W. Service was similarly romantic. Along with the American author Jack London, Service is still a celebrated literary figure in contemporary Yukon.

Storytellers and actors

Neither the Inuit nor the First Nations population have a written literature. Instead, theirs is an oral history, relayed not by writers and poets, but by storytellers. The long winter evenings provided

George Copway (1818–69) was one of the leading First Nation writers – his book *The Life, History and Travels of Kah-ge-ga-gah-bowh* (published in 1847) was extremely successful. Several generations later, in 1985, Jeanette Armstrong enjoyed similar success with *Slash*.

Music

When it comes to contemporary culture, it is Canada's musicians who stand out the most. Singer-songwriter, poet,

Everyday art: First Nation peoples in Victoria often use the pavement as a canvas for their street art.

A collection of larger than life sculptures in a Calgary park.

cially in the upmarket galleries of Vancouver and Victoria.

Literature

Early Canadian literature largely comprises the stories recorded by the explorers, fur traders, missionaries, and the military officers who traveled beyond the frontier or took part in the campaigns that decided the map of Canada. The reports and diaries they wrote tend to be fairly dry, and are rarely of great literary merit. Yet their recollections nonetheless provide a raw

romanticized view of settler life. The same might be said of the work of Grey Owl, who for decades claimed to be a member of the Native North American Ojibwe, but was in fact exposed as an English immigrant whose real name was Archibald Stansfield Belaney. Leaving the comforts of life in England behind him, he arrived in Canada in the early 20th century in order to live out his years as a white member of the First Nations in the Canadian wilderness. His book *Pilgrims of the Wild* was a bestseller. The poetry of

an occasion to gather round the fire and listen to the legends and fairytales that lie at the heart of Native North American culture. Many of the storytellers were natural actors, using gestures and sounds to bring their stories to life in ways that made each rendition unique. They would interrupt the stories with long breaks for smoking, which added to the tension. It is only since the beginning of the 19th century that the Inuit and First Nation peoples have begun to write down their stories.

and musician Leonard Cohen and fellow pop legend Neil Young have enjoyed immense popularity since the 1960s, along with the jazz-rock sound of Joni Mitchell. Other Canadian musical luminaries include jazz-pianist and composer Oscar Peterson, Grammy Award-winner Anne Murray, and Paul Anka, who, although now a naturalized US citizen, was born in Ottawa. New stars on the country music scene include artists like k.d. lang, the Cowboy Junkies, and Shania Twain, who are all pushing the boundaries of the genre.

WESTERN CANADA PROFILE: THE LAND OF THE MAPLE

Cowboy culture is still very much alive in British Columbia. The cattle "roundups" demand great skill of both horse and rider. The cattle can be spread out for miles in rough country, over rocky mountains, forest clearings, and valleys. They usually take place twice a year – first in spring, when the newborn calves have to be branded, and again in autumn, when the animals are split from the main herd in order to be sold on the market.

The great Canadian outdoors

Canada has been called the land of a thousand adventures, and there are certainly plenty of opportunities to experience nature in all its unspoiled glory in the vast, seemingly endless wilderness stretching north of the Trans-Canada Highway. The areas that have been opened up – above all in the national parks like Jasper and Banff – are

A snowy paradise: the Rocky Mountains.

superb for hiking, climbing, and winter sports. Expert skiers enthuse about the incredibly fine, powdery snow found in the Rocky Mountains. Once the long highways have been left behind, there is an extensive network of hiking trails and a good chance of seeing mountain goat, elk, and bear. Experienced climbers will also find suitably challenging terrain. The locals in these parts ride snowmobiles as city dwellers ride cars and bicycles, and there are well-marked routes across the pistes and through the deep snow. A ride on a dog sled is equally exciting.

From untamed wilderness to city action

The western part of Canada – British Columbia, Alberta, and, up in the far north, the Yukon Territory – is surely the real Canada, a land of enchanting snow-capped mountains and endless forests that is well known from the movies. The Rocky Mountains are probably Western Canada's single most impressive feature. Beyond the towns and villages in the valleys, the mountain landscape still looks exactly as it would have done when the first European explorers discovered it. Most of the mountain peaks are lonely and untouched. The tranquil valleys and lakes are breathtakingly beautiful, and the views from the remote mountain crests are just magnificent. What really sets the landscape apart is the sheer scale of its features. The distances involved are immense, and even if certain towns such as Banff and Jasper, and areas along the banks of Lake Louise, clearly have tourism and commercialism in mind, it hardly seems to matter when placed in the context of such unending vastness. Wherever you go in Canada, the real wilderness is never far away. Beyond Vancouver, Victoria, and the Trans-Canada Highway lies a massive, natural, untouched landscape that cannot fail to captivate visitors. It is hard to think of a place where the heart of nature beats as loudly as it does here. This is not to say that Western Canada is devoid of urban amusements. Vancouver is one of the world's most beautiful cities. Surrounded by picturesque bays and the majestic

Coast Mountains, the city has it all, from the skyscrapers of its dynamic central district to the shops and street-side cafés of its romantic old town, its large open green spaces, 18-km (11-mile) long sandy beach, and the buzzing recreation area on Granville Island. Victoria, the British metropolis on Vancouver Island, feels very British, complete with afternoon teas, shortbread, and even a replica of Anne Hathaway's cottage. The red double-decker buses parked

gan Lake – both dotted with the bright sails of the boats navigating across them.

Cultural diversity

Two-thirds of British Columbia's population of 3.4 million are of British descent; there are also Scandinavian, German, Ukrainian, Indian, Chinese, Japanese, and Italian communities. First Nation peoples – mostly from the Salish, Kootenay, and Tlingit groups – make up just three percent of

An Inuit man photographed in the early 20th century.

outside the Empress Hotel could just as easily be in London, and while the Royal British Columbia Museum is no match for London's British Museum in size, it is just as interesting. There are also the blossoming fruit orchards of the Okanagan Valley, as well as Shuswap Lake and Okana-

the population. The First Nation community in Alberta is slightly larger, forming five percent of the population, primarily drawn from the proud Blackfoot Nation. Around two-fifths of Alberta's population of 2.8 million are descended from the British, with the remainder of German and eastern European descent. The Yukon Territory's population amounts to just 32,000, one-third of which is of First Nations descent. The north is also home to a significant number of German and Swiss expatriates.

Cultural diversity runs right through Canadian society, and the Canadians' respect for one another makes them much more liberal and open-minded than Americans across the border. This is a place where people live and let live. While other countries are proud of their "melting pot" of different cultures, the Canadians aspire to a mosaic in which each ethnic group retains its own unique identity. The clearest line of cultural demarcation is the enduring divide between Canada's British and French descendents, but there are over sixty other ethnic groups, including, of course, the Inuit and First Nations. Canadian Native North Americans, with the exception of the Inuit and the Métis, are also known as First Nations.

From Inuit to First Nations

The aboriginal people are believed to have arrived in Alaska from Siberia some 30,000 years ago, when the two continents were still joined by a land bridge. The Siberian hunters simply followed their prey to the new world, their new environment largely determining the path of their subsequent cultural development. The word "Eskimo" is a corruption of the Cree (a First Nations language) word for "raw meat eater". In fact, the Arctic peoples do eat cooked meat, only resorting to raw meat when

there is no fuel to make a fire. Their own name for themselves is not Eskimo but Inuit, meaning "the people" or "human beings". Their clothes are mostly made from caribou furs, which are warm and naturally water resistant, and can easily be brushed clear of ice. The Inuit wear their anoraks (an Inuit word) and trousers loose and baggy, so that heat can collect in the air pockets inside. They hunt using dog sleds made from driftwood or bone, always with a harpoon at hand in case they encounter seals. To hunt whales, the Inuit use umiaks – boats made from animal skins stretched over a wooden frame. In Inuit society, all food is shared, and it is this that assures their survival, but the influence of white society has gradually begun to undermine this traditional culture. Other aspects of traditional life have been affected too. The snowmobile has supplanted the dog sled, small supermarkets have started to sell groceries at high prices, and the Inuit are now wearing anoraks made from synthetic materials. Unfortunately, alcoholism and unemployment have also become serious problems. Canada's First Nations population comprises several tribes and groups, whose individual cultures reflect their particular environment and local climate, but hunting and fishing are central to all of them. The First Nation peoples of Western Canada in particular established their villages on the banks of local rivers, from where they hunted caribou, elk, and bear. Salmon and trout were dried and smoked to be stored for the winter. When the snows arrived, the tribesmen would don snow

shoes for the hunt. They were organized in clans led by the most experienced warriors and hunters. As in the Inuit community, belief in the supernatural was a significant part of the culture. Houses and boats were built from the bark of birch trees, and tools and clothes were fashioned from bone and animal skins. At potlatch ceremonies, it was the practice of community leaders to give away their possessions, a way of impressing other hunters that continues today.

A big catch: a chinook caught in the Pacific.

By contrast, the Native American peoples who settled the coastal regions lived from fishing and whale hunting.

Culinary Canada

Canadian cuisine, especially in the big cities, draws heavily on the country's ethnic diversity, with Asian influences predominating in the coastal city of Vancouver. Exotic and spicy noodle soups sold at Vietnamese stalls, tasty Chinese dim sum, and sushi and tempura served in the Japanese restaurants and sushi bars are just some of the most popular fare. Many restaurants serve

fusion dishes, combining Asian cooking with the cuisine of far-flung places such as South America and California. The combination of fresh Pacific coast ingredients with the ethnic recipes introduced by the many Asian immigrants forms the style of cuisine known as Pacific Rim. Salmon, including the red sockeye, chinook (or spring salmon), and fat coho, is without a doubt the most popular fish, but halibut, trout, and tuna also make frequent appearances on local menus.

Salmon is traditionally grilled or smoked over an open log fire, and served with fresh fruit and vegetables from the Fraser and Okanagan valleys. For diners who prefer meat dishes, Alberta is the place to go for a particularly tender steak. Game is eaten much less frequently than might be expected, thanks to the strict regulation governing the sale of elk and deer meat. Local beers such as Molson and Moosehead or wine from the Okanagan valley are the perfect accompaniment to a meal, and the odd glass of whisky (Canadian, of course) does not go amiss either.

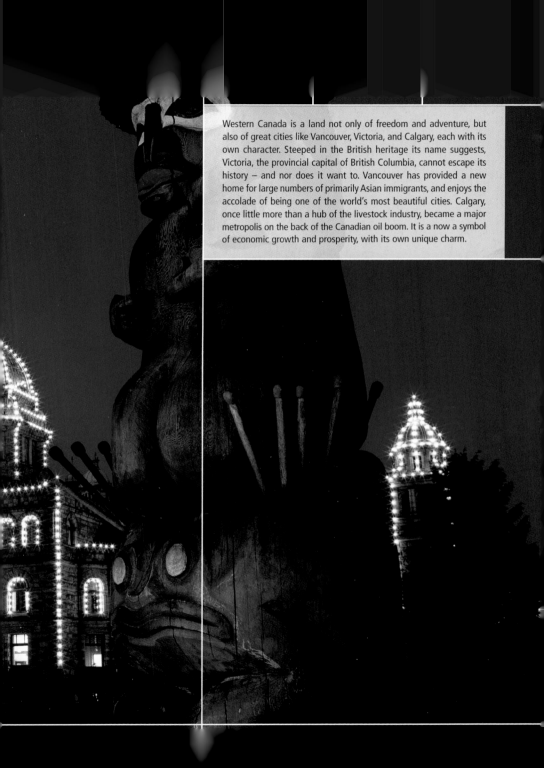

Western Canada is a land not only of freedom and adventure, but also of great cities like Vancouver, Victoria, and Calgary, each with its own character. Steeped in the British heritage its name suggests, Victoria, the provincial capital of British Columbia, cannot escape its history – and nor does it want to. Vancouver has provided a new home for large numbers of primarily Asian immigrants, and enjoys the accolade of being one of the world's most beautiful cities. Calgary, once little more than a hub of the livestock industry, became a major metropolis on the back of the Canadian oil boom. It is a now a symbol of economic growth and prosperity, with its own unique charm.

Sights

❶ Gastown

Vancouver's old town has enjoyed protected status since 1971. Its name is a tribute to "Gassy" Jack Deighton, who opened a saloon in the future port district in 1867. Local businesses have funded the restoration of the historic buildings, turning the old port into a vibrant area of boutiques, restaurants, antique shops, and street cafés. The Steam Clock on the corner of Cambie Street and Water Street is unique, and has become a symbol of Gastown's regeneration. Every five minutes, a steam engine pulls the clock's ball weights back up to the top.

❷ Chinatown

Vancouver's Chinatown is the third biggest Chinese district on the American continent, outdone only by New York and San Francisco. The Chinese writing on the illuminated neon signs points the way to countless souvenir shops, bookstores, jewelers, and laundries. The signs are as central to the streetscape as the Chinese dragons and red pagoda roofs that adorn the doorways and telephone boxes. A significant number of Canada's early settlers were Chinese, and the Chinese community remains one of the biggest sectors of today's population.

❸ Canada Place

This futuristic commercial complex on the Burrard Inlet was built for the Expo 86 exhibition in 1986. It is home to the Vancouver Convention Centre, the Vancouver World Trade Centre, the extremely luxurious Pan Pacific Hotel, the CN IMAX Theatre, and numerous shops and restaurants. The white fabric sails that rise above the building are reminiscent of a windjammer, but it is cruise ships that moor alongside. From the promenade, you get a breathtaking view of the port, Coast Mountains, and the north of the city.

❹ Science World

South-east of the middle of town, the Science World building looks like a gigantic silver golf ball. It was built as the Expo Centre for Expo 86, and now houses an interactive museum that provides a fun way for young people to discover science. This ultramodern structure sits easily in the city skyline and creates an interesting contrast with the wilderness that extends either side of North Vancouver.

❺ Stanley Park

Stanley Park is Vancouver's "green lung". Its lush, proliferating rainforest, many bicycle routes, playgrounds, sports courts, seaside promenade, swimming pools, auditorium, picnic spots, and meadows are the perfect antidote to the stresses of city life. The city zoo and the Vancouver Public Aquarium are also located in the middle of the park.

❻ Robson Street

Sometimes known by its German name of *Robsonstrasse*, this famous shopping street was, until a few decades ago, the home of the city's German community. Today it enjoys a far greater ethnic diversity. A wide range of small shops, including the odd whacky boutique, specialist markets, and numerous restaurants all keep shoppers coming back.

❼ Granville Island

This artificial island beneath the highway bridges on the banks of False Creek is a major leisure area. Its warehouses have been turned into bars, restaurants, and shops, and you can watch artists and craftsmen – ranging from painters and sculptors to glassblowers, potters, and even totem-pole carvers – at work in the galleries. Musicians, jugglers, and clowns all perform on the streets, and there are any number of gastronomic delights to sample in Granville Market.

❽ Grouse Mountain

If a morning spent basking in the Vancouver sun leaves you hankering to go tearing down the pistes in the afternoon, then the Grouse Mountain ski area is just 3 km (2 miles) from the Lions Gate Bridge. There is a cable car to the top of the 1,211-m (3,973-feet) high mountain, although experienced hikers might like to try their hand at the steep, 3-km (2-mile) long trail instead. The ski runs range from beginner to advanced level, and some are illuminated at night. The view over Vancouver and the Coast Mountains from here is simply breathtaking.

❾ Museum of Anthropology

Opened in 1947, the museum has occupied its current building – designed by Arthur Erickson – since 1976. It is home to a fascinating and valuable collection of Native North American art, with a particular emphasis on the totem poles, sculptures, canoes, and carvings of the First Nation communities along the western Canadian and Alaskan coasts.

Eating and drinking

❶ Joe Fortes Seafood and Chop House

This famous rustic restaurant on English Bay is known for its excellent fish, which – like much of the shellfish on the menu – is sourced from the local waters. The Seafood Tower comes highly recommended.
777 Thurlow Street;
Tel (604) 669 19 40;
11.00–22.30 daily.
www.joefortes.ca

VANCOUVER

Surrounded by Pacific bays and the peaks of the Coast Mountains, Vancouver is the very epitome of urban chic. Its gleaming skyscrapers and picturesque old town provide a pleasing contrast to the vast wilderness that lies just beyond the city limits.

❷ Tojo's Restaurant

Tojo is one of North America's leading sushi chefs, and he has been hot property in Canada for years. The innovative food at this award-winning restaurant is among the best Japanese cuisine you will find this side of Tokyo – the raw fish literally melts in your mouth.
1133 West Broadway;
Tel (604) 872 80 50;
Mon–Sat 17.00–22.00.
www.tojos.com

❸ Imperial Chinese Seafood Restaurant

This place has been serving its celebrated Cantonese dishes since 1989. Peking duck and steamed lobster are two of the most popular choices, and the excellent selection of dim sum is much in demand at lunchtime.
355 Burrard Street;
Tel (604) 688 81 91;
Mon–Fri 11.00–22.30,
Sat–Sun 10.30–22.30.
www.imperialrest.com

Accommodation

❹ Pacific Palisades Hotel

With its bright decor, this jazzy hotel really stands out from the crowd. The spacious suites are superbly equipped.
1277 Robson Street;
Tel (604) 688 04 61.
www.pacificpalisadeshotel.com

❺ Sunset Inn

This good-value hotel is just a few blocks from English Bay.

The decoration of the suites and apartments might not be to everyone's taste, but the beds are comfortable and all the rooms have balconies.
1111 Burnaby Street;
Tel (604) 688 24 74.
www.sunsetinn.com

❻ Lonsdale Quay Hotel

The Lonsdale Quay Hotel is just opposite Canada Place Pier. The SeaBus ferry stops right outside, and the lift from the adjacent Quay Market takes you straight into the lobby. Good value for money.
123 Carrie Cates Court;
Tel (604) 986 61 11.
www.lonsdalequayhotel.com

Shopping

❼ Granville Island Market

This is the place to buy fresh fruit from the Okanagan Valley and other top quality produce. It is worth a visit even if you are staying in a hotel. The benches at False Creek are a perfect place for a picnic.

❽ Salmon Village

Traditional smoked salmon is one of Vancouver's most popular souvenirs. This store supplies unusual variations such as smoked salmon marinated in maple syrup, and Salmon Jerky.
779 Thurlow Street;
Tel (604) 685 33 78.
www.salmonvillage.com

❾ Lonsdale Quay Market

There are all sorts of things to buy at this large market, which spans two floors of the modern SeaBus terminal on the north bank of the Burrard Inlet.
123 Carrie Cates Court;
Tel (604) 985 62 61;
Sat–Thurs 9.30–18.30,
Fri 9.30–21.00.

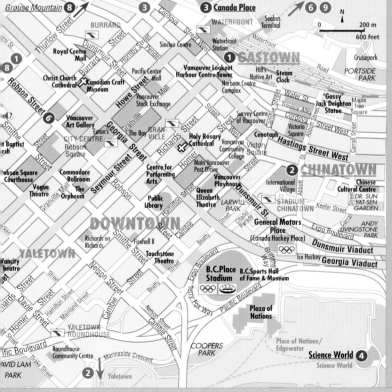

Sights

❶ Calgary Tower

Originally known as Husky Tower, Calgary Tower has dominated the city skyline since 1968. The distance to the top of the antenna is 191 m (627 feet), but it only takes a minute to get to the viewing platform in one of the two lifts. There are spectacular views of the Rocky Mountains and the Olympic ski jumps. Thanks to the solid glass floor, you can literally stand right above Ninth Avenue.

❷ Devonian Gardens

Access to the year-round indoor garden on the fourth floor of the Toronto Dominion Square complex (TD Square) is via a glass lift. There are 16,000 tropical and 4,000 indigenous plants, representing 138 different species. Waterfalls, fountains, and small bridges create a truly romantic mood. Established in 1977, the gardens closed for renovation in 2008 and reopen fall 2010. The shopping complex has 110 retailers over three floors.

❸ Chinatown

Over in the east of the city, Calgary's Chinatown is home to about 2,000 people. There was a significant wave of Chinese immigration here in the 1880s, when Chinese workers helped build the transcontinental railway. Modeled on Peking's Temple of Heaven, the Calgary Chinese Cultural Centre, established in 1993, documents the cultural history of the area's Chinese immigrants. The most stunning feature is the Dr Henry Fok Cultural Hall, with its massive murals and golden dragon.

❹ Eau Claire Market

This covered market is located opposite Prince's Island Park. It is as popular with the locals as it is with visitors. Alongside top-quality Albertan meat, you can buy delicious fresh fruit and vegetables from British Columbia and fresh seafood from the Pacific. A wide range of cafés and restaurants, all sorts of craft stalls, and multi-screen cinemas (including an IMAX screen) mean there is always something to do here – and street entertainers are usually on hand to perform for the passing crowds.

❺ Heritage Park Historic Village

Heritage Park is situated on a peninsula on the Glenmore Reservoir. The old Canadian west is brought back to life in the shape of some 150 original buildings, brought here from all over Western Canada and faithfully reconstructed to create a real pioneer town. There are over 45,000 individual exhibits, all dating from the period 1880–1914. Among the attractions are three old steam locomotives and an amusement park, and visitors are transported around the village by two historic trams.

❻ Glenbow Museum

Spread over four floors, Alberta's largest museum explores the history of Western Canada. Its interesting displays and regular temporary exhibitions skilfully recreate the days of the pioneers. The permanent exhibition "Niitsitapiisinni – Our Way of Life" documents the culture of the Blackfoot. The displays include clothes, weapons, tools, and even an original tipi. The exhibits of Cree embroidery show the extent to which First Nations decorative art has influenced contemporary artists and designers.

❼ Canada Olympic Park

Calgary's sports facilities bring memories of the 1988 Winter Olympics flooding back. From the top of the ski jump, there is a stunning view of the Rocky Mountains. The ski runs are open in winter, but if you would rather stay indoors, try virtual ski jumping in one of the simulators, for all the thrills but none of the danger. The Olympic Hall of Fame, meanwhile, tells the story of the winter games in a display that features over 1,500 exhibits.

❽ Telus World of Science

Though aimed at a young audience, this science complex has plenty to interest older visitors. There are over thirty exhibitions, each exploring different scientific phenomena in a fun and innovative way. The giant book of mirrors, the music area, and the human sundial are three of the most popular attractions, and children can let their imagination run wild in the Creative Kids Museum.

❾ Fort Calgary Historic Park

The North West Mounted Police base at Fort Calgary was established at the confluence of the Bow and Elbow rivers in 1875. Today, the Fort Calgary Historic Park pays tribute to the adventures of this famous police force. Inside the reconstructed living quarters, RCMP veterans recall the trials of life in the wild Canadian west.

Eating and drinking

❶ Murietta's West Coast Grill

The ability to appreciate a good steak is almost a professional obligation in cowboy country, and there is no better place for this than the grill of the Alberta Hotel.

808 First Street SW;
Tel (403) 269 77 07;
Mon–Wed 11.00–24.00,
Thurs 11.00–1.00, Fri–Sat
11.00–2.00, Sun 4.00–22.00.

CALGARY

On the western edge of the prairie, Calgary city is now home to the headquarters of almost all the Canadian oil companies, though its country roots are not forgotten. The black gold has turned this once sleepy cowtown into a thriving hub of glistening corporate palaces.

② River Café
The River Café lies on the bank of the Bow river. Its rustic decor is reminiscent of an old fishing lodge. Situated in the middle of Prince's Island Park, this restaurant serves seasonal Canadian cuisine. The roast pheasant and smoked fish both come highly recommended.
Prince's Island Park;
Tel (403) 261 76 70;
Mon–Fri 11.00–23.00,
Sat–Sun 10.00–23.00.
www.river-cafe.com

③ Tribune
Sitting in this former newspaper newsroom, you could be forgiven for thinking that you have gone back to the early 20th century. The substantial dishes, however, appeal to more contemporary tastes. Highlights include daube of bison and shoulder of lamb.
118 Eighth Avenue SW;
Tel (403) 269 31 60;
Mon–Thurs 17.00–22.00,
Fri–Sat 17.00–23.00.
www.thetribunerestaurant.ca

Accommodation

④ Calgary Marriott Hotel
The Marriott is close to both the Convention Centre and attractions such as the Glenbow Museum. The rooms are generously proportioned.
110 Ninth Avenue SE;
Tel (403) 266 73 31.
www.calgarymarriott.com

⑤ Hotel Arts
This is a sophisticated boutique hotel. The rooms are brightly decorated, the furniture modern, and the beds comfortable. The two hotel restaurants – the Raw Bar and the St Germain – are both excellent.
119 Twelfth Avenue SW;
Tel (403) 266 46 11.
www.hotelarts.ca

⑥ Sandman Hotel
When it comes to reasonably priced accommodation in a central location, the Sandman Hotel is hard to beat. The spacious rooms even have their own kitchenette.
888 Seventh Avenue SW;
Tel (403) 237 86 26.
www.sandmanhotels.com

Shopping

⑦ Alberta Boot Company
If you want to go home looking like a real cowboy, this is the place to buy your cowboy boots. It is the province's only boot manufacturer.
614 Tenth Avenue;
Tel (403) 263 46 05.

⑧ Mountain Equipment Co-op
This outdoor equipment specialist stocks tents, sleeping bags, kayaks, and anoraks at extremely reasonable prices.
830 Tenth Avenue;
Tel (403) 269 24 20.
www.mec.ca

Festivals and events

⑨ Calgary Stampede
Every July, the local cowboys mount their broncos and bulls to show their mettle in the rodeo. Add the program of supporting attractions, and you have an event that no western fan will want to miss.
Stampede Park (17th Avenue/Second Street SE).
www.calgarystampede.com

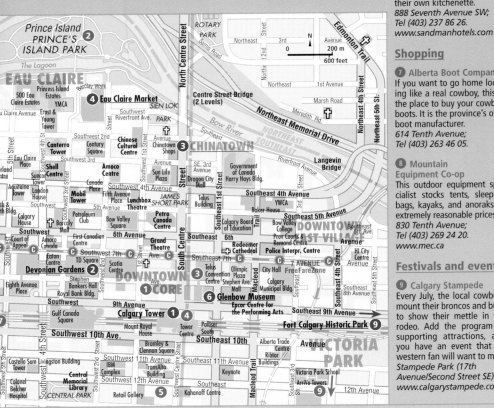

Sights

❶ Royal British Columbia Museum

The realistic displays at this museum bring Canada's natural history vividly to life, from the prehistoric animals of the primeval landscape to the steamy rainforest and the ocean bed. The First Peoples Gallery explores the First Nations cultures before and after the arrival of the Europeans, while in the Modern History Gallery you can wait for a steam train at the turn-of-the-century station, see how lumber from the northern forests was processed at the sawmill, and find out what a grand hotel would have looked like around 1900. There is also a replica of the stern of explorer George Vancouver's ship *Discovery*.

❷ Butchart Gardens

These enchanting gardens date back to 1908, when Jennie Butchart, the wife of a wealthy businessman, planted the Sunken Gardens in an old quarry. Rose, Japanese, and Italian gardens followed. Today, the circular beds in the rose garden contain varieties from all over the world, marble pillars separate the hedges in the Italian garden, and bridges and steps link the exotic flowerbeds in the Japanese garden. In the summer, eco-friendly electric boat trips explore Tod Inlet and Brentwood Bay where you can see seals, otters, and eagles in their natural habitat.

❸ British Columbia Aviation Museum

Housed in a small hangar next to the main airport, the museum documents a century of aviation history. Enthusiasts can see examples of nearly all of Canada's most important aircraft, from the very first plane to take to the Canadian skies, to bombers and helicopters. There are also a number of bush planes, putting the spotlight on the era of Canada's pioneering aviators. Some of the aircraft are original, while others are accurate reproductions.

❹ Craigdarroch Castle

This magnificent building was the brainchild of the millionaire industrialist Robert Dunsmuir. Built in 1889, it bears a strong resemblance to the historic castles of its creator's Scottish homeland. The mix of different architectural styles, including both Romanesque and Gothic elements, as well as the multitude of turrets and oriels and the extensive use of stained glass, is a testament to Dunsmuir's vivid imagination. The castle now houses a museum, including an extremely valuable collection of stained-glass windows. The rooms are furnished with original Victorian furniture.

❺ Parliament Buildings

Erected between 1893 and 1898, the palatial British Columbia Parliament Buildings are located at Victoria's Inner Harbour. They are particularly impressive after dark, when thousands of small bulbs trace the buildings' silhouette in the night sky. The commission to design the Parliament Buildings was won by the British architect Francis Rattenbury when he was just 25 years old. A statue of George Vancouver is mounted over the central dome, while one of Queen Victoria stands on the front lawn.

❻ Crystal Garden

Reminiscent of the design of London's Crystal Palace, the Crystal Garden is also the work of Francis Rattenbury – the architect behind the Parliament Buildings. The Crystal Garden was constructed in 1925 to accommodate the largest saltwater swimming pool in Canada. The pool has since given way to a beautiful tropical garden, inhabited by some rare species of ape as well as all kinds of exotic birds. Large numbers of free-flying butterflies flit about the Conservatory during the summer months.

❼ Helmcken House

One of the oldest houses in British Columbia is situated on Elliot Square. It belonged to John Sebastian Helmcken, a long-serving Hudson's Bay Company surgeon. Helmcken had the house built with local Douglas spruce. Most of the original furniture is still in place and you can also see Helmcken's medical kit. Some of the family's old clothes and shoes are also on display, providing a fascinating glimpse of the fashions of the era. There is also a fun exhibit of antique dolls.

❽ Art Gallery of Greater Victoria

West of Craigdarroch Castle, this modern gallery is home to an impressive collection of important historic and contemporary Canadian art. Works by the famous Canadian artist Emily Carr (1871–1945) form the highlight of the exhibition. Carr captured the melancholy of the coastal region and the daily lives of its First Nation inhabitants perfectly.

Eating and drinking

❶ The Blue Crab Bar and Grill

This fish restaurant is well worth visiting for the incredible view of the bay alone. The fish and shellfish served here are all caught in the local waters, and the seafood chowder and crab sandwiches are particularly tasty.
*146 Kingston Street;
Tel (250) 480 19 99;
6.30–22.00 daily.*

From left: A view of the Fairmont Empress Hotel; the Empress Hotel's Buckingham Meeting Room; a shopping paradise on the many levels of the Bay Centre.

VICTORIA

Victoria remains thoroughly British. Its gabled houses with neat front gardens might be in suburban London, and the old district – or Olde Towne, as the locals call it – feels more like an English city than one on the western coast of the North American continent.

❷ Camille's
David Mincey, the owner of this romantic restaurant, is also a co-founder of the Vancouver Island Farm Cooperative, whose guiding principle is that local food should be prepared with ingredients sourced within a radius of no more than 100 km (62 miles). The innovative menu changes daily.
45 Bastian Square;
Tel (250) 381 34 33;
Tues–Sun 17.30–22.00.
www.camillesrestaurant.com

❸ Canoe
There is more to this rustic brewpub than its own beers. The highlights include tasty burgers, some first-rate fish dishes, and pizzas with unusual toppings like grilled lamb, all elegantly presented. The view over the port towards Johnson Street Bridge is just magnificent.
450 Swift Street;
Tel (250) 361 19 40;
11.00–24.00 daily.
www.canoebrewpub.com

Accommodation

❹ The Fairmont Empress
The Empress recalls the grand hotels of old, and more than a few monarchs have laid their royal heads on its soft pillows. Many of the rooms contain fine antiques, and the most luxurious of the suites feature Victorian-style four-poster beds.
721 Government Street;
Tel (250) 384 81 11.
www.fairmont.com/empress

❺ The Haterleigh Heritage Inn
A bed and breakfast with more than a hint of old England – Queen Victoria herself would surely have appreciated the antique furniture and stained-glass windows. The bathrooms and whirlpools add a welcome touch of contemporary luxury.
243 Kingston Street;
Tel (250) 384 99 95.
www.haterleigh.com

❻ Swans Suite Hotel
Minutes from Victoria's Inner Harbour, this comfortable boutique hotel has its own restaurant and nightclub. The spacious suites each feature a fully equipped kitchen.
506 Pandora Street;
Tel (250) 361 33 10.
www.swanshotel.com

Shopping

❼ The Bay Centre
Clothing, cosmetics, household goods, electronics, and much more, all under one roof at the Bay Centre. The complex takes its name from the legendary Hudson's Bay Company, Canada's oldest department store, which dates back to the 18th century.
Between Government Street and Douglas Street;
Tel (250) 952 56 80.
www.thebaycentre.ca

❽ Alcheringa Gallery
This well-known gallery is the place to buy a wide range of Native North American art. There is a particular emphasis on the carvings and paintings of the coastal First Nations, but Cowichan textiles are also well represented.
665 Fort Street;
Tel (250) 383 82 24.
www.alcheringa-gallery.com

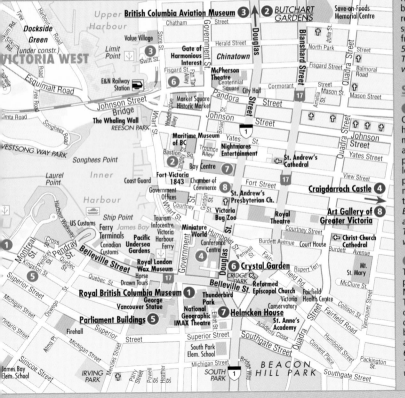

SMART START

ROAD TRIPS

The sheer range of Western Canada's natural beauty has people reaching for superlatives – from the Pacific coast and its offshore islands to the majestic peaks of the Rocky Mountains and the enchantingly beautiful lakes that lie beneath them. The three routes described in this section also take in some of the region's urban areas, including modern and busy regional cities and towns steeped in the country's more recent heritage, but the culture of the First Nation peoples is also very much in evidence here. There is plenty to do en route, from whale watching and hiking to exploring the vineyards and fruit plantations of the sunny Okanagan Valley.

Sights

① Prince Rupert
Known as the "City of Rainbows", Prince George is a deep, ice-free natural port on the north-west coast, and the focal point of the Yellowhead Region economy. An industrial city and regional transport hub, the port is the city's main attraction for visitors. Wooden walkways line the water's edge beside the moorings for vessels and tempting seafood restaurants – all serving freshly caught fish. On a good day, the view out to sea is superb.

② Terrace
Continue along the route beside the shores of the local lakes, and follow the Skeena river to the small community of Terrace. It lies in the shadow of Sleeping Beauty Mountain, which towers over both the town and the surrounding wilderness. Heading south, Highway 25 leads on to Lakelse Provincial Park, a romantic landscape with lakes and rivers that are an angler's paradise. Nass Road culminates at one of northern Canada's most beautiful areas.

③ New Hazelton
East of Prince Rupert lie the Hazeltons – New Hazelton, South Hazelton and Hazelton. In South Hazelton, the road turns north to cross Bulkley River. The area beneath the modern suspension bridge was, some 4,000 years ago, the location of the First Nation settlement of Hagwilget. Passing a First Nation chapel, you reach 'Ksan, a reconstruction of a Gitksan village, its houses overshadowed by huge totem poles. A little farther up the road, Hazelton is an old pioneer town with covered walkways and restored heritage buildings. Follow the Bulkley River into Moricetown Canyon, where you can watch people fishing for salmon. Harpoons are hurled into the bubbling water and the fish then pulled back to shore.

Eating and drinking

① Waterfront Restaurant
Situated beside the port, this supremely elegant restaurant serves mostly seafood – in all its different varieties. The salmon, which is all sourced from local waters, is first rate, and the halibut and scallops are delicious culinary treats.
222 First Avenue West (in the Crest Hotel), Prince Rupert;
Tel (250) 624 67 71,
6.30–22.00 daily.
www.cresthotel.bc.ca

② Waddling Duck Restaurant
The fireplace and the rustic decor give this restaurant the atmosphere of a British pub. The steaks and burgers are well up to standard, and there is an all-you-can-eat buffet at lunchtime.
1157 Fifth Avenue, Prince George;
Tel (250) 561 55 50;
11.00–22.00 daily.

Accommodation

③ Crest Hotel
Set high on a promontory above the Inner Harbour, this hotel has splendid views out over the bay and the surrounding mountains. You can relax in the steam room or in the outdoor hot tub on the terrace in the hotel's fitness center.
222 First Avenue West, Prince Rupert;
Tel (250) 624 67 71.
www.cresthotel.bc.ca

④ Goldcap Travelodge
An unusually reasonable and centrally located hotel which scores top marks for its spacious guest rooms, each of which has its own fridge and – for an extra supplement – microwave. Family friendly and part of the well-known hotel chain.
1458 Seventh Avenue, Prince George;
Tel (250) 563 06 66.
www.travelodgeprince george.com

From left: Skyscrapers and advertising banners on Calgary's Stephen Avenue; a cute pika in one of Canada's national parks; drive for miles through the stunning scenery of the Rockies.

FROM THE COAST TO THE ROCKY MOUNTAINS

If you really want to experience the Canadian wilderness, hire a motor home and catch the ferry from Vancouver Island to Prince Rupert. From there, take the Yellowhead Highway to Prince George. Passing Mount Robson, continue on through Jasper and Banff, the two big national parks in the Canadian Rockies, making Calgary your final destination.

❹ Smithers
A surprise awaits visitors from Switzerland in the town of Smithers (the residents are known as "Smithereens"), where the town's symbol, a statue of a Swiss alpenhorn player, looms large at the end of Main Street. The Alpine theme is echoed in the flags of the Swiss cantons that fly from

❺ Prince George
Named after the English king George III, Prince George lies right in the middle of British Columbia at the confluence of the Nechako and Fraser rivers. The Fort George trading post was originally established here by the explorer Simon Fraser. Now an important commercial hub, the town has a lively cultural scene, from art galleries to the Fraser Fort George Regional Museum and Prince George Symphony Orchestra.

❻ Bowron Lake Provincial Park
The park is a wildlife sanctuary with hiking, boating, camping, and fishing facilities.

Canoeists come from all over the world to paddle the Bowron Lake Canoe Circuit, 11 lakes connected by a system of streams and portages to form a 116-km (72-mile) circuit that takes around a week to complete. The starting point, Kibbee Lake, connects with Indianpoint Lake. From here, you paddle across the Isaac Lake and Isaac River to the McCleary, Lanezi, Sandy, and Unna Lakes.

❼ Mount Robson Provincial Park
Usually hidden behind thick cloud, Mount Robson – British Columbia's tallest mountain (3,954 m/12,972 feet) – towers above the valleys of the beautiful park that bears its name. The First Nations called it "Yuh-hai-has-hun", meaning "mountain of the spiral road".

❽ Jasper National Park
Jasper is Canada's largest national park. Over 800 lakes lie within its boundaries, fed by the surrounding glaciers. Maligne

Lake is one of the most photographed of the entire Rocky Mountains, while Lac Beauvert is a jade green glacial lake. Follow the hiking trail to the top of Whistler Mountain or take the mountain railway.

❾ Columbia Icefields
The 230-km (143-mile) Icefield Parkway is a scenic route through wild mountain landscape, with magnificent massifs and shimmering glaciers. The route is named after the nearby ice features such as the vast Columbia Icefield that feeds eight major glaciers. Fitted with extra soft tyres, snowcoaches allow visitors onto the icefield and the glaciers in summer.

❿ Banff National Park
With secluded valleys, crystal clear rivers, magnificent glaciers, and high, snow-covered mountains, Banff National Park is a place of unspoiled natural beauty – especially in the hinterland. Apart from the scenery, the hot springs are the park's biggest attraction. The resort of Banff lies beneath Cascade Mountain.

⓫ Calgary
Almost all of Canada's oil companies are based in Calgary, an old prairie town that has been transformed into a major city by the oil boom. At 191 m (627 feet), Calgary Tower has the best views of the city and the nearby Rocky Mountains.

the windows of Main Street's timber-framed buildings. But that is not all that Smithers has to offer. Follow the gravel track that leads out to the west of town to reach the Twin Falls and the craggy rocks of Glacier Gulch.

Dawson Creek 2499 △ Sentinel Pk.
Parsnip R.
2286 △
Willow River
Red Deer Cr.
Yellowhead Highway
Sinclair Mills
Kakwa Prov. Park
Kakwa R.
Mt. Sir Alexander
Penny
3274 △ Rocky
Grande Cache
Crescent Spur
Isaac Lake
16
2653 △
McBride
Willmore Wilderness Provincial Park
Barkerville
❻ Bowron Lake Provincial Park
Fraser R.
Mt. Robson 3954 △ Mt. Robson Provincial Park
Edmonton
Hinton
❼
16
Likely
Tête Jaune Cache
Jasper Lake
Pocahontas
Quesnel Lake
Valemount
Maligne Canyon/Lake
Horsefly
2548 △
Whistler Mt.
2181 △
Jasper
Cadomin
❽ Jasper National Park
Wells Gray Prov. Park
Murtle Lake
Athabasca Falls
Mountains
Nordegg
Blue River
3219 △
Icefield Parkway
Panamericana
Mica Creek
Columbia Icefield ❾
Abraham Lake
Rocky Mtn. House
Kamloops
Avola
3747 △ Mt. Columbia
93
Forest
Saskatchewan River Crossing
Caroline
Columbia Reach
3533 △
Kinbasket Lake
3628 △
Kicking Horse Pass (1627)
Innisfail
Edmonton
Olds
Wimborne
Glacier National Park
Yoho Nat. Park
Three Hills
(1327)
Donald
Golden
Cascade Mt. 2998
Carstairs
Rogers Pass
Lake Louise
Linden
Sasskatoon
Revelstoke
Leanchoil
93
Banff National Park ❿
Banff
Airdrie
Kootenay Nat. Park
Seebe
Beiseker
Harrogate
Banff Springs Hotel
1
95
Radium Hot Springs
Mt. Assiniboine 3618 △
Reserve
Priddis
⓫ Calgary
Hussar
Mt. Farnham 3457 △
Ta Ta Creek
Lethbridge
Gleichen
1
Regina

Western Canada 27

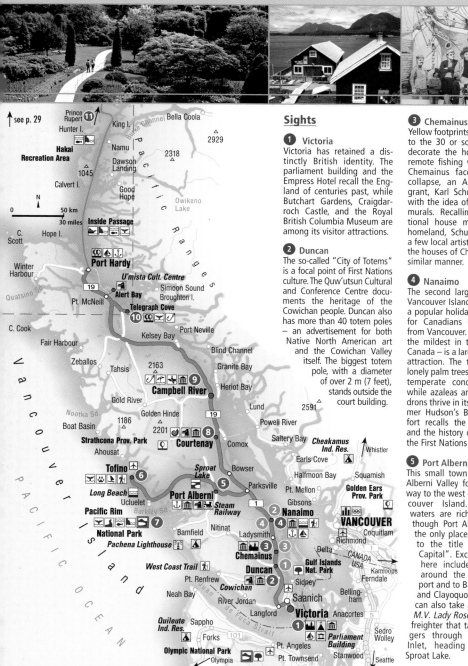

↑ see p. 29

Sights

1 Victoria

Victoria has retained a distinctly British identity. The parliament building and the Empress Hotel recall the England of centuries past, while Butchart Gardens, Craigdarroch Castle, and the Royal British Columbia Museum are among its visitor attractions.

2 Duncan

The so-called "City of Totems" is a focal point of First Nations culture. The Quw'utsun Cultural and Conference Centre documents the heritage of the Cowichan people. Duncan also has more than 40 totem poles – an advertisement for both Native North American art and the Cowichan Valley itself. The biggest totem pole, with a diameter of over 2 m (7 feet), stands outside the court building.

3 Chemainus

Yellow footprints lead the way to the 30 or so murals that decorate the houses of this remote fishing village. When Chemainus faced economic collapse, an Austrian emigrant, Karl Schulz, came up with the idea of painting the murals. Recalling the traditional house murals of his homeland, Schulz persuaded a few local artists to decorate the houses of Chemainus in a similar manner.

4 Nanaimo

The second largest town on Vancouver Island, Nanaimo is a popular holiday destination for Canadians coming over from Vancouver. Its climate – the mildest in the whole of Canada – is a large part of the attraction. The town's seven lonely palm trees testify to the temperate conditions here, while azaleas and rhododendrons thrive in its parks. A former Hudson's Bay Company fort recalls the pioneer era and the history of trade with the First Nations peoples.

5 Port Alberni

This small town in the rural Alberni Valley forms a gateway to the west coast of Vancouver Island. The local waters are rich in salmon, though Port Alberni is not the only place to lay claim to the title of "Salmon Capital". Excursions from here include boat trips around the picturesque port and to Barkley Sound and Clayoquot Sound. You can also take a trip on the *M.V. Lady Rose* – a historic freighter that takes passengers through the Alberni Inlet, heading west past Sproat Lake.

From left: A pleasant stroll through Victoria's Butchart Gardens; fishing huts and canoe hire in Tofino; a mural painted on a house in Chemainus.

EXPLORING VANCOUVER ISLAND

Vancouver Island is one of the world's last remaining natural paradises. This route begins in Victoria, the capital of British Columbia, and continues along the island's western coast – with its Native North American cultural attractions and romantic ports – through small towns and fishing villages to Prince Rupert.

Eating and drinking

1 Equinox Cafe
This pleasant restaurant in central Duncan is – in its own words – an invitation to "Taste the Cowichan Valley". Ingredients are all locally sourced, and the fish is especially good.
79 Station Street, Duncan;
Tel (250) 746 64 52;
Tues 10.30–15.00,
Wed–Fri 10.30–15.00 and
17.00–21.30, Sat 10.00–15.00
and 17.00–21.30.
www.equinoxcafe.com

2 Wesley Street Cafe
The chef at this top-quality restaurant in the heart of Nanaimo is famous for his innovative cooking.
321 Wesley Street, Nanaimo;
Tel (250) 753 60 57;
Tues–Fri 11.30–14.30
and 17.30–22.00,
Sat 12.00–14.30,
Sun 11.30–14.30.
www.wesleycafe.com

Accommodation

3 Bird Song Cottage Bed & Breakfast
With its piano, bird-themed decor, and antique-laden guest rooms, the interior is reminiscent of a 19th-century Victorian lodging house. It is close to the beach, shops, and restaurants.
9909 Maple Street,
Chemainus;
Tel (250) 246 99 10.
www.birdsongcottage.com

4 Coast Bastion Inn
Part of a chain, this contemporary style hotel is notable for its central location (close to the BC Ferry Terminal) and spacious rooms, with many extras.
11 Bastion Street, Nanaimo;
Tel. (250) 753 66 01.
www.coasthotels.com

6 Tofino
The fishing village of Tofino is characterized by quaint houses and cozy inns. Whale watching is a popular pastime here. Around 20,000 gray whales pass this section of coast between March and May each year, stopping off for a while in Clayoquot Sound. There are a number of companies offering whale-watching trips.

7 Pacific Rim National Park
Established in 1970, this is the oldest national park on Canada's west coast. It protects the wild landscape north of Ucluelet and also takes in the approximately 100 islands of the Broken Group archipelago in Barkley Sound, which are accessible only by boat or plane. The West Coast Trail, from Barnfield to Port Renfrew, can be reached from Port Alberni.

8 Courtenay
Recently named by a Canadian magazine as "the most charming small town on Vancouver Island", Courtenay is a romantic town on the island's east coast. Largely dependent on fishing and tourism, it lies within what was once the territory of the K'omok people.

9 Campbell River
Campbell River also claims to be the "Salmon Capital of the World". Salmon making their way toward the inland rivers in search of spawning grounds swim past the town's saltwater fishing pier. The chinook salmon caught here can weigh as much as 30 lbs (14 kg).

10 Telegraph Cove
The painted houses of Telegraph Cove are built on stilts and linked by wooden walkways. In spring and autumn, whale watching in the Queen Charlotte Strait is a popular activity.

11 Prince Rupert
Passing fjords, bays, and channels, the Inside Passage (a coastal route between the islands and mainland) runs from Vancouver Island up to Alaska. Local ferries setting off from Port Hardy sail through some spectacular scenery, and whales and dolphins frequently swim alongside the boat. The port of Prince Rupert marks the end of the route.

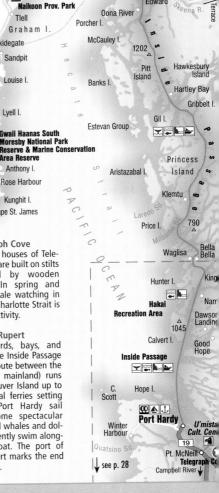

↓ see p. 28

Sights

❶ Vancouver

Situated on the picturesque Pacific coast, Vancouver is one of the world's most attractive cities. Protected from the Pacific Ocean by Vancouver Island, it is Canada's third largest city and the venue of the 2010 winter Olympics. Vancouver's citizens come from a wide range of ethnic and religious backgrounds, the multicultural nature of the city's society being evident in many of its districts.

❷ Whistler Blackcomb

The Whistler Blackcomb Ski Resort, approximately 120 km (75 miles) north of Vancouver, takes in the slopes of Mounts Whistler and Blackcomb. The superb range of slopes caters for skiers from novice to professional level. Mount Blackcomb features the steepest piste in North America. The ski lifts are right next to the hotels. The area is also a popular summer destination for mountain bikers and walkers.

❸ Lillooet

In the days of the Fraser Canyon gold rush, which took place in the mid-19th century, Lillooet was one of the largest settlements in Canada. Until the construction of the Cariboo Wagon Road, it was the starting point of the long trek to the northern gold fields – a journey that took weeks to complete. A milestone in central Lillooet still marks

the beginning of the trail. The Bridge of 23 Camels commemorates another, rather curious episode of gold rush history, when camels were used to transport heavy loads to Barkerville. The shops, bars, and saloons of Main Street still form the heart of the town today. In 1981, the Hotel Victoria was rebuilt in the style of the original hotel on this site.

❹ Kamloops

Not far from the lake of the same name, the town of Kamloops lies at the confluence of two branches of the Thompson River. It owes its rapid growth to the gold rush that took place along the Fraser River and the construction of the Canadian Pacific Railway. Today, sport plays an important part in the life of Kamloops – the city has excellent

golf, riding, and mountain-biking facilities. The nearby Sun Peaks resort offers superb downhill and cross-country skiing, while the fast currents of the Thompson River attract white-water rafting enthusiasts.

❺ Salmon Arm

The town of Salmon Arm calls itself the "Northern Gateway to the Okanagan". It began life as a camp for construction workers on the Canadian Pacific Railway, but is now primarily dependent on tourism. It lies at the heart of a paradise for water sports enthusiasts formed by the four large lakes (Shuswap Lake, Adams Lake, Mara Lake, and Mabel Lake), and it also benefits

from an extremely mild climate. Though it is the region's largest town, Salmon Arm has maintained its rural character – despite the influx of tourists who come to sun themselves on the beaches every summer.

❻ Penticton

It was Penticton's Salish inhabitants who gave the town its name, meaning "a place to stay forever". The Salish recognized the value of the town's location in the fertile Okanagan Valley long before the first vines were brought here in 1859. The area is now home to a large number of excellent vineyards and fruit plantations. Thanks to the mild climate, conditions are perfect for both.

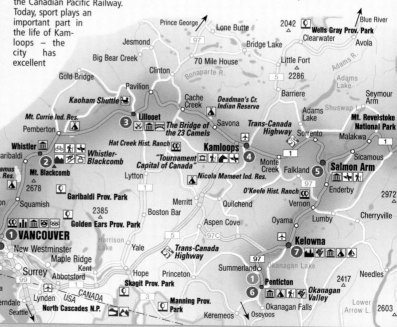

From left: A classic Cadillac, at home on the highway; a Native North American temple with totem pole in Vancouver's Stanley Park; the Minto Manor Bed & Breakfast in Revelstoke.

THE TRANS-CANADA HIGHWAY

Follow the Trans-Canada Highway from Vancouver to Lake Louise in Banff National Park across some spectacularly beautiful landscape. The road passes giant mountains and glaciers like those in Glacier National Park, and glacial lakes of an intense green. A trip to the vineyards of the fertile Okanagan Valley makes an enjoyable detour.

➐ Kelowna
Kelowna, the largest town on Lake Okanagan, also boasts numerous wine estates. The vast lake and mild climate mean Kelowna is primarily a summer holiday destination with a relaxed atmosphere, attracting large numbers of tourists to its beaches, yachting marina, shops, restaurants, and green parks.

➑ Mount Revelstoke National Park
This national park, established in 1914, covers 260 sq km (100 sq miles) of the Clachnacudainn Range of the Columbia Mountains. It takes in several glaciers, including the Clachnacudainn Icefield. A 26-km (16-mile) road leads up to the mountain meadows of

Mount Revelstoke, which rises to 1,938 m (6,358 feet). In summer, at higher altitudes, the meadows form a carpet of bright flowers, with a spectacular view over a panorama of glaciers and snow-covered slopes. The Columbia Mountains are among the most imposing in Canada.

➒ Rogers Pass
Between the towns of Revelstoke and Golden, the Trans-Canada Highway follows the 1,330-m (4,364-foot) high Rogers Pass through the Selkirk Mountains. The pass lies within the Glacier National Park, which was established in 1886 and includes over 400 glaciers. The best views are from the Abbot Ridge and Avalanche Crest trails, while the Copperstain trail leads to the meadows of Bald Mountain. The Rogers Pass visitor information office is just off the highway.

➓ Golden
Yoho National Park is a stone's throw from the town of Golden, just off the Trans-Canada Highway. The park is a patchwork of jagged mountain peaks, deep ravines, thick cedar forests, and raging waterfalls such as the Wapta Falls and Takakkaw Falls. At a height of 384 m (1,260 feet), the latter is the second highest waterfall in Western Canada. Branching off the Trans-Canada Highway, a side road leads to the green waters of Emerald Lake. A hiking trail encircles the whole lake.

⑪ Lake Louise
Set in the magnificent mountain landscape of Banff National Park, Lake Louise is around 5 km (3 miles) from the Trans-Canada Highway. Emerald green thanks to the fine rock (glacial) flour carried into the lake by water melting from the surrounding glaciers, it is positively overrun with tourists in high season, but you can escape the masses by following one of the hiking trails.

Eating and drinking

➊ Granny Bogners
Popular with the locals, this restaurant focuses on hearty fare – including one or two traditional, or even slightly old-fashioned dishes. The best tables are in the garden.
302 West Eckhardt Avenue, Penticton;
Tel. (250) 493 27 11;
Tues–Sun 17.30–21.30.

➋ Eagle's Eye Restaurant
You take the ski gondola to this restaurant, famed as Canada's highest restaurant (altitude 2,410 m/7,907 feet). The meat dishes are especially good and the fish is also excellent.
Dyke Road, Golden,
Tel (250) 344 86 26;
summer 10.00–22.00 daily,
low season Mon–Thurs
10.00–15.30, Fri–Sun
10.00–21.00, closed
mid-Oct–mid-Dec
and mid-Apr–mid-May.
www.kickinghorseresort.com

Accommodation

➌ Minto Manor Bed & Breakfast
This historic manor house has retained much of its original Victorian charm. The rooms are generously proportioned.
815 MacKenzie Avenue, Revelstoke;
Tel. (250) 837 93 37.
www.mintomanor.com

➍ Alpine Meadows Lodge
Situated high above Golden, this pleasant lodge enjoys a fantastic view over Glacier National Park. The guest rooms are rustic and cosy.
717 Elk Road, Golden;
Tel (250) 344 58 63.
www.alpinemeadowslodge.com

THE HIGHLIGHTS

BRITISH COLUMBIA
VANCOUVER AND
SURROUNDINGS

Surrounded by the picturesque bays of the Pacific and the majestic mountains of the Coast Range, the jewel that is Vancouver lies on the western mainland and blends seamlessly into the virtually untouched natural landscape of British Columbia. The city boasts impressive futuristic buildings such as Canada Place and historic quarters like Gastown, and is also home to a large number of museums and art galleries. Its Chinatown is atmospheric and exuberant, with a hint of the exotic. And the hustle and bustle of the shopping district of Granville Island can be contrasted with a relaxing visit to the extensive Stanley Park.

1 Downtown

2 Gastown

3 Chinatown

4 False Creek

5 Granville Island

6 English Bay

7 Stanley Park

8 Fort Langley

9 Garibaldi
Provincial Park

Hakai Recreation
Area 1045
Calvert I.
Dawson Lan

Queen

Charlotte

Rivers Inle

Queen Charlotte St

Sound

580

Hope

Channel

C. Scott

Bear l

Port Hardy

YZT

Winter Harbour

1272

Port Ali

Quatsino Sd.

C. Cook

Kyuqu

Fair Ha

Vancouver Islan

P A C I F I C   O C E A N

N

0   40 km

20 miles

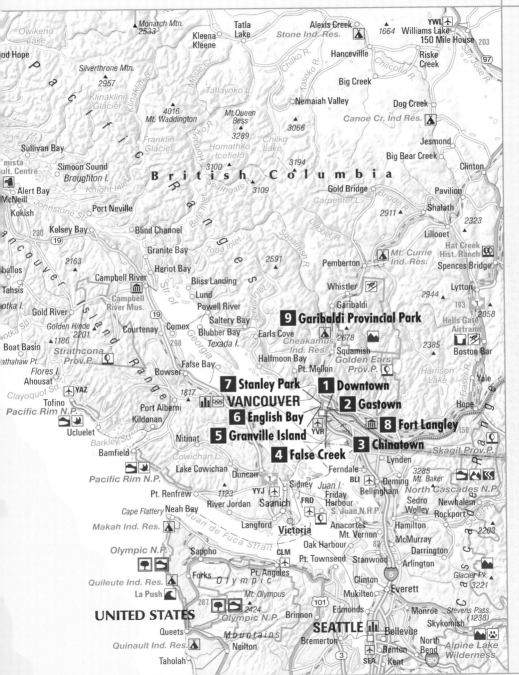

Monarch Mtn.
2533
Tatla Lake
Kleena Kleene
Stone Ind. Res.
Alexis Creek
1664
Williams Lake
YWL
150 Mile House
203
Owikeno Lake
od Hope
Silverthrone Mtn.
2957
Hanceville
Riske Creek
97
Klinaklini Glacier
4016
Mt. Waddington
Mt.Queen Bess
3289
Big Creek
3066
Nemaiah Valley
Dog Creek
Jesmond
Clinton
Sullivan Bay
Franklin Glacier
Homathko Icefield
Chilko Lake
3194
Canoe Cr. Ind. Res.
Big Bear Creek
mista
ult. Centre
Simoon Sound
Broughton I.
3100
3109
B r i t i s h   C o l u m b i a
Gold Bridge
Carpenter L.
Pavilion
Shalath
Alert Bay
McNeill
Kokish
Knight Inlet
Port Neville
2911
Lillooet
2323
Kelsey Bay
19
230
Blind Channel
Granite Bay
Toba Inlet
2591
Mt. Currie Ind. Res.
Hat Creek Hist. Ranch
Spences Bridge
2163
Heriot Bay
Pemberton
ballos
Campbell River
Bliss Landing
Lund
Whistler
2944
193
Lytton
2058
Tahsis
otka I.
Gold River
Campbell River Mus.
19
Powell River
Saltery Bay
Garibaldi
9 Garibaldi Provincial Park
Hells Gate Airtram
Golden Hinde
2201
1186
Courtenay
Comox
298
Blubber Bay
Texada I.
Earls Cove
Cheakamus Ind. Res.
2678
Squamish
2385
Boston Bar
Boat Basin
athaw Pt.
Strathcona Prov.P.
Halfmoon Bay
Pt. Mellon
Golden Ears Prov.P.
Harrison Lake
Flores I.
Ahousat
Bowser
False Bay
YAZ
Yale
Clayoquot So.
Tofino
Pacific Rim N.P.
1817
7 Stanley Park
VANCOUVER
1 Downtown
Hope
Port Alberni
6 English Bay
2 Gastown
Ucluelet
Kildonan
YVR
8 Fort Langley
150
Barkley Sd.
Nitinat
5 Granville Island
3 Chinatown
Skagit Prov.P.
Bamfield
Cowichan L.
4 False Creek
Lynden
Pacific Rim N.P.
Lake Cowichan
Duncan
Ferndale
3285
Mt. Baker
North Cascades N.P.
Pt. Renfrew
Neah Bay
1123
Sidney
Juan I.
BLI
Deming
Cape Flattery
River Jordan
YYJ
Saanich
Friday Harbour
Bellingham
Sedro Wolley
Newhalem
Rockport
2203
Makah Ind. Res.
Langford
FRD
S. Juan N.H.P.
Hamilton
Olympic N.P.
Sappho
Victoria
Anacortes
Mt. Vernon
McMurray
Darrington
Quileute Ind. Res.
Forks
Oak Harbour
Stanwood
Arlington
Glacier Pk.
3221
La Push
Olympic
Pt. Angeles
CLM
Pt. Townsend
5
287
Mt. Olympus
2424
Clinton
Mukilteo
Everett
UNITED STATES
Olympic N.P.
Brinnon
101
Edmonds
Monroe
Stevens Pass (1238)
Skykomish
Queets
M o u n t a i n s
SEATTLE
Bellevue
North Bend
Alpine Lake Wilderness
Quinault Ind. Res.
Neilton
Bremerton
Renton
3
90
Taholah
SEA
Kent

INFO Capilano Suspension Bridge

The view from the Vancouver Lookout (below), a viewing platform on the roof of the Harbour Centre, extends past the skyscrapers downtown to False Creek. In the harbour (right), ocean liners and freighters from eastern Asia pass formidable cliffs as they put in to dock.

The suspension bridge across the Capilano River was built in 1889 and leads to a park. Attractions include totem poles and the Treetops trail where you can walk suspended 30 m (100 feet) above the ground.
Capilano Road; Tel (604) 985 74 74; May–Sept 9.00–20.00, Dec 9.00–21.00, otherwise 9.00–18.00.

Vancouver is a busy Canadian metropolis. Its heart beats loudest downtown, on Robson Square and Robson Street, the legendary shopping thoroughfare named after the German immigrants who once dominated this area of the city. Today, its ethnic diversity is remarkable. A wealth of small stores, fancy boutiques, markets, and restaurants entice visitors through their doors. Opposite the Pacific Centre, a two-level concrete landscape with pretty flowerbeds, sparkling waterfalls, and fountains has been transformed into a blossoming city oasis. The historic art gallery is reflected in the glass façades of the office buildings. The most eye-catching of these is Canada Place, the futuristic commercial complex in Burrard Inlet. Huge teflon-coated white plastic sails extend over the complex forming a striking skyline and landmark. Canada Place houses the Vancouver Convention and Exhibition Centre and is also the region's main cruise ship terminal. (See p.18)

Gastown begins just behind the Harbour Centre. The most historic part of the old town, its side streets are perfect for a leisurely stroll (right). Today, the Steam Clock (below) is powered by steam fed through underground pipes from the district heating grid. It chimes the hour with whistles rather than bells.

TIP Angel of Vancouver

The cheerful art of Angel Paint was born in Vancouver over 20 years ago. Jackie Haliburton's hand-painted fashions for children and adults, vibrant accessories, wall hangings, and wearable artworks are world-renowned.
No 2 Powell; Tel (604) 681 09 47; 11.00–18.00 daily.

Vancouver's oldest buildings are found in Gastown, the city's restored old quarter. It was established by the British settler John ("Gassy" Jack) Deighton, who arrived here in September 1867 with a canoe full of barrels of whisky and opened the first saloon in what is now Maple Tree Square. Taking advantage of the Burrard Inlet location, a seaport grew up here and soon developed into an important base for trade. It was incorporated as the City of Vancouver in 1886; much of it burned down in the same year but was quickly rebuilt. Gastown has been a listed area since 1971. Shrewd businesspeople restored the historic buildings and created a district with a nostalgic feel with boutiques, restaurants, antique shops, and street cafés. The steam-operated clock on the corner of Cambie Street and Water Street, which emits white plumes of steam every 15 minutes, has become the symbol of the new Gastown. (See p.18)

STEAM CLOCK
T-SHIRTS & SOUVENIRS
Canadian Gifts
Hockey Jerseys
Smoked Salmon
Film

ANIE BABIES

321 WA
ORIA PIZ

E MA
FUDGE

TIP Chinatown Night Market

The Millenium Gate (below, left) marks the western entrance to Vancouver's Chinatown. A participant dressed in traditional costume in a parade in Chinatown (below, right), where old and new and East and West go hand in hand. Nature's timeless beauty in the Dr. Sun Yat-sen Chinese Garden (right).

The night market in Chinatown is one of Vancouver's summer highlights. There are countless stalls selling Asian arts and crafts along with clothes, accessories, and novelties, as well as food.
Keefer Street/Main Street; 14 May–5 Sept, Fri–Sun 18.30–23.00.

After San Francisco and New York, Vancouver's Chinatown is the third largest Chinese settlement on the American continent. Vivid neon signs in Chinese characters and building entrances decorated with fanciful dragons and pagoda-style roofs characterize the district. The Chinese accounted for a significant proportion of Canada's original settlers, and are still among the dominating immigrant ethnic groups today. As a symbol of the bond between the Canadians and Chinese, the Dr. Sun Yat-sen Chinese Garden was created by Chinese craftsmen from Suzhou. It is named after the revolutionary and politician Sun Yat-sen (1866–1925), considered the "Father of modern China", who visited Vancouver on several occasions. Chinatown hosts various events every year, including the Chinatown Festival in August, the Mid-Autumn Moon Festival, and the Winter Solstice Lantern Processions. (See p.18)

INFO False Creek Ferries

The skyline on the eastern bank of False Creek with the striking geodesic dome of the TELUS World of Science museum – Telus is an Alberta-based national telecommunications company, which donated money to the museum. False Creek with the multi-lane Granville Street Bridge in the backround (right).

Electric boats have been a city sight for 30 years, offering everything from mini-cruises to sightseeing tours. Romantic sunset trips are particularly popular and must be booked in advance.
Sunset Beach, Davie Street, Science World, Quayside Marina; May–Sept; Tel (604) 684 77 81.

"False Creek" is the inlet that separates downtown Vancouver from the rest of the city and is connected to the Burrard Peninsula by three bridges. It was named by George Henry Richards, who surveyed the area in around 1859. During World War I, the Great Northern Railway and Canadian Northern Pacific Railway filled in the easternmost part of the creek to create space for their railyards. A large sawmill and storage depots were also built. False Creek was the industrial heart of the city until the 1950s, when its importance declined. In the 1970s a city development program was conceived, reinvigorating and transforming the area into an attractive residential and commercial hub. In the 1980s Expo 86 provided further impetus for new building work. The creek is also the venue for the Canadian International Dragon Boat Festival, which has been taking place here since 1986 and attracts huge crowds. (See p.18)

Numerous restaurants cater to passers-by as they stroll along the promenade at False Creek, while high above cars race along Granville Street Bridge (below). Stock up with delicious fresh fruit and vegetables at Granville Island Public Market (right). The large houseboats in the harbor are a typical sight (below, inset).

TIP Public Market

The daily market is a place of culinary pilgrimage, with over one hundred stands selling all kinds of fresh and homemade produce. Foodies might like to book a place on a chef-guided tour of Edible British Columbia.
Tel (6 04) 812 96 60; Johnston Street, 9.00–19.00 daily.

This island is located beneath the southern end of Granville Street Bridge, which links Vancouver's downtown with the southern suburbs. A former industrial district, in the 1970s its storage depots and factory buildings were restored and divided up into small restaurants, boutiques, and shops. Painters, potters, and other craftspeople set up studios and workshops, and a host of small art galleries and various performance venues also sprang up. Buskers often perform in front of the Market Courtyard. As an experiment in town planning, Granville Island has been held up as a successful example in Canada and elsewhere. The island became a popular tourist attraction and now draws several million visitors a year. Concerts and musicals are staged here, and the Granville Island Public Market stocks a sumptuous range of fresh fruit and vegetables as well as exquisite specialties. (See p.18)

The Museum of Anthropology is the main attraction on the campus of the University of British Columbia (UBC). Over 30 totem poles measuring up to 10 m (33 feet) in height are exhibited here (below). (Below, inset): Also on display in the museum, which was designed by Arthur Erickson, is *The Raven and the First Man* by Bill Reid (1920–98). The fountain in front of the Vancouver Museum features the crab that, according to legend, watches over the city's port.

THE MUSUEMS OF VANCOUVER

The citizens of Vancouver feel especially indebted to the history of Western Canada: the art and culture of the Coastal First Nations and the lives of the first immigrants are documented and commemorated in a number of museums here. One such is the Museum of Vancouver, situated in Vanier Park to the west of Granville Island. Its design is reminis-cent of the conical head-dresses made from cedar bark once worn by the First Nations. The largest munici-pal museum in the province, Vancouver Museum docu-ments the history of the Pacific Northwest Coast First Nations, from the first set-tlements to the present. Right next door, at the H. R. MacMillan Space Centre, visitors can learn about the history of space exploration. The most important exhibit in the Maritime Museum, also situated in Vanier Park, is the restored *St Roch*, the two-masted schooner of the Royal Canadian Mounted Police on which Henry Larsen first navigated the Northwest Passage between the Pacific and Atlantic Oceans from west to east (that is, starting from the Pacific), between 1940 and 1942. The Museum of Anthropology, on the Cam-pus of the University of British Columbia, is home to one of the best and most important art collections of the Northwest Coast First Nations, and includes totem poles and historic carvings as well as contemporary art. A Haida Indian house stands in front of the museum.

INFO Fantastic fireworks

Situated directly to the west of the inner city, English Bay is part of the Strait of Georgia, a stretch of water that all Vancouver-bound ships have to cross (below). The lights of the nearby suburb of Kitsilano (known locally as "Kits") as seen from English Bay Beach (right).

At the end of July each year, the best fireworks artists in the world come to the Olympics of pyrotechnics in Vancouver to light up the night sky for four days of symphonies of synchronized rockets and music.

Vancouver Fireworks Festival Society; Tel (604) 642 68 35.

Located to the west of the inner city, English Bay opens out into Burrard Inlet and False Creek. English Bay Beach is popular with the city's residents who come here to relax, swim, and watch the sun set from one of its many street cafés and inviting bistros. A pathway for cyclists and inline skaters runs along the Vancouver Seawall, which hugs the shoreline between Stanley Park and West Point Grey, one of the westernmost city districts with a large student population. In the 1890s the beach was only accessible via trails through the bush. It was divided into two by a large rock, with women restricted to one side and men the other – mixed bathing was not allowed. Today, the bay's calendar of events includes the Polar Bear Swim on 1 January, when Polar Bear Swim Club members brave the icy waters, and the HSBC Celebration of Light, held on the beach in summer – four nights of fabulous firework displays with music.

THE HIGHLIGHTS: BRITISH COLUMBIA: VANCOUVER AND SURROUNDINGS

Highlights of Stanley Park include the Vancouver Aquarium. White or Beluga whales, which can reach a length of up to 6.5 m (21 feet), impress visitors to the aquarium (below). Canadian icons: intricate totem poles carved by the members of various Northwest Coast First Nations tribes (right).

INFO Vancouver Aquarium

The Marine Science Centre works with Canada's largest aquarium to protect marine life, and every visit supports the organization's work. Over 70,000 creatures can be seen here. Try the 4D Experience, a film show with extra sensory effects.
845 Avison Way; Tel (604) 659 35 52; 9.30–17.00 daily.

Named after Lord Stanley, the Governor General of Canada from 1888 to 1893, this city park covers an area of 400 ha (988 acres) of former First Nations territory. Containing around half a million trees, much of the park is forested. The centuries-old redwoods, hemlock trees, and Douglas firs in the western part of this park escaped the axes of the lumberjacks because they were identified as being suitable to provide the wood for repairs to the ships of the British naval fleet, and so were protected for that purpose. Also, Vancouver's city council, newly formed in 1886, had the foresight to order that the land be converted into a park and installed a network of roads. It had previously been used as a strategically located military reserve. The park was designated a National Historic Site in 1988 and is popular with cyclists, inline skaters, and joggers, who run along the seawall, and people who just come here to get closer to nature. (See p.18)

The fort was originally built, in 1827, a few miles downriver from its present location, on the bank of Fraser River. It was moved to its current location 12 years later. Right: The Community Hall. Reconstructed rooms, including an original 1840s storehouse, in the Fort Langley National Historic Site (below).

INFO Langley Centennial Museum

The Museum and the National Exhibition Centre document the history of the founding fathers of British Columbia. There is a large collection of historic photographs.
9135 King Street, Fort Langley, V1M 2S2; Tel (604) 888 39 22; Mon–Sat 10.00–16.45, Sun 13.00–16.45.

About 40 km (25 miles) east of Vancouver, the Fort Langley National Historic Site is on the location of a former Hudson's Bay Company trading post. Today Fort Langley is an outdoor museum that recreates the early 19th-century trading post and the time when the company's trappers hunted beaver for their hides, which were used to make the hats that were popular at the time. The site includes a train station, farm, and many other historic buildings, as well as two museums. The life of the 19th-century settlers is also re-enacted in original costume. In around 1858, the gold rush on the Fraser River brought countless settlers to this area, creating further business for the trading post. It was on 19 November of the same year, in Fort Langley that Sir James Douglas, a former Company employee and the first governor of British Colombia, declared the province of British Columbia a British crown colony (which it remained until 1866).

INFO Wedgemount Lake Trail

The light blue water of Garibaldi Lake (below) creates a stunning contrast with the dark jagged mountains rising in the background. Some of the park's truly beautiful scenery can be seen from the Garibaldi Lake Trek (9 km/5.6 miles). You can also camp near to the lake at one of the designated sites.

One of the most spectacular trails in the park leads over 1,200 m (3,937 feet) up to the glacial Wedgemount Lake and its waterfalls. Requiring around seven hours to complete, the trail is open from July to September.

Signposting from Highway 99 north of Whistler, info: Tel (604) 898 36 78. w.magnoliahoTelcom

Situated at the end of Howe Sound around 13 km (8 miles) north of the old lumberjack settlement of Squamish, this park covers an area of nearly 1,950 sq km (753 sq miles) in the Coast Mountains and is characterized by startlingly blue-green lakes, forests, alpine meadows, glaciers, and mountain peaks created by prehistoric volcanic eruptions. At a height of 2,678 m (8,786 feet), Mount Garibaldi is a stratovolcano. Like the park itself, it was named after the Italian freedom fighter; however, the highest peak in the park is Wedge Mountain at 2,891 m (9,482 feet). A number of roads lead into the park from Highway 99 (also known as the Sea to Sky Highway, between Squamish and Whistler). It is divided into five main recreational areas: Black Tusk/Garibaldi Lake is the most beautiful; the others are called Wedgemount Lake, Singing Pass, Cheakamus Lake, and Diamond Head. On-site camping is available and there are plenty of hiking trails.

Vancouver

🏛 Commodore Ballroom

This art deco-style dance hall first opened its doors in 1929. Since then, it has been known mainly for its live events. The performances given here over the years by Sammy Davis Jr, James Brown, Tina Turner, and The Police are legendary. In 1996 the hall closed for renovation and reopened again three years later. Since then, a host of contemporary artists such as Franz Ferdinand, Lady Gaga, and Snoop Dogg have appeared. The Commodore is also known for its fine sprung dance floor.
868 Granville Street;
Tel (604) 739 45 50.

🏛 Vancouver Opera

The Vancouver Opera enjoys a countrywide reputation. Classical and modern operas are staged in their original language, and English subtitles help the audience to understand the action and lyrics.
500–845 Cambie Street;
Tel (604) 683 02 22.
www.vancouveropera.ca

🔍 Dr. Sun Yat-sen Classical Chinese Garden

This full-size Chinese garden was designed according to Chinese feng-shui principles by experts from Suzhou. It features all the typical contrasting elements of classical Chinese garden design: delicate water plants curl around craggy rocks, white pebbles lie between dark stones, and bamboo canes undulate in front of bare stone – yin and yang are wherever you look. Guided tours are available, explaining the use of materials and the symbolism in the garden design.

578 Carrall Street;
Tel (604) 689 71 33; May–14 June, Sept 10.00–18.00 daily, 15 June–Aug 9.30–19.00 daily, Oct–April Tue–Sun 10.00–16.30.
www.vancouver chinesegarden.com

🔍 English Bay

A popular destination for Vancouver residents and a place for city workers to come and relax after a hard day in the office, English Bay lies north-west of the city, just a few minutes from downtown. People also come here to exercise and jog or cycle along the seawall, or play beach volleyball on the gleaming white sand of the beach. After their exertions, thanks to Vancouver's mild climate, the sports enthusiasts are tired but not too tired to sip a welcome refreshing drink in one of English Bay's many street cafés and bars.

🔍 Vancouver Aquarium Marine Science Centre

One of the largest in North America, the aquarium is home to thousands of sea creatures, ranging from the Beluga whale to the fearsome piranha and not forgetting microscopic lifeforms. A realistic tropical downpour is simulated every hour in an artificial rainforest. The Pacific Canada Pavilion contains marine life from the local habitat.
Stanley Park;
Tel (604) 659-3400;
summer 9.30–19.00 daily, winter 10.00–17.30 daily.
www.vanaqua.org

🔍 Vida Spa

This oasis of wellness was voted the best spa in Vancouver in numerous surveys.

Offering tranquility and a pleasant atmosphere in its modern rooms, refreshing cucumber water is always available. Most of the treatments aim to relieve tense city dwellers (and holiday-makers) of fatigue and stress. Beauty treatments such as facials, wraps, and exfoliations are available, many of which are based on Ayurveda, the ancient Indian medicine system.
Sheraton Vancouver Wall Centre Hotel, 1088 Burrard Street; Tel (604) 682 84 10.
www.vidawellness.com

♣ La Baguette & L'Echalote

The secret has long been out about this small bakery on Granville Island. Its crisp, freshly baked baguettes of French quality are first class, although baked goods of all kinds are on offer, including organic and sourdough breads or others containing figs, pecans, and rosemary – not to mention their delicious tiramisu and hazelnut chocolate cake. The founder, Mario, is also a fine sculptor. You will often find some of Granville Island's buskers performing nearby.
1680 Johnston Street;
Tel (604) 684 13 51.
www.labaguette.ca

♣ Charlie's Chocolate Factory

This small factory has been a paradise for those with a sweet tooth since 1970, with chocolate and candy as far as the eye can see. A small river of chocolate even flows through the store. You can buy kits to start your own mini chocolate factory, but of course you can also buy it

ready-made – in all kinds of forms: flowers, animals, and even computers for technology fans. There are also chocolate fountains to suit every occasion, from weddings to birthdays.
3746 Canada Way;
Tel (604) 437 82 21.
www.charlieschocolate factory.com

♣ Hill's Native Art

Opened in 1946, this gallery has the largest and most interesting selection of Indian art to be found anywhere. Sourced from the northwest coast of the North American continent, you will find sculptures, masks, paintings, jewelry, drums, rattles, clothing, and even totem poles – although the latter cost an eye-watering $30,000.
165 Water Street;
Tel (504) 686 42 49.
www.hillsnativeart.com

♣ Imperial Salmon House

Smoked salmon gift boxes are sold in just about every souvenir shop in Canada, but if you managed to miss out during your trip, you can still buy it on your way home at the airport. However, this large mail order firm offers truly high-quality salmon and sells in small quantities if desired. Imperial Salmon House will also package up your order for sending home if required. The short detour to the shop is worth the effort.
1632 Franklin Street;
Tel (604) 251 11 14.

♣ Leone Fashions

Fans of the latest designer fashions come to this store near the cruise ship terminal. Local designers are found

From left: Indulge in true luxury – the lobby, entrance, and breakfast terrace on the sunny side of the Wedgewood Hotel; fish delicacies are served at the Coast Round Bar.

VANCOUVER AND SURROUNDINGS

The insider tips listed here refer to the sights described on pages 32–55.

The Listel Hotel
A mixture of first-class hotel, art gallery, and ethnological museum. The walls of the corridors and suites are adorned with paintings from the Buschlen Mowatt Gallery, and Northwest Coast Indian artefacts from the Anthropology Museum are exhibited on one floor. But comfort is essential too: the rooms were renovated just a few years ago and are very spacious, with some overlooking the port. Apart from its central location, other bonuses include a swimming pool and free yoga classes.
1300 Robson Street;
Tel (604) 684 84 61.
www.thelistelhotel.com

Opus Hotel
The emphasis is on modern style at the elegant Opus Hotel. The decor features vibrant hues, merging futuristic aspects with comfort and useful extras such as ergonomic chairs. The bathrooms are also luxurious with spacious walk-in showers. The cruiseship terminal, Stanley Park, and the entertainment district are not far away.
322 Davie Street;
Tel (604) 642 67 87.
www.opushotel.com

Shangri-La Hotel
This Asian hotel chain is known for its elegant ambience. Half of the spacious rooms, decorated in modern Asian style, have a balcony with a magnificent view of the city and the mountains in the distance. Another special feature is the enormous bathrooms with integrated TV and luxury shower.
1128 West Georgia Street;
Tel (604) 689 11 20.
www.shangri-la.com

Wedgewood Hotel
Situated on Robson Square, the Wedgewood Hotel is reminiscent of a high-end European lodging house from the early 20th century, though the service and furnishings are top notch. Five stars for the tasteful ambience, the discreet service, and the multi-award-winning hotel restaurant.
845 Hornby Street,
Tel. (604) 689 77 77.
www.wedgewoodhotel.com

West End Guest House
Antique furniture and old photographs in the nine rooms of this pleasant bed and breakfast bring historic Vancouver to mind. There is no trace here of the commotion outside in what is a busy commercial district. Each of the rooms is comfortably appointed, and every bathroom has an old-fashioned tub. The breakfast is opulent, and sherry and iced tea are served in the afternoon. Utterly civilized!
1362 Haro Street;
Tel (604) 681 28 89. www.
westendguesthouse.com

Fort Langley

ℹ️ Tourist information
Fort Langley, a village to the east of Vancouver, was the first European settlement in Fraser Valley. The Fort Langley National Historic Site, on the bank of the river, has its origins in the Hudson's Bay Company trading post that was previously here – it played a prominent role in the settlement history of British Columbia. The first fort was erected in 1827. In 1858, British Columbia was made a British crown colony, which it remained for a number of years. In 1886 the Hudson's Bay Company ceased operating here, and in 1923 the site was recognized as having national historic importance. The site has been open to the public since May 1955.
Tel (604) 888 88 35.
www.fortlangley.com

Mount Seymour Provincial Park

🗺️ Park management
Named after Frederick Seymour, the Governor of British Columbia between 1864 and 1869, the park extends through the north of the city. From the top of Mount Seymour (1,455 m/4,774 feet), you can enjoy a breathtaking view of Vancouver and Fraser Valley. Dense forests containing Douglas firs and cedars cover the mountainside, and in the early summer the alpine meadows near the summit are in full bloom. Numerous hiking trails crisscross this wild natural habitat, and in the winter cross-country skiers take advantage of the deep snow that usually falls here. Racoons, eagles, and brown bears are all indigenous to this conservation area.
Tel (604) 986 93 71.
www.env.gov.bc.ca/bcparks

Whistler

ℹ️ Tourist information
Whistler was just a quiet backwater until the early 1960s when Vancouver businessmen, spotting its potential, began to develop the area. Now the most famous skiing area in British Columbia (the Winter Olympics and ski world championships have been held here), it lies 120 km (78 miles) north of Vancouver and can be reached along the particularly scenic coastal and mountain Highway 99. The magnificent slopes of Mount Whistler and Mount Blackcomb have won several awards from ski magazines. Blackcomb also has the steepest ski slope in North America. The ski lifts begin right beside the hotels. A wide range of superb hiking trails are open in the summer months, which are normally warm and dry, and sports equipment from mountain bikes to inline skates is available to hire in many places.
www.whistleronline.ca

❌ Tandoori Grill
This restaurant in Whistler is famed for its East Indian fare and its relaxed atmosphere. Vegetarians and curry-lovers in particular will appreciate the meals on offer here, but there are plenty of other options on the menu if you are not a fan of spicy food. Enhanced with all kinds of exotic sauces, the meat dishes are particularly tasty.
201-4368 Main Street;
Tel (604) 905 49 00.
www.tandooriwhistler.com

Summit Lodge & Spa
A modern aparthotel in the Whistler ski resort with large suites and studios. The wellness area is luxurious, one of the best spas in this upmarket location where you can relax in style. Use of the pool, sauna, and fitness suite is included as standard. The two restaurants are also excellent, one offering Spanish dishes, the other sushi creations.
4359 Main Street;
Tel (604) 932 27 78.
www.summitlodge.com

THE HIGHLIGHTS

BRITISH COLUMBIA
VANCOUVER COAST,
VANCOUVER ISLAND

The Vancouver coastline and Vancouver Island form a true natural paradise. British Colombia's rugged west coast is typical of Canada's wild beauty. The largest of British Colmbia's islands, Vancouver Island is around 450 km (280 miles) long and up to 100 km (62 miles) wide and enjoys a mild climate. Indented with numerous fjord-style inlets, the central part of the island is occupied by a mountain range, while creeks and lakes full of fish are found along the well-forested east coast. Beaches such as Duncan, Chemainus, and Nanaimo attract hordes of visitors in summer. Victoria, British Colombia's capital, has retained its very British charm.

THE HIGHLIGHTS:
BRITISH COLUMBIA: VANCOUVER COAST, VANCOUVER ISLAND

10 Johnstone Strait, Queen
Charlotte Strait

11 God's Pocket Marine
Provincial Park

12 Victoria:
Inner Harbour,
Parliament Buildings
Royal British Columbia
Museum
Thunderbird Park
Butchart Gardens

13 Goldstream Provincial
Park, Cowichan Valley

14 Strathcona Provincial
Park

15 Pacific Rim
National Park

16 Tofino,
Nootka Sound

17 Tweedsmuir
Provincial Park

Sandpit
Alliford Bay
Louise I.
Hecate Strait
1082
San Christoval Ra.
Lyell I.
Gwaii Haanas South More
National Park Reserve
Moresby I.
Marine Conservation
Area Reserve
749
Anthony I.
Rose Harbour
Kunghit I.
Cape St. James
Queen Charlotte Islands
Queen Charlott Sound
580

PACIFIC OCEAN

N
0   40 km
20 miles

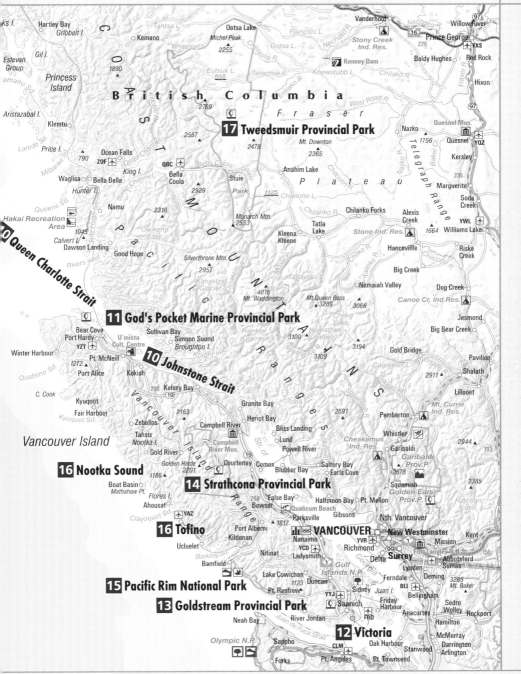

THE HIGHLIGHTS: BRITISH COLUMBIA: VANCOUVER COAST, VANCOUVER ISLAND

The waters of this region are home to Steller sea lions (below), the largest type of eared seals, and Pacific white-sided dolphins (below, inset). The aerial image shows part of God's Pocket Marine Provincial Park, characterized by the strong currents that occur around the bays of Vancouver Island.

INFO Whale watching

Around 200 of the enormous killer whales – the largest population in the world – live in Johnstone Strait in the summer months. Donna and Bill Mackay run whale-watching tours from June to October.

Mackay Whale Watching, 1514 Broughton Blvd, Port McNeill V0N 2R0; Tel (877) 663 67 22.

JOHNSTONE STRAIT, QUEEN CHARLOTTE STRAIT 🔟
GOD'S POCKET MARINE PROVINCIAL PARK 1️⃣1️⃣

The Johnstone Strait, approximately 110 km (68 miles) long and up to 5 km (3 miles) wide, separates Vancouver Island from the mainland. Farther north, it opens into the Queen Charlotte Strait and the Inside Passage, the route for ferries to Alaska. The waters between the many small islands are particularly popular with sea kayakers. The former home of the Kwakwaka'wakw First Nations is a haunt of orcas – over 150 of these killer whales come to the Johnstone Strait every year. Boughton Archipelago Pacific Marine Park in the north is a good place to see them, along with humpback whales. According to Jacques Cousteau, the waters of Browning Pass in God's Pocket Marine Provincial Park, which includes Crane Island and several other small islands in Johnstone Strait, are one of the best cold water diving locations in the world. The park also offers opportunities for wildlife viewing, with eagles and colonies of seabirds a common sight.

The well-plied route along the Inside Passage runs from Port Hardy on the northeast tip of Vancouver Island to Prince Rupert on Kaien Island, 60 km (37 miles) from the southern coast of Alaska. Leading through a labyrinth of densely forested islands, winding inlets, and channels, it offers protection from the bad weather of the open ocean. Douglas Channel seen from an observation point on Kitimat (below). Cruise liners in the Inside Passage (below, inset and right).

THE INSIDE PASSAGE

At 1,600 km/1,000 miles long, the legendary Inside Passage waterway is also known as the Alaska Marine Highway. It runs north-west from Seattle in the US state of Washington toward Skagway in Alaska, winding its way along the west Canadian coast through inlets, bays, and channels. Glacial activity resulting from the ice ages of thousands of years ago has left its mark on the land and given the coast its dramatic appearance. At one time, the Haida and Tlingit peoples manoeuvred canoes through these waters, explorers like James Cook and George Vancouver steered their ships along the coast, and fishermen of First Naton and European origin established colonies on the local islands and hunted salmon. Their descendents still live here, although the salmon have since disappeared from many bays. Most passengers on BC Ferries (British Colombia Ferries, the company that serves the coastal and island communities) now travel the Inside Passage purely for pleasure – and it is indeed one of the most beautiful landscapes on the planet. From the deck of a ferry, the shore almost seems close enough to touch at times, and the mighty firs and gigantic snow-covered mountains in the Coastal Range form an impressive panoramic backdrop. The channels and bays are just a few hundred feet wide in places. Whales and dolphins swim up close to the ships, and with a bit of luck you might even catch sight of some seals.

THE HIGHLIGHTS:
BRITISH COLUMBIA:
VANCOUVER COAST,
VANCOUVER ISLAND

The major "must-see" sights in Victoria, along with the best shops and restaurants, are to be found around the Inner Harbour area (below) and in the nearby old town. The illuminated parliament buildings (right) at the southern end of the port add to the light show in the evenings.

TIP Tea in the Fairmont Empress

This legendary hotel, a study in Edwardian elegance, is the traditional setting for classic five o'clock tea, when dainty sandwiches and cakes are served. Smart casual wear is obligatory.
721 Government Street;
Tel (2 50) 384 81 11;
reservations daily from 12.00.

The city of Victoria was founded in 1843 as a Hudson's Bay Company trading post and fort, and it became the capital of the crown colony of British Columbia in 1868. It was named after Britain's Queen Victoria. The historic buildings of the Inner Harbour, which include the Empress Hotel and the British Colombia Parliament Buildings, still recall Britain's colonial era. The imposing parliament building were designed by English architect Francis Rattenbury and date from the late 1890s. In the nearby old quarter, which has been carefully restored in recent years, you could almost be walking through the streets of England's university towns of Oxford or Cambridge. In a superb location on the waterfront, the Empress Hotel was also designed by Rattenbury as a terminus hotel for the Canadian Pacific Railway's steamship line. It was carefully restored in the late 1980s. Five o'clock tea is still served every afternoon from silver teapots. (See p.23)

INFO Thunderbird Park

Symbolic of Canada and the First Nation peoples, totem poles served various purposes from celebrating cultural beliefs to telling legends. Below: Modern totem poles from Thunderbird Park – original examples are preserved in the museum. The museum's displays also include the life-size model of a mammoth (right).

This fascinating open-air museum exhibits totem poles and many other cultural artefacts of the First Nations – such as the house of the Kwakwaka'wakw chief Mungo Martin.

675 Belleville Street;
Tel (250) 356 72 26.

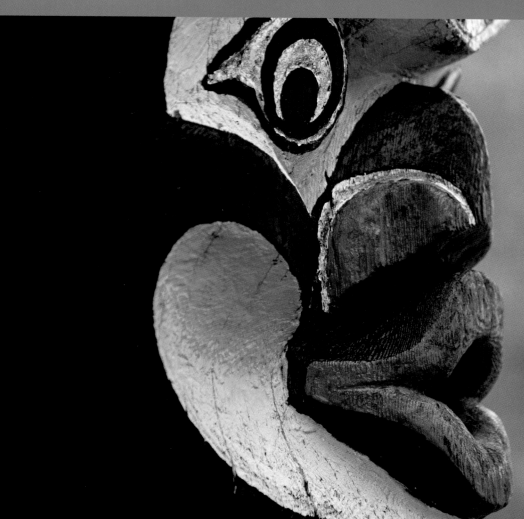

VICTORIA: ROYAL BRITISH COLUMBIA MUSEUM, THUNDERBIRD PARK 12

Situated in downtown Victoria, near the parliament buildings and the Empress Hotel, the Royal BC Museum has the best natural history and cultural exhibits in Western Canada. Founded in 1886, it has three permanent galleries and also hosts major temporary exhibitions. State-of-the-art technology is used to illustrate the evolution of British Columbia – from the prehistoric landscape, via the rainforest, to early First Nation villages and a colonial pioneer town from the 19th century. The sights, sounds, and smells of the past are vividly recreated in realistic settings, such as Captain George Vancouver's ship HMS *Discovery* in Nootka Sound, a pioneer family homestead, and a turn-of-the-century city street with hotel and shops. In Thunderbird Park, in the grounds of the museum, you will find a long house of the Coastal First Nations, in which traditional dances of the Kwakiutl are performed, and contemporary totem poles. (See p.22)

Open year-round, the five main areas of Butchart Gardens – the Sunken Garden, the Rose Garden, the Japanese Garden, the Italian Garden, and the Mediterranean Garden – are linked by painstakingly maintained lawns and paths that wind their way between the herbaceous borders and exotic plants.

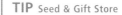

TIP Seed & Gift Store

By 1920, Jennie Butchart was selling her seeds around the world. The store in Butchart Gardens still sells a wide range of seeds, garden equipment, and local crafts.

800 Benvenuto Ave, Brentwood Bay V8M 1J8; Tel (2 50) 652 52 56; June–Sept daily 9.00–22.00, Dec. 9.00–21.00.

VICTORIA: BUTCHART GARDENS

Situated in Brentwood Bay on the Saanich Peninsula, 22 km (14 miles) north of Victoria, Butchart Gardens began life as a Japanese garden, created in 1908 by Jennie Butchart. The wife of a quarry merchant, she transformed a bleak redundant quarry pit into a green haven. An Italian garden was soon added, then a rose garden. In spring, thousands of tulips, forget-me-nots, rhododendrons, and dogwood bushes are in flower; in summer the air is heavy with the scent of roses, fuchsias, and begonias, while in autumn the dahlias and chrysanthemums come into bloom. The remains of a tall chimney can still be seen from the Sunken Garden Lookout, evidence of the garden's origins. The gardens have their own microclimate, slightly warmer in summer and cooler in winter than the surrounding area. Today, over 50 gardeners are required to tend the grounds and maintain interest throughout the seasons. (See p.22)

THE HIGHLIGHTS: BRITISH COLUMBIA: VANCOUVER COAST, VANCOUVER ISLAND

INFO Chemainus murals

Signposted trails in Goldstream Provincial Park (below) lead deep into primeval forest, with Douglas firs, giant cedars, and tumbling waterfalls. Here – and in Strathcona Provincial Park – you may be lucky enough to spot bald eagles soaring high above (below, right). Right: Autumn comes to Cowichan Valley.

Chemainus hit the headlines when the construction of a highway hit tourism heavily, causing the residents to take action to promote their community. They decorated the walls of the town with over 40 murals illustrating the culture of the First Nations and the story of the early settlers.

GOLDSTREAM PROVINCIAL PARK, COWICHAN VALLEY 🔢
STRATHCONA PROVINCIAL PARK 🔢

The wilderness is close at hand in Goldstream Provincial Park, though just 16 km (10 miles) north-west of Victoria. Amid the jungle-like forests of Douglas firs and red cedars, with the sound of rushing waterfalls, civilization seems a world away. Between October and December, thousands of salmon swim upstream to their spawning grounds. The First Nation tradition lives on in Cowichan Valley on the west coast of Vancouver Island. There is a range of things to do and see, from exploring wine country trails to fishing, kayaking, and hiking. The main town is Duncan, some 60 km (37 miles) north of Victoria, where you can see more than 80 totem poles. Founded in 1911, in the central part of Vancouver Island, Strathcona Provincial Park is the oldest nature reserve in British Columbia – and the largest on Vancouver Island at nearly 2,500 sq km (965 sq miles). It contains the Elk River Mountains with the Golden Hinde, the island's highest peak.

THE HIGHLIGHTS:
BRITISH COLUMBIA:
VANCOUVER COAST,
VANCOUVER ISLAND

INFO Storm watching

In the dense rainforest of the Pacific Rim National Park, branches are overgrown by moss and wooden walkways protect the forest floor (below). Red-breasted nuthatches, house finches, Stellar's jays, and pine siskins demonstrate the diversity of bird life – not to be outdone by grey squirrels (below, inset, from top).

The wave-battered tip of the peninsular is named after the Ucluelet tribe ("people from the safe harbour"). Massive breaking waves during winter storms (right).

Info from Tourism Ucluelet;
Tel (250) 726 24 85.

The Pacific Rim National Park was established in 1970 and is situated on the west coast of Vancouver Island. A remote natural paradise, it is served by Highway 4. Before the arrival of the Europeans, it was the territory of the Nuu-Chah-nulth people. The park comprises three main areas: Long Beach, the Broken Group Islands, and the West Coast Trail. The broad sandy Long Beach region stretching between Tofino and Ucluelet is a popular rest stop for migrating birds in the winter. The Broken Group Islands consist of over 100 tiny islands in Barkley Sound, the Loudoun Channel, and the Imperial Eagle Channel. It is the perfect spot for adventure-seeking kayakers. The West Coast Trail, one of the most demanding hiking trails in all of Canada, leads along the rugged coast in the southernmost part of the Pacific Rim National Park. It was originally built as a telegraph maintenance trail and was also used to help rescue shipwrecked sailors.

THE HIGHLIGHTS:
BRITISH COLUMBIA:
VANCOUVER COAST,
VANCOUVER ISLAND

The beaches of Tofino (below and below, right, from top: MacKenzie Beach, Long Beach, Chesterman's Beach) are much prized by surfers. James Cook's first encounter with West Coast First Nations people, in 1778, is commemorated In Friendly Cove, Nootka Sound (below, inset, left).

INFO Whale Centre

Explore the region's natural world at John Forde's Whale Centre & Museum. Sturdy Boston whaler boats depart daily at 10.30, 14.00, and 17.00 on 2–3 hour whale-watching tours.
411 Campbell Street, Tofino, V0R 2Z0; Tel (250) 725 21 36; 9.00–20.00 daily.

On a small peninsula between Tofino Sound and the Pacific Ocean, the town of Tofino is a Mecca for whale-watchers. Over 20,000 whales pass by the coast each year between March and May, and rest in Clayoquot Sound during their migration from Mexico to Alaska. The Pacific Rim Whale Festival held here in March celebrates these huge marine creatures. In summer Tofino is full of hikers, campers, water sports enthusiasts, and anglers. A number of former lumberjacks live here, and the villages of the Tla-o-qui-aht and Ahousath people are nearby. The two tribes clashed in the past, but today they benefit jointly from tourism in the area and have been reconciled to an extent. Attractions close to Tofino include the hidden bays, inlets, and straits of the surrounding area – such as Nootka Sound, where British Captain James Cook was the first European to arrive in March 1778, on his third voyage around the world.

Schools of orca make their way between Vancouver Island and the Canadian mainland (right). Catching sight of a killer whale as it leaps from the water is a rare stroke of luck – the entire body frequently breaches the water (below). Their dorsal fins can be up to 2 m (7 feet) high. The marine life of the region also includes this little hermit crab who has made an empty snail shell its home, starfish, and sea anemones (below, inset, from top).

WILDLIFE ON THE CANADIAN PACIFIC COAST

Schools of gray whales and orcas romp in the waters off the Pacific coast, while sea lions and seals can be seen near the off-shore islands. Gray whales grow to around 15 m (49 feet) in length and up to 34 tonnes (37 tons) in weight. Orcas feed mainly on sea lions, fish, and seabirds. The name "killer whale" was coined to describe the brutal hunting technique in which they use their high dorsal fin like a sword. Weighing between 5 and 9 tonnes (5.5–10 tons) and measuring up to 8 m (26 feet) in length, the whales travel in family groups, in schools. The social structure of each group is based around the matriarch and her descendents. The best-known fish in the Pacific is the salmon – the largest of which, the chinook, can reach over 1 m (40 inches) in length. Once fully grown, they habitually spend three to four years in the ocean and then return to their home rivers to spawn, after which they die – salmon do not assimilate food in fresh water. The female lays her eggs in the gravel of the riverbed where they are fertilized. The hatchlings remain in the fresh water for a time before making their way to the ocean. White-tailed sea eagles, with impressive wingspans, circle majestically above at great height. The coastal vegetation consists primarily of dense forest with lush undergrowth, and forest floors covered with mosses and lichens. Moose appear at the forest edge, and black bear search hungrily for salmon in the rivers.

INFO Grizzly safari

Part of the Rainbow Range mountains lie in Tweedsmuir South Provincial Park (right). Canoeists can paddle their way through seven interconnecting lakes, rivers, and creeks on the Turner Lake Canoe Circuit, amid spectacular mountain scenery. It normally takes around 3–5 days. Below: Turner Lake.

From the beginning of September to mid-October, under the supervision of experienced guides, you can watch large grizzly bears hunting salmon. Tweedsmuir Park Lodge offers grizzly safaris that require no special level of fitness.
Bella Coola, V0T 1C0;
Tel (877) 982 24 07.

This conservation area off Highway 20 was named after Canada's 15th Governor General, John Buchan Tweedsmuir. After riding through the park in August 1937, he noted: "I have now traveled over most of Canada and have seen many wonderful things, but I have seen nothing more beautiful and more wonderful than the great park which British Columbia has done me the honor to call by my name." Almost 500 km (311 miles) to the north-west of Vancouver, it is the largest provincial park in British Columbia, at 9,819 sq km (3,791 sq miles) and roughly triangular in shape. With the Dean River acting as a natural boundary, the park is divided into a southern section, which is relatively well-developed, and a northern section, generally less developed and bordered by several reservoirs. The starting point for explorations is the small ferry port of Bella Coola, at the end of a long inlet off the Inside Passage. (See p.96).

Campbell River

ℹ Tourist information
Somewhat worryingly for the "Salmon Capital of the World", on the Strait of Georgia, salmon stocks have been declining here for a number of years, as they have been elsewhere. The paper mill shut in 2009 but the area's mineral mines are still open.
1235 Shoppers Row;
Tel (250) 287 31 03.
www.northcentralisland.com

🏛 The Museum at Campbell River
The carvings and other artefacts on display here illustrate the varied history and culture of the First Nations people. Other exhibits, such as the pioneer log cabin that stands in front of the museum, illustrate how the early settlers lived. The 1920s floathouse is a portable home that could be moved from one location to another, rather like a houseboat. The museum also has other permanent and temporary exhibits.
470 Island Highway;
Tel (250) 287 31 03.
www.crmuseum.ca

✕ Lookout Seafood Bar & Grill
Naturally, salmon from regional waters are one of the highlights of this restaurant, but the hamburgers here are delicious too. The view of the bay is simply breathtaking.
921 Island Highway;
Tel (250) 286 68 12.

🛏 Anchor Inn
Every room here has a clear view of the ocean. As well as standard rooms, there are suites decorated in African, Arabic, or Arctic themes.

261 Island Avenue;
Tel (250) 286 11 31.
www.anchorinn.ca

Duncan

ℹ Municipality of Duncan
The aptly named "City of Totems", a small town in the Cowichan Valley, has over 40 totem poles as a reminder of the region's First Nations cultural heritage. If you are feeling a little peckish after completing the town's self-guided walking tour, try one of the cafés or bakeries offering delicious pastries and breads. Cowichan Valley is also one of the most fertile areas on Vancouver Island.
381A Trans-Canada Highway;
Tel (250) 746 46 36.
www.city.duncan.bc.ca

🏛 The BC Forest Discovery Centre
This open-air museum is dedicated to exploring the history of the timber industry. The timber barons and environmentalists have been in dispute for many years, so the preservation of forest stocks is one of the themes in the museum. A historic train steams nostalgically through the extensive forest beside the highway.
2892 Drinkwater Road;
Tel (250) 715 11 13.

✕ Rock Cod Café
A cozy eatery situated directly on the waterfront, Rock Cod Café serves the best fish and chips outside the UK, accompanied by freshly tapped beer. The ocean view is sublime.
4-1759 Cowichan Bay Road, Cowichan Bay;
Tel (250) 746 15 50.

🛏 Travelodge Silver Bridge Inn
This basic but very economical motel is located on the bank of the Cowichan River and offers spacious, clean rooms. The large honeymoon suites include an open fireplace and jacuzzi as standard. The adjoining pub is in a historic country house.
140 Trans-Canada Highway;
Tel (250) 748 43 11.
www.travelodgeduncan.com

Nanaimo

ℹ Tourist information
The second-largest city on the island is known for its picturesque port, where the ferries from Vancouver also dock. A wealth of restaurants, hotels, and souvenir stores cater to the large numbers of tourists who come here.
2290 Bowen Road, Beban House; Tel (250) 756 01 06.
www.tourismnanaimo.com

🏛 Nanaimo District Museum
This regional museum is dedicated to the history of the city. The main focus is on the culture of the Snunéymuxw First Nations people and the boom years of the 20th century, when Nanaimo's main industrial site was a large coal mine. There is an old log cabin that once belonged to the Hudson's Bay Company on the museum's grounds.
100 Museum Way;
Tel (250) 753 18 21.
www.nanaimomuseum.ca

◉ Gabriola Island
A small island located in the Strait of Georgia, a few miles from Nanaimo, Gabriola Island is a popular excursion destination. The Folklife Village

Shopping Centre has a number of restaurants and retail stores and is also renowned for its art galleries. Hiking trails in the small Sandwell Provincial Park at Lock Bay in the north-east of the island lead to secluded beaches and hidden picnic areas. The beach in Drumberg Provincial Park is also popular, especially among divers. There are two more beautiful sandy beaches in Gabriola Sands Provincial Park, which form an isthmus. They are also popular with swimmers and picnickers.

✕ Wesley Street Cafe
Seafood dishes making use of fish caught in regional waters are just some of the delights served at this restaurant. Recommended dishes include the mussels cooked in a pear cider broth and the chicken breast served with mushrooms and risotto.
321 Wesley Street;
Tel (250) 753 60 57.
www.wesleycafe.com

🛏 Grand Hotel Nanaimo
The Grand Hotel is one of the plushest places to stay in Nanaimo. The deluxe rooms come with an open fireplace and an extra-large bathtub as standard. The impressive hotel lobby features an enormous chandelier and comfortable armchairs.
4898 Rutherford Road;
Tel (250) 758 30 00. www.thegrandhotelnanaimo.ca

🛏 Pepper Muffin Country Inn
This cozy bed and breakfast is located by an idyllic river. All the rooms are furnished with antique furniture and have a balcony. The spicy pepper muffins from which the inn

From left: Haida carving in Campbell River; Duncan in Cowichan Valley – self-appointed "City of Totems"; surfers love Tofino's Long Beach; water taxis waiting outside a waterfront restaurant in Nanaimo.

VANCOUVER COAST, VANCOUVER ISLAND

The insider tips listed here refer to the sights described on pages 60–83.

gets its intriguing name are served at breakfast.
3718 Jingle Pot Road;
Tel (250) 756 04 73.
www.peppermuffin.com

Tofino

ℹ️ **Tourist information**
The town of Tofino lies at the edge of the Esowista Peninsula and so is part of Clayoquot Sound. People come here to join whale-watching tours, hoping to see the gray whales that rest in nearby Clayoquot Sound on their journey from Mexico to Alaska, and to storm-watch in winter. The whales sometimes come in quite close to the shore. Bears also roam around nearby, but are more wisely observed from the water (from the safety of a boat). During the summer months the waters off Tofino are also popular with surfers.
1426 Pacific Rim Highway;
Tel (250) 725 34 14.
www.tourismtofino.com

🏛️ **Reflecting Spirit Gallery**
This gallery sells First Nations arts and crafts, particularly pottery and carvings, as well as souvenirs such as medicine wheels and crystals.
441 Campbell Street;
Tel (250) 725 42 29.

Ucluelet

ℹ️ **Tourist information**
Ucluelet, located on Barkley Sound on the west coast of Vancouver Island, means "safe harbour" in the language of the local people, the Yu-cluth-aht. Like Tofino, Ucluelet is also a departure point for whale-watching trips off the coast. Every year

in spring, gray whales pass along the coast, their backs majestically breaking the surface of the water and then disappearing beneath again. Hiking enthusiasts can follow the trails through the nearby temperate rainforest.
100 Main Street;
Tel (250) 726 46 41.
www.ucluletinfo.com

🗙 **Boat Basin Restaurant**
Situated opposite the port, the menu in this popular restaurant includes an ambitious selection of fish dishes. Naturally, the fish is sourced from the local coastal waters. Some of the dishes have an Asian influence.
1971 Harbour Drive;
Tel (250) 726 46 44.

🛏️ **Canadian Princess Resort**
This hotel with a difference, as some of the rooms are on board a decommissioned ship, but guests must share a bathroom and toilet. The hotel restaurant is also situated on board. Rooms are available too in the shoreside fishing lodge. Fishing trips set off from the hotel to the nearby bays.
1943 Peninsula Road;
Tel (250) 726 77 71.
www.canadianprincess.com

Victoria

📷 **Beacon Hill Park**
With its rare Garry oaks, which thrive only on Vancouver Island and a few of the smaller islands off its coast, Beacon Hill Park lies between Southgate Street, Dallas Road, Douglas Street, and Cook Street. Wide lawns alternate with flamboyant flowerbeds and secluded

ponds. Climb Beacon Hill itself for a superb view over the ocean.
www.beaconhillpark.ca

🏛️ **The Aerie Resort and Spa**
This is a high-end resort located to the north of Victoria, which offers every conceivable luxury. The grand villa, reminiscent of those that line the French Riviera, is surrounded by extensive forests and parks. Many of its opulently appointed rooms have a balcony and an open fireplace. Extras in the rooms include CD players, fresh flowers every day, and, delicious truffles left on the pillow in the evening.
600 Ebedora Lane, Malahat;
Tel (250) 743 71 15.
www.fivestaralliance.com

🏛️ **Roger's Chocolates**
Roger's chocolate emporium has been a place of pilgrimage for chocoholics for years. He sells a vast array of chocolate treats from all over the world, as well as his own homemade chocolates. Of course, this is obviously not the best place for the diet-conscious calorie-counter.
913 Government Street;
Tel (250) 384 70 21.
www.rogerschocolates.com

🗙 **Café Brio**
This restaurant's fish dishes have enjoyed a good reputation for more than a decade. Salmon, caught in the nearby coastal waters, and oysters, also harvested on Vancouver Island, are served with delicious – homemade – Italian pasta and fresh vegetables.
944 Fort Street;
Tel (250) 383 00 09.
www.cafe-brio.com

🗙 **J&J Wonton Noodle House**
Don't let the rather stark atmosphere in this family-run Chinese restaurant put you off – they say the best noodles on Vancouver Island are served here. You can observe the cooks at work through a glass window – the kitchens are a real hive of activity. The lunch dishes are particularly tasty and extremely good value. Look out for the daily specials, too.
1012 Fort Street;
Tel (250) 383 06 80.

🛏️ **Spinnakers Guest House**
A moderately priced bed and breakfast belonging to the Spinnakers Brewpub chain. The guest house occupies two separate buildings. The rooms in the main property on Catherine Street, which was built in 1884, are luxuriously appointed and each have a jacuzzi and an open fireplace. In the other building, on Mary Street, there are four apartments which are ideal for longer stays.
308 Catherine Street;
Tel (250) 384 27 39.
www.spinnakers.com

🛏️ **The Magnolia**
This luxurious but nonetheless reasonably priced boutique hotel is quite English in atmosphere – the rooms and communal spaces are reminiscent of a British stately home. All the bathrooms are opulently appointed with marble tiling and ultra modern fittings. The hotel also has its own brewpub and an elegant new spa.
623 Courtney Street;
Tel (250) 381 09 99.
www.magnoliahotel.com

BRITISH COLUMBIA
QUEEN CHARLOTTE
ISLANDS/
HAIDA GWAII

The First Nations peoples, Canada's pre-colonial inhabitants, named Canada's westernmost island group Haida Gwaii, which roughly translates as "Islands of the People". They were renamed the Queen Charlotte Islands much later, when the English explorer and sea captain George Dixon discovered them in 1785. Dixon was on a mission to establish the islands' potential value for the fur trade, which the British were keen to develop. Along with Moresby Island in the south and Graham Island in the north, the archipelago comprises over 150 smaller islands. They are home to many different animal species, including black bear and raccoons.

18 Graham Island

19 Moresby Island

20 SGang Gwaay
(Anthony island)

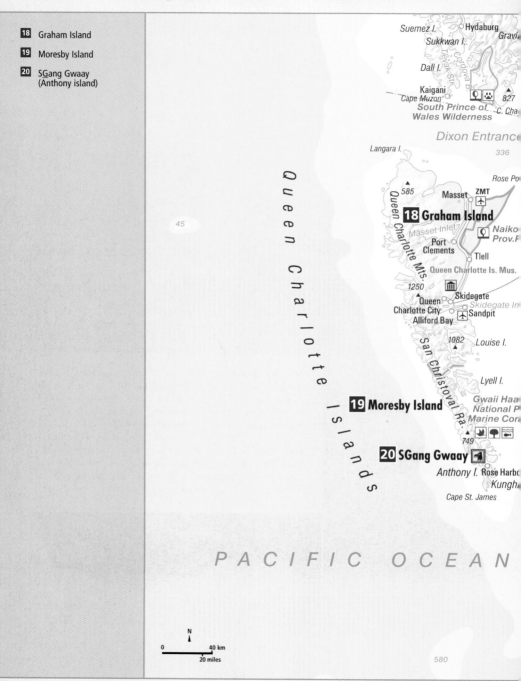

Suemez I.   Hydaburg
Sukkwan I.   Gravi
Dall I.   Cordova Str.
Tlevak Str.
Kaigani
Cape Muzon   827
South Prince of   C. Cha
Wales Wilderness

Dixon Entrance

Langara I.   336

Rose Po

585
Masset   ZMT

18 Graham Island

Masset Inlet   Naiko
Prov.P
Port
Clements
Tlell
Queen Charlotte Is. Mus.

1250
Skidegate
Queen   Skidegate In
Charlotte City   Sandpit
Alliford Bay

1082   Louise I.

Lyell I.

19 Moresby Island   Gwaii Haa
National P
Marine Cor
749

20 SGang Gwaay

Anthony I.   Rose Harbo
Kungh
Cape St. James

PACIFIC   OCEAN

N
0   40 km
20 miles   580

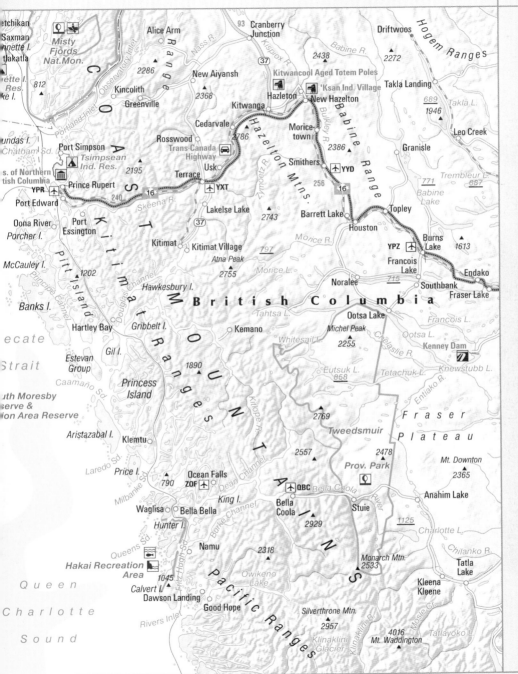

Ketchikan
Saxman
...nnette I.
...tlakatla
Misty Fjords Nat. Mon.
...lette I.
... Res.
...ke I.
812

Alice Arm
New Aiyansh
Kincolith
Greenville
2286
2368
Cedarvale
Kitwanga
2786
Rosswood
Trans-Canada Highway
Usk
Terrace
YXT
240
16
Port Simpson
Tsimpsean Ind. Res.
2195
YPR
Prince Rupert
Port Edward
Oona River
Porcher I.
Port Essington
Kitimat
Kitimat Village
Atna Peak
2755
797

Cranberry Junction
93
Nass R.
Kispiox R.
37
2438
Babine R.
2272
Driftwoos
Hogem Ranges
Kitwancool Aged Totem Poles
Hazleton
'Ksan Ind. Village
New Hazelton
Takla Landing
689
1946
Takla L.
Leo Creek
Morice-town
2386
Smithers
YYD
256
16
Barrett Lake
Houston
Granisle
Trembleur L.
771
687
Babine Lake
Topley
Burns Lake
1613
YPZ
Francois Lake
Noralee
715
Southbank
Endako
Fraser Lake

Range
Observatory Inlet
Portland Inlet
Skeena R.
Zymoetz R.
Hazelton Mtns.
2743
Morice R.
Morice L.
Babine Range
Bulkley R.

COAST
Kitimat Ranges
MOUNTAINS

...undas I.
Chatham Sd.
s. of Northern ...tish Columbia
McCauley I.
1202
Pitt River
Douglas Channel
Princip Channel
Hawkesbury I.
Banks I.
Hartley Bay
Gribbelt I.
Gil I.
Estevan Group
Princess Island
1890
Aristazabal I.
Klemtu
Laredo ...
Price I.
790
Ocean Falls
ZOF
King I.
Waglisa
Bella Bella
Hunter I.
Namu
Hakai Recreation Area
1045
Calvert I.
Dawson Landing
Good Hope

British Columbia

Kemano
Whitesail L.
Michel Peak
2255
Chelaslie R.
Ootsa L.
Kenney Dam
Knewstubb L.
Eutsuk L.
858
Tetachuk L.
Entiako R.
Tahtsa L.
Ootsa Lake
Francois L.
Fraser Plateau
Mt. Downton
2365
2769
Tweedsmuir
2557
2478
Prov. Park
QBC
Bella Coola River
Anahim Lake
Stuie
1125
2929
Charlotte L.
Chilanko R.
2318
Monarch Mtn.
2533
Tatla Lake
Kleena Kleene
Owikeno Lake

Killope R.
Dean Channel
Burke Channel
Fritz Hugh Sd.
Milbanke Sd.
Queens Sd.
Bella Coola River

Queen
Charlotte
Sound
...ecate
Strait
...uth Moresby ...serve & ...ion Area Reserve

Pacific Ranges
Silverthrone Mtn.
2957
Klinaklini Glacier
Mt. Waddington
4016
Mosle Cr.
Tatlayoko L.
Klinaklini R.
Rivers Inlet

THE HIGHLIGHTS: BRITISH COLUMBIA: QUEEN CHARLOTTE ISLANDS/HAIDA GWAII

Gwaii Haanas National Park is on Moresby Island. The plant and animal life here are quite unique (below, left). Bathing in one of the park's thermal pools (right) is just one of the attractions on offer. Diverse landscape, unusual features, and beautiful views in Naikoon Provincial Park on Graham Island (below, right).

INFO Ed Jones Haida Museum

Old Masset is a chance to experience Haida culture, both in the town itself and in the Ed Jones Haida Museum, with its displays of Haida art (totem poles in particular).

For opening times, contact the Old Masset Village Council, Masset V0T 1M0;
Tel (250) 626 51 15.

The largest settlements on Graham Island are Queen Charlotte City (the achipelago's administrative hub), Skidegate, and Masset. The ferries that connect Graham Island with Moresby Island arrive at Skidegate, also the location of the Haida Gwaii Museum, which documents the history and culture of the First Nations people who settled these islands long before the arrival of the first white inhabitants. Some very beautiful scenery is to be found in Naikoon Provincial Park, in the north-eastern corner of Graham Island. Most of the two islands' population of 5,000 is concentrated on Graham Island. Moresby Island is largely untouched, but the many abandoned Haida villages provide evidence that this was not always the case. The entire island is part of the Gwaii Haanas National Park Reserve and Haida Heritage Site, jointly managed by the Canadian government in Ottawa and the local Haida authorities.

Views of Graham Island: a traditional dance (right) and a canoe dedication ceremony (far right). The raven plays an important role in Haida mythology, as do many other creatures. Some totem poles – properly known as mortuary poles – have an opening for the ashes of the dead, and bear the family's crest at the top. Mythical creatures that are important to the Haida are carved into the totem poles (below, right). Further evidence of the Haida people's artistic skills is on show in these extraordinary carved masks (below, left).

THE HAIDA NATION

Before white fur hunters discovered the Queen Charlotte Islands, the archipelago was already home to some 8,000 Haida people. The population was split between the raven and eagle clans, divided into 22 and 23 families respectively, each comprising about 40 members. The villages, together with their hunting and fishing grounds, were passed down through the generations, along with countless legends and songs. Even the names, style, and appearance of the Haida's elaborate tattoos were handed down by tradition. According to Native North American mythology, the raven created mankind, cleverly picking out the first humans from among the clams he found on the beach. Then the cunning bird flew up into the skies to steal the sun, moon, and stars. Legend also tells how the raven taught man to build houses, having stolen the art of house-building from the beaver. The Haida lived in solid houses built from cedar, each with a totem pole outside. Their large, ocean-going canoes were made from the trunk of a single cedar. Skilled fishermen, the Haida used them to hunt whales. They also hunted on foot in the forests and mountain foothills. Fearsome warriors, their well-built canoes gave the Haida the upper hand in sea battles against their enemies. The Haida, whose territories include parts of Alaska and British Colombia, are also known for their traditional Chilkat weaving, using complex techniques.

INFO Haida Tours

SGang Gwaay (or Anthony Island, right), one of the small islands off the southern tip of Moresby Island, is part of the Gwaii Haanas National Park Reserve and Haida Heritage Site. The remains of Haida totem poles outside the village of Ninstints (below) stand defiantly, their paint faded by the wind and rain.

The daily tours of the Haida Heritage Centre in Kaay Llnagaay explore the roots of Haida culture. The institute also helps arrange local excursions.

Skidegate, Haida Gwaii V0T 1S1;
Tel (250) 559 78 85;
May–Jun Mon–Sat 10.00–18.00,
Jun–Sept 10.00–18.00, daily,
Sept–Apr Tues–Sat 11.00–17.00.

SGANG GWAAY (ANTHONY ISLAND)

The Haida civilization was already thousands of years old by the time the last inhabitants of the village of Ninstints left the small island of SGang Gwaay (Anthony Island) in 1880. They left behind them the remains of their cedarwood longhouses and totem poles. Skilfully carved and decorated, the tall totem poles document the history of an ancient people who did not come into contact with white settlers until the end of the 18th century. When they did, the consequences were catastrophic. With the Europeans came epidemics of smallpox and other diseases that ravaged the Haida population. In 1787 there were around 8,000 Haida living on the island but by 1835 this figure had fallen to around 6,000. Some 80 years later, the Haida population was not even a tenth of this number. Today, their numbers on SGang Gwaay have risen to around 2,000, and the island has been designated a World Heritage Site.

Chilcotin Country

ℹ️ Tourist information
The Chilcotin Country spans the area between the Coast Mountains and the central highlands of south-western British Columbia. Mountains, glaciers, lakes, rivers, and hilly pastures typify the landscape. Highway 20 serves as a vital artery, and wends its way from Williams Lake in the east, through the Chilcotins to Bella Coola on the western Pacific coast.
204-350 Barnard Street,
Williams Lake;
Tel (250) 392 22 26.
www.landwithoutlimits.com

🏛 Tweedsmuir Provincial Park
The park protects an area of wild and unspoilt landscape. Magnificent glaciers, crystal clear lakes, and remote valleys are the dominant features of this natural paradise, a refuge for the wildlife of Canada's far north. Even grizzly bear and caribou are found here. Eutsuk Lake (80 km/50 miles long) is a major water sports location. Most of the park is only accessible by seaplane or on foot. Popular activities include fishing, hiking the wilderness trails, canoeing, and horseback riding. Campsites are also available.
Highway 20.

Kleena Kleene

🛏 Clearwater Lake Lodge
Bernhard and Gisela Kalbhenn are the owners of one of the Chilcotin's most attractive lodges. Guests stay in either the main house or in one of the cosy log cabins. Motorboats and canoes are available for exploring the lake,

and Gisela serves hearty Canadian and German food. On request, your hosts will also organize horse riding, canoe trips, hiking, and even flights to see the glaciers of Tweedsmuir Provincial Park.
19579 Highway 20;
Tel (250) 476 11 50.
www.clearwaterlakelodge
.com

Masset

❌ Sea Breeze Restaurant
Top-quality fish is served in most restaurants on the Queen Charlotte Islands, and this one is no exception. The steamed and grilled fish recipes are particularly tasty. Alternatively, try one of the restaurant's famous cheeseburgers. A popular local meeting place for locals.
1675 Main Street;
Tel (250) 626 37 79.

🛏 Eagle View House
This impressive cedar log house gets its name from the rare bald eagles that are nevertheless a common sight here in the romantic wilderness of the Delkatla Inlet. With four bedrooms, a gym, and a fully equipped kitchen, Eagle View House is good for small groups. Golf and fishing trips can be arranged.
1650 Delkatia Street;
Tel (250) 557 24 15.
http://eagleviewhouse.ca

🛏 Singing Surf Inn
Behind its slightly underwhelming exterior, this motel provides very comfortable accommodation. The rooms have large beds, kitchenettes, and cable television with free sports and movie channels.
1504 Old Beach Road,
Tel (250) 626 33 18.
www.singingsurf.com

Queen Charlotte City

🐋 Anvil Cove Charters
Take a leisurely trip in a small schooner around the Queen Charlotte Islands, or you might prefer to head inland on a guided kayak tour. Trips to Native North American villages and whale-watching excursions are also available – both led by knowledgeable guides.
P. O. Box 454;
Tel (250) 559 82 07.
www.queencharlotte
kayaking.com

🐋 Gwaii Haanas Guest House and Kayaks
The owners of this remote lodge organize tours of the surrounding bays in kayaks and Zodiac inflatable boats, as well as half-day trips to the historic Haida settlement of Ninstints, where you can see the island's oldest totem poles. The Zodiac boats allow you to get right alongside gray whales.
P. O. Box 578; Rose Harbour
via Queen Charlotte City.
www.gwaiihaanas.com

🐋 Gwaii Haanas National Park Reserve
Management of this huge national park in the southern Queen Charlotte Islands is shared between the Council of the Haida Nation and the Canadian government. The reserve is accessible only by seaplane or boat but it is well worth the effort. Its isolated bays and coastline form part of a landscape of outstanding natural beauty. SGang Gwaay llnagaay (Ninstints), a historic Haida settlement, is one of the most popular sights.
Tel (250) 559 88 18.
www.pc.gc.ca/pn-np/bc/
gwaiihaanas

🛒 Isabel Creek Store
This wonderful shop mostly sells dairy products and organic groceries, including bread that is freshly baked on the islands and – of course – salmon and halibut, delivered daily by the fishermen themselves.
3219 Wharf Street;
Tel (250) 559 86 23.

❌ Oceanview Restaurant
Though this might look like your average country eatery, the food is anything but. The fish is outstanding, but the burgers also deserve a special mention – seasoned fast-food eaters will be amazed at how juicy these can really be. The perfect place for breakfast.
3301 Third Avenue;
Tel (250) 559 85 03.

❌ Purple Onion Deli
A small delicatessen that also serves food to eat in. The delicious soups and other healthy snacks are really very good indeed. If you are about to set off on a walk or boat trip, take one of the Purple Onion's sandwiches with you – there's a great range of fillings to choose from.
1-3207 Wharf Street;
Tel (250) 559 41 19.

🛏 Premier Creek Lodge
This lodge has been one of the best and most popular places to stay on the Queen Charlotte Islands ever since it opened in 1910. It is located right on the bay, and there is a fantastic view from the hotel veranda – you can see the boats in the port and watch majestic eagles soaring high above. The rooms are generously proportioned and well-appointed – standard features include fridge, microwave, coffee machine, and internet access.

From left: Roam free in Chilcotin Country; an idyllic scene on the Queen Charlotte Islands; the port at Queen Charlotte City, at the foot of the San Cristoval Mountains; serenity in Tweedsmuir Provincial Park.

QUEEN CHARLOTTE ISLANDS/ HAIDA GWAII

The insider tips listed here refer to the sights described on pages 86–99.

P. O. Box 268;
Tel. (250) 559 84 15.
www.qcislands.net/premier

🛏 Sea Raven Motel
The biggest hotel in town, the Sea Raven Motel is located right on Skidegate Inlet and enjoys a fantastic view over the picturesque bay. The rooms are modest, but – all importantly – very clean. Facilities include cable television and free internet access.
3301 Third Avenue;
Tel (250) 559 44 23.
www.searaven.com

🛏 Dorothy & Mike's Guest House
The owners, Dorothy and Mike, have lived on the Queen Charlotte Islands for many years, and the warm welcome they extend to their guests exemplifies the islands' legendary hospitality. The guest house is decorated in traditional style and the rooms are immaculately presented, each with its own unique character, and most have great views of the bay. The superb breakfast spread alone is reason enough to stay here.
3127 Second Avenue;
Tel (250) 559 84 39.
www.qcislands.net/doromike

🛏 Spruce Point Lodging
The rooms here are typical of the fairly modest accommodation offered by most hotels on the Queen Charlotte Islands. That said, the rooms all come equipped with cable television, a fridge, and their own bathroom. Snow-capped mountains overlook the hotel to the rear, with the attractive bay to the front.
609 Sixth Avenue;
Tel (250) 559 82 34.
www.qcislands.net/sprpoint

Queen Charlotte Islands

ℹ Visitor Information Centre
Sometimes known as the Misty Islands, the Queen Charlotte Islands lie 100 km (62 miles) off the coast of British Columbia. The low-lying Naikoon Provincial Park – with its hiking trails, clam-rich beaches, and even the odd shipwreck – is in the north-east of the islands. Near the village of Port Clements, golden spruce lends a magical glow to the banks of the Yakoun River. South of the village, a gravel trail leads to a forest clearing where you can see a historic Haida canoe. Take a sip from St Mary's Spring and you will surely return to the Queen Charlotte Islands – at least, so the legend goes.
3220 Wharf Street,
Queen Charlotte City;
Tel (250) 559 83 16.
www.qcinfo.ca

🏞 Naikoon Provincial Park
The park's landscape was formed by glacial activity in the ice age. At just 150 m (492 feet) above sea level, Argonaut Hill is the highest point on the island, while on the northern coast an outcrop of basalt columns at Tow Hill form a notable landmark. Migratory birds stop to nest at both the Tow Hill and Rose Hill Ecological Reserves, before continuing their journey south. The park can be accessed via Masset and Tlell in the northern part of Graham Island.

Sandspit

✖ Dick's Wok Inn
Dick Leung serves the Cantonese cuisine of his Chinese homeland, but he dishes up good salmon and hamburgers, too. If you fancy a change, this place will not disappoint.
388 Cooper Bay Road;
Tel (250) 637 22 75.

🛏 Sandspit Inn
A small hotel with modest, country-style rooms at reasonable rates. Anglers can hire a full range of equipment on site as well as decent fishing boats. Guided fishing trips are also available.
P. O. Box 469;
Tel (250) 637 53 34.
www.westcoastresorts.com

🛏 Northern Shores Lodging
This cosy lodge on the rocky coastline is a particularly good family choice. The spacious suites each have their own kitchenette and bathroom, and you can play billiards or darts in the communal recreation room. Given the islands' rather frequent bad weather, the washing machines and the drying room could also come in very handy.
455 Alliford Bay Road;
Tel (250) 637 22 33.

🛏 The Lodge at Tasu Sound
This secluded fishing lodge is situated in a dramatic setting "on the edge of the wilderness". The sheltered bay and the waters beneath the 1,000-m (3,281-feet) high basalt cliff can yield sizeable salmon – making it very popular with angling enthusiasts. The comfortable rooms are furnished in a rural style, and the food is excellent. Accessible only by plane.
Tasu Sound (travel via Sandspit);
Tel (604) 278 31 30.

Skidegate

🏛 Haida Gwaii Museum
This museum forms part of the Haida Heritage Centre at Second Beach, Kaay Llnagaay. Its exhibits and many photographs document the history of the First Nations people in the area. One of the most valuable items is the Loo Taas canoe, displayed at the 1986 Expo exhibition in Vancouver. Carved from the trunk of a red cedar, it is 15 m (49 feet) long. The totem poles outside the museum include both historic and modern examples.
2 Second Beach Road;
Tel (250) 559 78 85.
www.haidaheritage centre.com

✖ Dave's In The Village
This casual eatery with an equally casual name is famous for its tasty fish and chips – tuck into the finest, locally caught halibut. The milkshakes are also famous.
112 Front Street;
Tel (250) 559 87 82.

✖ Jags Beanstalk
Great coffee, delicious homemade cakes, and a breathtaking sea view. Sitting on the terrace, you might even catch a glimpse of a passing whale. A seasonal flower and garden supply shop is adjacent.
100 Highway 16;
Tel (250) 559 88 26.

✖ Keenawii's Kitchen
Native North American chef Roberta Olsen – otherwise known as Keenawii – serves traditional Haida fare. Roberta comes from a long line of traditional food gatherers. By appointment only.
237 Highway 16;
Tel (250) 559 83 47.

THE HIGHLIGHTS

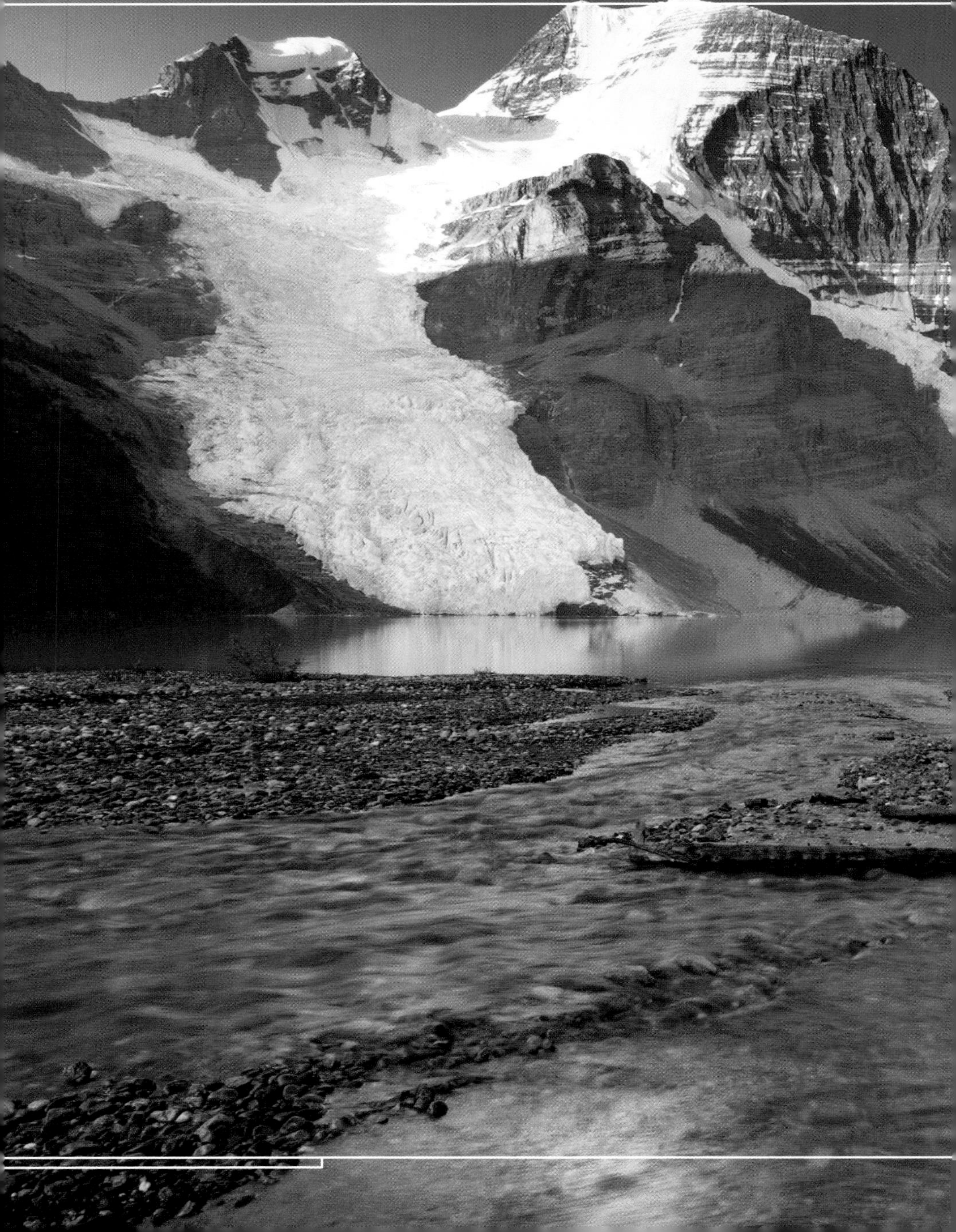

BRITISH COLUMBIA
THOMPSON
OKANAGAN
CARIBOO

The pale, cobalt-blue tones of the waters and mountains of British Colombia form a somewhat chilly palette, but one that is warmed by the reddish glow of the sun during the day. The Thompson plateau dominates the Thompson Okanagan region in this central part of British Columbia, its mountains including the Columbia, Cariboo, and Skeena ranges. Two magnificent rivers – the Fraser and the Columbia, which rises in the Rocky Mountains – have also left their mark on the landscape. The Okanagan Valley, stretches from Vernon to Osoyoos, near the US border. Famed for its wine and high-quality fruit, Okanagan's main towns are Kelowna and Penticton.

21 Fraser River Valley

22 Chilliwack River Valley

23 Okanagan Valley

24 Shuswap Lake Area

25 Mount Revelstoke National Park

26 Glacier National Park

27 Wells Gray Provincial Park

28 Mount Robson Provincial Park

29 Barkerville

30 Quesnel Museum

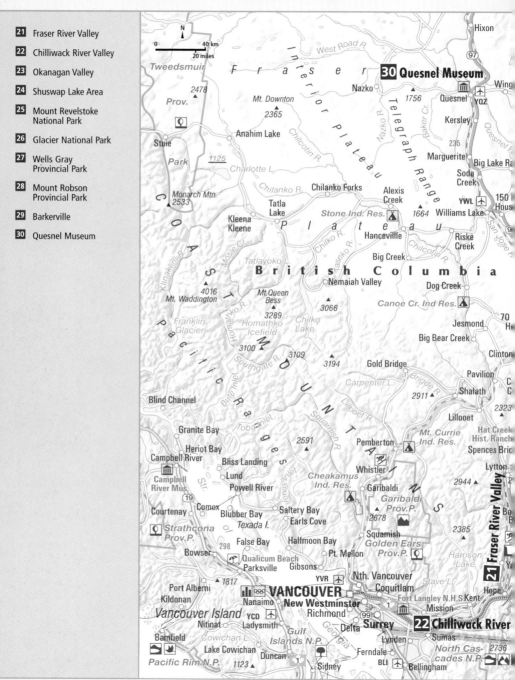

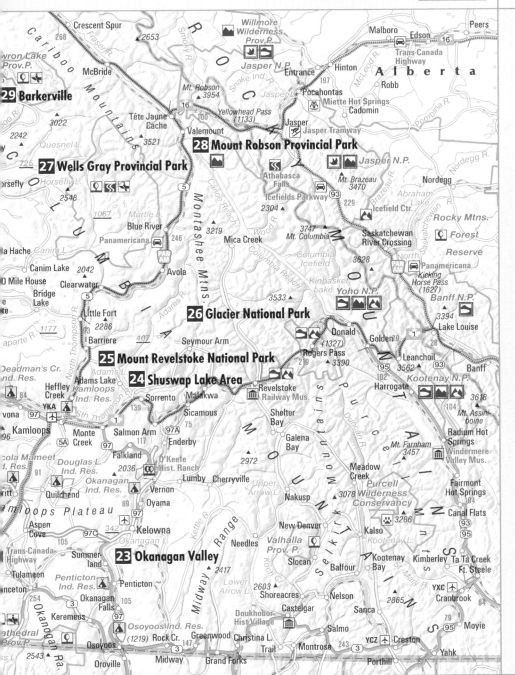

THE HIGHLIGHTS:
BRITISH COLUMBIA:
THOMPSON OKANAGAN,
CARIBOO

The source of the Fraser River is at Mount Edith Cavell. From here, the 1,375-km (854-mile) river flows past Mount Robson (below, right) before flowing into the Pacific. The Chilliwack River is an important tributary, fed by forest streams (below, left). The Alexandra Bridge spans the Fraser River at Yale (right).

INFO Hell's Gate Airtram

This cable railway spans the Fraser Canyon. Twice as much water flows through Hell's Gate as cascades down Niagara Falls. Salmon climb the artificial fish ladders in September.

43111 Trans-Canada Highway;
Tel (604) 867 92 77,
Apr–Oct 10.00–16.00,
May–Sept 10.00–17.00.

FRASER RIVER VALLEY 21
CHILLIWACK RIVER VALLEY 22

Like the adjacent Chilliwack River Valley, Fraser River Valley is one of the region's primary agricultural areas. The deep gorge known as Hell's Gate is situated in the northern part of Fraser River Valley. Just 35 m (115 feet) wide at its narrowest point, this spectacular gorge was declared the "gate of hell" by cartogra- pher Simon Fraser in 1808. Fraser mapped large parts of modern-day British Columbia, and the Fraser River is named after him. The canyon and its val- leys, which cut deep into the landscape, were formed during the ice age, and the area was already widely settled by the time the first Europeans arrived. The dis- covery of gold in the Thompson River in 1857 sparked a gold rush that further accelerated the area's settlement. Sev- eral new towns grew up around the mooring places for the steamers from Vancouver. Chilliwack was one of them; situated in the southern part of Fraser Valley, it is a now a major city.

Between the months of June and November, adult salmon swim distances of up to 30 km (19 miles) every day, finding their way from the Pacific Ocean to their home rivers in British Columbia. Once in the confines of the rivers, during the spawning season, altercations between rival males are not unusual (below). There are many idyllic fishing locations on the Fraser River Valley (below, inset). An impressive catch of sockeye salmon (right).

COMMERCIAL SALMON FISHING

There are five different salmon species to be found in the lakes and rivers of Western Canada, namely the pink, coho, chum, chinook, and sockeye. The latter – also known as the red salmon – is the most common. Frequently exceeding 14 kg (30 lb), when it is known as tyee, the chinook is the biggest, while the coho – or silver salmon – is the most prized by anglers.

The chum and pink salmon are less fatty, so they lack the intensity of taste that is typical of the other three species. There are more salmon in the Fraser River system with its many tributaries than anywhere else on the North American continent. Throughout the spawning season, Shuswap Lake (which drains into a smaller lake and river) is an important safe haven for

the young fish before they set off on their journey to the sea. Salmon Arm, a town on the shores of the lake, gets its name from the traditional fishing methods used by its Shuswap inhabitants, who would hurl long spears into the water to catch the fish. An early blow was dealt to the area's commercial fishing industry in 1913, when major landslides at Hell's Gate in the

Fraser River Canyon blocked many local access routes. Today, over-fishing is the main problem. As a result, there are severe restraints on commercial fishing, and most of the salmon sold locally in stores comes from large salmon farms. Despite the introduction of temporary fishing bans and a complete ban on the use of driftnets, stocks of wild salmon continue to fall.

THE HIGHLIGHTS: BRITISH COLUMBIA: THOMPSON OKANAGAN, CARIBOO

TIP Okanagan Wine Route

The Okanagan Valley is Canada's best-known wine region (below). Salmon Arm Wharf projects out into the water sports lover's paradise that is Shuswap Lake (below, inset). In October, you can see huge schools of migrating salmon here.

From Osoyoos to Salmon Arm, the Okanagan Wine Route takes in some 60 different estates. Predefined itineraries like the Great Estates of the Okanagan tour will take you straight to the region's top wineries. Alternatively, just follow your nose!
Tel (877) 433 04 51.
www.greatestokanagan.com

OKANAGAN VALLEY 23
SHUSWAP LAKE AREA 24

Traversed by the Okanagan River, the Okanagan Valley is one of the most fertile regions in the whole of Western Canada. Father Charles Marie Pandosy planted the first vines here in 1859, and by the turn of the century there were over a million fruit trees in the area. The dry climate helps the fruit to ripen, creating ideal conditions for both fruit plantations and vineyards. Today, there are over twenty wine estates in the fertile lands between Osoyoos, Winfield, and Keremeos. Thanks to several large lakes – Shuswap Lake, Adams Lake, Mara Lake, and Mabel Lake – this is a water sports paradise, with plenty of beaches. Situated amid some truly beautiful scenery, Salmon Arm is the region's main town, while Sicamous, at the junction of Shuswap and Mara lakes, is known as "House Boat Capital of Canada", due to the number of houseboats available for rent. The name Okanagan Valley can be traced back to that of one of the First Nations peoples.

INFO Giant Cedars Boardwalk Trail

The alpine meadows of Mount Revelstoke National Park are at their most stunning in summer, when all kinds of wild flowers bloom, including lupin, arnica, and many species of *Castilleja* ("Indian Paintbrush"). The park authorities frequently close off sections of the parkway to help protect the ecosystem.

This boardwalk trail lies about 30 km (19 miles) east of Revelstoke, on the Trans-Canada Highway. It leads right through the rainforest, passing giant red cedar trees up to 500 years old. Get your breath back – or just struggle to take it all in – on one of the benches along the way. The trail starts at the Giant Cedars Picnic Area.

MOUNT REVELSTOKE NATIONAL PARK 25

Established in 1914, this national park in the Selkirk Mountains covers an area of approximately 260 sq km (100 sq miles). The Meadows in the Sky Parkway (26 km/16 miles long) – also known as Summit Road – branches off the Trans-Canada Highway about 1.5 km (1 mile) east of Revelstoke, winding its way north through the park's woodland and mountain meadows, with panoramic views at every turn. Hemlock trees (*Tsuga*) grow here (a misnomer as they are not poisonous) but are now under threat from a sap-sucking insect, and tall red cedars thrive, some up to 1,000 years old. Birds and squirrels also flourish in the sub-alpine pine forests. Higher up, the alpine meadows are a vivid carpet of flowers. From the top of Mount Revelstoke itself, the view below is over snow-covered rock faces and jagged crevasses. The park's dark valleys, meanwhile, provide a safe haven for grizzly bear, mountain goat, and caribou.

INFO Rogers Pass Discovery Centre

The vivid hues of autumn in Rogers Pass (below) form a contrast with the mountain landscape and its evergreen conifers. From the pass, there is a good view of Illecillewaet Neve, the largest of Glacier National Park's snow and ice fields, which is still growing today (below, inset).

The Rogers Pass Discovery Centre is a one-stop shop for information on trails, weather, and bear movements. There are also natural history displays and the Glacier Circle Bookstore, which stocks a good range of titles.
Tel (250) 837 68 67; Jun–Sept 7.30–20.00, daily, Oct–Nov 8.30–16.30, closed Tues–Wed.

GLACIER NATIONAL PARK 26

Glacier National Park, established in the Columbia Mountains in 1886, covers an area of approximately 1,350 sq km (521 sq miles). With its 400 glaciers, much of the park is permanently covered in ice. The park is a popular destination for mountain climbers and hikers. The small town of Golden serves as a base for the various sporting activities available in this area – hiking, horseback riding, and notably whitewater rafting on the Kicking Horse and Columbia rivers, which meet here. The Trans-Canada Highway is the only road through the park, leading up to the 1,330-m (4,364-foot) high Rogers Pass. Surrounded by steep mountains that rise to heights of over 3,000 m (9,843 feet), the pass was discovered during the construction of the Canadian Pacific Railway in 1881. Just west of the pass, the Nakimu Cave system is one of the most extensive in Canada – *nakimu* means "grumbling spirits" in Shuswap.

THE HIGHLIGHTS:
BRITISH COLUMBIA:
THOMPSON OKANAGAN,
CARIBOO

Spectacular waterfalls are just one way that nature attracts our attention in Wells Gray Provincial Park. At Helmcken Falls (below, left), the Murtle River thunders down from the plateau around 140 m (459 feet) into the gorge below, framed by black basalt cliffs. Below, right: Canim Falls, also in the park.

INFO Salmon spawning

During the latter half of August, the search for the perfect spawning grounds brings thousands of salmon to Raft River. You can watch this extraordinary natural spectacle from the viewing platform near Highway 5, north of Clearwater.
Wells Gray Information Centre; Tel (250) 674 33 34.

Established in 1939, this spectacular park in the Cariboo Mountains spans over 5,000 sq km (1,930 sq miles). It takes in majestic mountains and glaciers, clear, tranquil lakes, rushing rivers, thundering waterfalls, and deep canyons created by meltwater during the last ice age. Much of the park is densely forested and dotted with alpine meadows. Parts of the park have not yet been fully explored, and it is with good reason that the park authorities issue visitors with a leaflet on "Bear Watching Etiquette". Beaver, mule deer, and elk are – alongside the grizzly bear – some of the other animals you may spot here. The Wells Gray-Clearwater volcanic field is in the southern part of the park. Formed some 3.5 million years ago, the field has been increasing in size gradually ever since. The volcanoes (both extinct and dormant), basalt columns, cooled lava flows, and mineral springs are a striking reminder of the region's eventful geological history.

THE HIGHLIGHTS:
BRITISH COLUMBIA:
THOMPSON OKANAGAN,
CARIBOO

Berg Lake Trail is one of the most beautiful in the whole of Western Canada (below). It starts by following the Robson River, continuing past Kinney Lake and the Valley of a Thousand Waterfalls. On the western bank, ice breaking off the Berg Glacier on the side of Mount Robson calves into the lake below (right).

INFO Four-wheel drive tours

These tough, all terrain vehicles allow you to explore beyond the established trails. All the tours are guided. You can drive if you are over 20 and hold a driving licence. Passengers must be at least 12.

Mica Mountain Lodge, 15658 Tete Jaune Road, Valemount V0E 2Z0; Tel (250) 566 98 16.

At 3,954 m (12,972 feet) above sea level, Mount Robson is easily the highest mountain not only in the park that bears its name but in the whole of the Canadian Rockies. It towers over Mount Fitzwilliam, which – at 2,911 m (9,551 feet) – is the next highest summit. The First Nations people named it Yuh-hai-has-hun, meaning "mountain of the spiral road" – a reference to the layers of rock that wind their way up to the summit like a snake. The white settlers, meanwhile, named it after John Robson, prime minister of British Columbia from 1889 to 1892. Mount Robson Provincial Park was created in 1913. Bordering Alberta's Jasper National Park to the east, the park covers an area of over 2,200 sq km (849 sq miles). In 1990, it was declared a UNESCO World Heritage Site along with other national and provincial parks in the Rockies. Wildlife to look out for include grizzly bear, caribou, and 182 bird species.

THE HIGHLIGHTS:
BRITISH COLUMBIA:
THOMPSON OKANAGAN,
CARIBOO

Yesteryear is brought to life at Barkerville Historic Town, one of British Colombia's most popular tourist attractions, where scenes from the days of the gold rush are re-enacted. Watch the town judge mete out justice, see a Cornish Waterwheel in action, or join a lesson in an 1880s-style classroom.

INFO Cottonwood House

East of Quesnel, this old roadhouse and post office dates from 1864. It once played an important role in the gold rush, serving the prospectors who stopped off here. Today, it offers wagon rides and tours.
Barkerville Highway;
Tel (250) 992 20 71;
May–Sept 10.00–17.00 daily.

This former gold rush town was named after Billy Barker, a sailor from Cornwall in England, who struck large quantities of gold here in 1862. Barkerville rapidly became a boomtown, as prospectors combed the river bed for more gold, and Barker made a fortune. Unfortunately, he and his fun-loving wife spent it all, and were buried in a pauper's grave in Victoria. The boom lasted for 20 years before the prospectors moved on to try their luck elsewhere – leaving Barkerville to fall into decline. Around an hour's drive east of Quesnel, the town was restored and opened as a historic town and tourist attraction at the end of the 1950s. There are tours, activities, and events throughout the day, such as stagecoach rides and gold panning, with actors in costume bringing the days of the gold rush vividly to life. Visit the nearby Quesnel Museum for more information and exhibits on the era.

Barkerville

🏛 **Barkerville Historic Town**
This reconstructed gold-rush town looks much as it would have done in the 1860s. A variety of tours and activities cater to young and old alike. Watch a period production at the Theatre Royal, pan for gold outside the souvenir shop, or visit the historic stores, blacksmith, and saloons. Barkerville also has its own cemetery. Tour guides dressed in period costume, will show you around town.
P. O. Box 19;
Tel (250) 994 33 32;
sunrise to sunset daily.
www.barkerville.ca

Cariboo Country

ℹ️ **Tourist information**
The wild west is alive and well in Cariboo Country, British Columbia. The landscape here ranges from alpine meadows to thick forests and vast prairie. The highway follows the course of Fraser River, retracing the steps of the gold prospectors of old.
204-350 Barnard Street,
Williams Lake;
Tel (250) 392 22 26.
www.landwithoutlimits.com

Kelowna

ℹ️ **Tourist information**
Situated in the heart of the Okanagan Valley, Kelowna is one of the most popular holiday destinations in British Columbia. The town is famous for its temperate climate and long hours of sunshine, and – like most places in the valley – is known for its lakeside beaches, fruit plantations, and excellent wine.

544 Harvey Avenue,
Tel (250) 861 15 15.
www.tourismkelowna.com

🏛 **Father Pandosy Mission**
The mission dates back to 1859 and has been restored as a museum. It was Father Pandosy who planted the first vines and fruit trees in the Okanagan Valley.
3685 Benvoulin Road;
Tel (250) 860 83 69.

🏛 **B.C. Orchard Industry Museum**
Housed in a former commercial fruit-packing house, this museum is devoted to the Okanagan Valley fruit industry. There are all sorts of facts and figures about the different varieties of fruit, and how they are cultivated and packed. The photography archive provides an interesting insight into the region's wider history.
1304 Ellis Street;
Tel (250) 868 04 41;
Mon–Sat 10.00–17.00.
www.kelownamuseum.ca

🌺 **Summerhill Estate Winery**
Among the many wine estates in the Okanagan Valley, Summerhill has really made a name for itself. It is a "Certified Organic Vineyard", meaning that it does not use harmful pesticides or chemical fertilizers. Summerhill's fertile soil plays an important part in producing the estate's eminently drinkable wines.
4870 Chute Lake Road;
Tel (250) 764 80 00; guided tours 12.00–14.00 daily.
www.summerhill.bc.ca

🌺 **Appleberry Farm Ltd**
Take a guided tour of one of the vast fruit plantations that

are typical of this region. You can buy fresh fruit, jam, and juices in the Orchard Store.
3193 Dunster Road,
Tel (250) 868 38 14;
guided tours Apr–May Tues–Sun 10.00–17.30, Jun–Aug 10.00–17.30 daily, Sept–Dec Tues–Sun 10.00–17.30.

❌ **Christophers**
This elegant restaurant is the place to sample a superbly tender Alberta steak. The chicken and pasta dishes, though equally delicious, seem to pale in comparison.
242 Lawrence Avenue;
Tel (250) 861 34 64.

🛏 **The Grand Okanagan Lakefront Resort**
With its private beach and stylish Atrium Lobby, there is more than a hint of a retro Florida about this grand hotel. The rooms are enormous, and luxuriously appointed – some even include a kitchen and an open fireplace. You can choose from numerous treatments available at the hotel spa, and there is a yachting marina outside.
1310 Water Street;
Tel (250) 763 45 00.
www.grandokanagan.com

Naramata

🛏 **Naramata Heritage Inn & Spa**
This former girls' school is one of the most romantic places to stay in Okanagan wine country. Though relatively small, the rooms are exquisitely furnished, and there is a real air of 19th-century elegance. The restaurant stands out for its excellent wine list, and the spa is the perfect place to relax after a busy day.

3625 First Street;
Tel (250) 496 68 08.
www.naramatainn.com

Penticton

ℹ️ **Penticton & Wine Country Chamber of Commerce**
The city of Penticton lies at the southern end of Okanagan Lake. Life here is relaxed, with superb beaches along both Okanagan Lake and Lake Skaha. Peach, apple, and cherry trees thrive in the surrounding area, as do the local vineyards. The town hosts a peach festival, the Okanagan Wine Festival, the Okanagan Fest-of-Ale, and, the Pacific Northwest Elvis Festival.
553 Railway Street;
Tel (250) 493 40 55.
www.tourismpenticton.com

🏛 **S.S. Sicamous**
Built by the Canadian Pacific Railway to connect the towns involved in the fruit industry, this last example of a historic paddle steamer is permanently moored on the banks of Okanagan Lake. It was in regular service from 1914 to 1935. Temporary exhibitions are often held on board.
1099 Lakeshore Drive West;
Tel (250) 492 04 03;
summer 9.00–21.00 daily, winter Mon–Fri 9.00–16.00.
www.sssicamous.com

❌ **Granny Bogners**
This old-fashioned restaurant is very popular, especially with the locals. The menu might look a little dated, but the cordon bleu steak is superb, the grilled salmon is excellent, and there is a choice of fine wines.
302 West Eckhardt Avenue;
Tel (250) 493 27 11.

THOMPSON OKANAGAN, CARIBOO

The insider tips listed here refer to the sights described on pages 98–117.

From left: Bathing fun on Shuswap Lake; Revelstoke's hydroelectric dam; an old building has been given a new lease of life at the B.C. Orchard Industry Museum; a summertime scene on Okanagan Lake.

Quesnel

🛏 Bowron Lake Lodge & Resort
Choose between a cozy room in the lodge or one of the traditional wood cabins on the banks of Bowron Lake – clean and functional, they have dramatic views of the distant mountains. Canoe hire is also available from the lodge.
672 Walkem Street;
Tel (250) 992 27 33.

Revelstoke

ℹ️ Tourist information
The former gold rush town of Revelstoke is situated between Rogers Pass and Eagle Pass in a magnificent setting. It forms the starting point for many excursions to the nearby glaciers and snow-covered mountains, and to the region's national parks and romantic valleys.
204 Campbell Avenue;
Tel (250) 837 53 45.

🏛 Revelstoke Railway Museum
Historic rolling stock, locomotives, and many other exhibits record the eventful history of the Canadian rail network. The museum also explains the challenges associated with its construction and the glory days of the first transcontinental routes.
719 Track Street West;
Tel (250) 837 60 60;
Jul–Aug 9.00–20.00 daily,
May–Jun, Sept–Oct
9.00–17.00 daily,
Nov–Feb Fri–Tues
9.00–17.00, Mar–Apr
Thurs–Tues 9.00–17.00.

🧭 Glacier National Park
As it crosses the park, the Trans-Canada Highway is overshadowed by jagged mountain peaks and over 400 glaciers. Established in 1886, Glacier National Park contains numerous hiking trails, including trails to Mount Tupper and the Rogers peaks. The trail along Connaught Creek and Cougar Creek leads to the Cougar Valley and the extraordinary glacial landscape of the Illecillewaet ice field.
P. O. Box 350;
Tel (250) 837 75 00.
www.pc.gc.ca/eng/pn-np/bc/
glacier/index.aspx

🛏 Three Valley Gap Lake Chateau
Located 19 km (12 miles) west of Revelstoke on the Trans-Canada Highway, this major hotel complex boasts over a hundred rooms, a swimming pool, and its very own western ghost town. The latter consists of around 25 original buildings brought here from towns across British Columbia by hotel owner Gordon Bell. The Three Valley Heritage Ghost Town recreates the pioneer days of the 1800s, while the Antique Autos Museum with its collection of classic cars jumps a hundred years or so into the future.
P. O. Box 860;
Tel (250) 837 21 09.
www.3valley.com

Salmon Arm

🛏 Salmon Arm Travelodge
A comfortable motel offering basic, clean accommodation. Amenities in the rooms include a fridge, microwave, and internet access. The lodge's heated pool and whirlpool are particularly popular in winter. Breakfast is included.
2401 Trans-Canada Highway West; Tel (250) 832 97 21.

Shuswap Lake Area

ℹ️ Thompson Okanagan Tourism Association
The Trans-Canada Highway runs alongside Shuswap Lake. With its many beaches, the lake is a popular spot for vacationers – especially families. You can take children rafting on the nearby Adams River. The small town of Salmon Arm, set amid beautiful scenery, is the region's largest settlement. Sicamous, meanwhile, is known as the "Houseboat Capital of Canada" – there are hundreds of houseboats for rent here.
2280-D Leckie Road, Kelowna;
Tel (250) 860 59 99.

Sicamous

🚤 Twin Achors Houseboat Rentals
It is hard to think of a better way to explore the local lakes than aboard a houseboat. Twin Anchors is one of the best-known rental firms, and there is a wide range of vessels to choose from. Inside, houseboats have the same kind of features you would expect to find in a motor home, and they are just as easy to manoeuvre. Features include a microwave, DVD player, and a dinghy for impromptu excursions.
101 Martin Street;
Tel (250) 836-24 50.

Vernon

ℹ️ Tourist information
North of Kelowna, the town of Vernon lies on the north bank of Okanagan Lake. White sandy beaches, seemingly endless fruit plantations, and richly stocked rivers and lakes are just some of the region's attractions.
701 Highway 97 South;
Tel (250) 542 14 15.
www.vernontourism.com

🏛 Historic O'Keefe Ranch
Established in 1867, this huge ranch once belonged to the cattle magnate Cornelius O'Keefe. The restored buildings include the ranch house, church, general store, and post office. Along with the accompanying museum, they bring the old west back to life.
9380 Highway 97;
Tel (250) 542 78 68;
9.00–17.00 daily.
www.okeeferanch.ca

🧺 The Farm Shop
Tasty organic food to take away, from organic bread to homemade ice cream, jams, and muffins with whole chunks of real fruit. Perfect for stocking the larder on your houseboat!
3005 39th Avenue,
Tel. (250) 545 25 49.

❌ Alexander's Beach Pub
This welcoming pub on the beach at Kalamalka Lake serves drinks and snacks. For the locals, it is a popular place to meet up after work.
12408 Kal Lake Road;
Tel (250) 545 31 31.

🛏 Best Western Vernon Lodge
The lobby forms part of the hotel's lovely tropical garden, which also includes a heated indoor pool. The generously sized rooms all have a Nintendo games console, internet access, and coffee machine.
3914 32nd Street;
Tel (250) 545 33 85.
www.bestwesternvernonlodge.com

Yoho National Park was established in 1886. Covering an area of 1,313 sq km (507 sq miles), it is the smallest of the four national parks included on the UNESCO World Heritage Site list in 1984 as the Canadian Rocky Mountains Parks (the others are Jasper, Banff, and Kootenay). The value of preserving this fascinating natural landscape, with its untouched flora and fauna, is easy to see. In 1990, the World Heritage Site was extended to take in the Mount Robson, Mount Assiniboine, and Hamber provincial parks as well. For many visitors, Yoho is the most beautiful of the four national parks. The two valleys created by the Kicking Horse and Yoho rivers form the heart of the park. The Takakkaw Falls are a particular highlight. Here, water melting off Daly Glacier, one of the principal outlet glaciers of the Waputik Icefield, cascades down a 254-m (833-feet) high rock face into the depths below. *Takakkaw* is Cree for "it is magnificent".

THE HIGHLIGHTS:
BRITISH COLUMBIA:
KOOTENAY ROCKIES

The Kootenay National Park protects not only the imposing mountain landscape of the high Canadian Rockies, but also the lakes, rivers, and wild-flower meadows that fall within the park's boundaries. Mountain goats (right) and bighorn sheep are found in the park. Below: Views of Kootenay River.

INFO Radium Hot Springs

Magnificent rock cliffs overlook Radium's hot pool. The water temperature is 39°C (102°F) and the air is pleasantly free of the usual sulphur smell.
Radium Hot Springs V0A 1M0; Tel (250) 347 94 85; May–Oct 9.00–23.00, Oct–May Sun–Thurs 12.00–21.00, Fri–Sat 12.00–22.00.

Established in 1920, Kootenay National Park covers a 1,406-sq km (543-sq miles) area in the south-western Canadian Rockies. The valleys of the Kootenay and Vermilion rivers form the heart of the park. From the 1,637-m (5,371-foot) high Vermilion Pass, you get a good view of Fireweed Trail. This short trail (1 km/0.6 mile) demonstrates nature's ability to recover from even the most devastating fires. South of the pass, the area around Stanley Glacier is famous for the many fossils found here. Marble Canyon, which cuts 37 m (121 feet) into the limestone, is another notable sight, as are the so-called Paint Pots, whose iron-rich soil the Native North Americans once used to make body paint. At the southern end of the park, the mildly radioactive thermal springs in the spa town of Radium Hot Springs are well worth a visit. The area's indigenous peoples were the first to attribute them with spiritual and healing powers.

Mount Assiniboine (below and right) is frequently referred to as the Canadian Matterhorn because of its similarity to the famous Alpine peak. The still waters of Lake Magog, right in the heart of Mount Assiniboine Provincial Park, are accessed via a 27-km (17-mile) long trail from bordering Banff National Park.

INFO Lake Magog

Lake Magog is at an altitude of 2,155 m (7,070 feet). The idyllic Lake Magog Campground is located in the forests overlooking the lake and its beaches. The site has all the necessary basic amenities, including cooking facilities.
BC Parks, Wasa V0B 2K0;
Tel. (250) 422 42 00.

Reaching an altitude of 3,618 m (11,870 feet), Mount Assiniboine is one of the highest peaks in the Canadian Rockies. The mountain is shaped a bit like a pyramid, and was named by the Canadian scientist George Mercer Dawson (1849–1901). Dawson journeyed through this part of the Rocky Mountains between 1883 and 1884 in order to map the highest peaks, passes, and rivers for the government. When he reached this particular giant, the clouds above the summit reminded him of the smoke he had seen rising above the Assiniboine people's tipis, and the mountain has been known as Mount Assiniboine ever since. Also named after the Assiniboine, the provincial park was founded in 1922. Covering an area of 390 sq km (151 sq miles), the park forms part of the Canadian Rocky Mountain Parks UNESCO World Heritage Site. There is no road access in the park, only hiking trails.

Cranbrook

ℹ Visitor Information Centre
Set in the foothills of the Rocky Mountains, Cranbrook itself does not really have much in the way of tourist attractions. Its location, however, makes it an ideal starting point for all sorts of excursions and hikes. If you are not venturing beyond south-eastern British Columbia, the town is actually a great base for your entire action-packed holiday.
2279 Cranbrook Street North; Tel (250) 426 59 14.
www.cranbrookchamber.com

🏛 Canadian Museum of Rail Travel
This railway museum recalls the heady days of the pioneer era, when the town of Cranbrook grew up at the end of the railway line. Look out for the luxurious trains that once carried various monarchs and financial tycoons. This opulent rolling stock includes 12 coaches lined with mahogany panels, previously operated by Trans-Canada Limited.
57 Van Home Street; Tel (250) 489 39 18.
www.trainsdeluxe.com

☒ Heidi's Restaurant
Heidi, your Canadian host, learnt about the joys of Germanic cuisine from her mother. The restaurant's top dishes include *Wiener Schnitzel* (pan-fried breaded pork), *Bratwurst* sausages as good as any you might taste in Berlin, beef roulade, and – a real treat – *Wiener Waltz Geschnetzeltes* (strips of pork in a creamy sauce).
821 C Baker Street; Tel (250) 426 79 22.
www.heidis.ca

▣ St Eugene Mission Resort
For much of the 20th century, these buildings housed a mission school for First Nations children. Now fully renovated, this is one the best resorts in south-eastern British Columbia. The guest rooms in this great complex are truly first-rate, and the resort has its own golf club and casino. There is also an exhibition devoted to the traditions of the local First Nations people.
7731 Mission Road; Tel (250) 420 20 00.
www.steugene.ca

🏛 Fort Steele Heritage Town
The days of the gold rush are brought back to life in this heritage town. The town was originally established in 1864 on a section of the Kootenay River that is navigable by ferry. Five years later, however, the Canadian Pacific decided to run its lines not to Fort Steele but to Cranbrook, leaving Fort Steele to become a ghost town. This reconstruction dates from the 1960s. The buildings are not entirely faithful copies of the originals, but the effect is totally authentic. Actors dressed in period costume interact with the visitors and portray life as it was in the pioneer towns of the late 19th century. Steam locomotives puff away noisily at the station.
9851 Highway 93/95, Fort Steele; Tel (250) 417 60 00.
www.fortsteele.ca

Golden

ℹ Tourist information
Conveniently poised between the Rocky Mountains and the Purcell Range, this Columbia River Valley town makes a perfect base for exciting trips to the major national parks like Kootenay, Glacier, Yoho, and Mount Revelstoke.
500 10th Avenue North; Tel (250) 344 71 25.

🏆 Kicking Horse Pass
East of Golden, the Kicking Horse Pass is the location of the Canadian Pacific Railway's famous Spiral Tunnels. The tracks wind their way up the steep mountain incline, passing through numerous tunnels along the way. When the longest goods train emerges from one of the tunnels near the top of the mountain, the last of its wagons will only just have disappeared into the tunnel opening 100 m (328 feet) below.

🏆 Northern Lights Wildlife Wolf Centre
Though the wolves in this outdoor enclosure were born in captivity, they still have much to teach us about the conduct and social interaction of their wild brethren. Experts are on hand to give lectures and lead guided tours.
1745 Short Road; Tel (250) 344 67 98.
www.northernlightswildlife.com

☒ Eagle's Eye Restaurant
This restaurant is accessible only by gondola, a 1,200-m (3,937-foot) ascent that is free to diners with reservations. The spectacular location is surely unmatched by any other Canadian eatery. The view is amazing, and the food is not at all bad, either. The meat dishes, in particular, come highly recommended.
Dyke Road, Kicking Horse Resort; Tel (250) 344 86 26.

☒ Cedar House
South of Golden, this restaurant enjoys superb views. The wooden cabin building is rather like a trapper's hut. The menu is contemporary, with an interesting range of dishes to suit all tastes. The wine list includes a good choice from Okanagan Valley vineyards.
735 Hefti Road; Tel (250) 344 46 79.
www.cedarhousecafe.com

▣ Prestige Mountainside Resort
This modern hotel on the Trans-Canada Highway is especially popular for its relatively large rooms and heated indoor pool. Some rooms have their own kitchenette. There is also a shopping arcade, fitness club, and a good restaurant.
1049 Trans-Canada Highway N.; Tel (250) 344 79 90.
www.prestigeinn.com

▣ Vagabond Lodge
Though part of the huge Kicking Horse Mountain Resort, this cozy lodge feels like a remote wood cabin up in the mountains. The lobby, dining room, and bar are extremely pleasant, and the rooms have all sorts of extras – notably the heated bathroom floors.
1581 Cache Close; Tel (250) 344 26 22.
www.vagabondlodge.ca

Kimberley

ℹ Rocky Mountains Visitors Association
The self-proclaimed "Bavarian City of the Rockies" woos visitors with its timber-framed architecture, oversize cuckoo clock, and Bavarian Platzl mall – home to all manner of suitably themed shops.

From left: The course at the Radium Springs golf resort; wild flowers near Cranbrook; enjoy a natural whirlpool bath at Radium Hot Springs; skiing fun in the Kootenay Rockies starts in the mountains around Kimberley.

The insider tips listed here refer to the sights described on pages 120–129.

The cheerful statue of Happy Hans is the town mascot, and its restaurants serve (almost) authentic German cuisine. The annual July Fest is held over the third weekend in July, while the Winterfest takes place in the second week of February. The nearby skiing areas, meanwhile, are popular with both experienced skiers and beginners.
495 Wallinger Avenue;
Tel (250) 427 48 38.

☒ The Old Bauernhaus
Opened by a German husband and wife team in 1989, this restaurant serves some very fine German dishes indeed. The *Schnitzel* – fried in clarified butter – is excellent, and the farmer's platter is as good as anything you might eat in Bavaria. Needless to say, the pretzels are baked on the premises.
280 Norton Avenue;
Tel (250) 427 51 33.

☒ Trickle Creek Lodge
This huge lodge is similar to an exclusive Swiss mountain hotel, combining rustic charm with a real sense of elegance. It enjoys magnificent views of the Rocky Mountains and is conveniently located for the nearby skiing areas. Its spacious suites all have their own kitchenette, fireplace, and balcony. There is no better place to stay in Kimberley.
500 Stemwinder Drive;
Tel (250) 427 51 75.
www.tricklecreeklodge.com

Nelson

ℹ Visitor Information Centre
Located in the Selkirk Mountains, this bustling city feels a lot livelier than some of the region's other mining towns. Its attractive, restored Victorian buildings have retained much of the distinctive character that first made Nelson a special place, in around 1900. The town's history began with the discovery of the Silver King Mine toward the end of the 19th century. There followed an intense but short-lived silver rush. When it ended, Stanley (as Nelson was then called) escaped decline by virtue of being the last station on the railway line – and it was the railway that brought renewed prosperity to the town.
225 Hall Street;
Tel (250) 352 34 33.

⛷ Whitewater Ski Resort
This attractive skiing area lies to the south of Nelson. Several of the surrounding mountains reach altitudes of over 2,000 m (6,562 feet), and the region is renowned for its light, powdery snow – and its virtually guaranteed snowfall. Most of the slopes, however, are suitable for experienced skiers only.
Tel. (250) 354 49 44.
www.skiwhitewater.com

☒ All Seasons Café
This romantic bistro in the old town certainly lives up to its name. Seasonal dishes prepared using locally sourced ingredients dominate the menu. The menu includes crispy fried breast of duck served with caramelized pear, watercress risotto, and plum chutney, as well as more exotic dishes like butter chicken cooked with Indian spices. It all tastes fantastic.
620 Herridge Lane;
Tel (250) 352 01 01.
www.allseasonscafe.com

☒ Dominion Café
This American-style diner serves a range of imaginative snacks and sandwiches, pastries (always fresh), and delicious sweet treats.
334 Baker Street;
Tel (250) 352 19 04.

⌂ Cloudside Inn
Close to historic Baker Street, this delightful hillside bed and breakfast overlooks Kootenay Lake. The individually furnished guest rooms have a real Victorian charm, and your hosts will go out of their way to make sure you have the best possible stay – including, of course, a deliciously sumptuous breakfast.
408 Victoria Street;
Tel (250) 352 75 73.
www.cloudside.ca

⌂ Hume Hotel
Located in the historic heart of Nelson, this has been one of the best hotels in town since 1898. The exterior might not be much to look at, but the traditional decor of the individually furnished guest rooms inside gives you a real taste of the old west. Most importantly of all, the beds are very comfortable.
422 Vernon Street;
Tel (250) 352 53 31.
www.humehotel.com

Radium Hot Springs

ℹ Visitor Information Centre
Famous for its hot springs, this slightly nondescript little town is very close to Kootenay National Park. A superb golf course is one of the main attractions here.
7685 Main Street West;
Tel (250) 347 93 31.
www.radiumhotsprings.com

♨ Radium Hot Springs Pool
The Radium Hot Springs sit beneath the sheer rock faces of Sinclair Canyon. The water temperature in the hot-water pool, the largest in Canada, is 39°C (102°F), and it is even a thoroughly respectable 27°C (81°F) in the cooler pool. The spa also has a sauna, and all manner of well-being treatments are available.
Sinclair Canyon, P O Box 40;
Tel (250) 347 94 85; summer
9.00–23.00 daily, winter
Sun–Thurs 12.00–21.00,
Fri–Sat 12.00–22.00.

☒ Angus McToogle's Restaurant & Bar
This lively eatery is located in Ivermere, not far from Radium Hot Springs. The friendly Scottish owner Angus and his son Fraser – among others – provide musical entertainment on certain evenings, while diners enjoy dishes such as the traditional Scottish shepherd's pie, the tasty salmon burger, or the "Braveheart" burger made from Angus beef. Plentiful supplies of dark Guinness are on tap.
1321 Seventh Avenue;
Tel (250) 341 68 68.
www.angusmctoogles.com

⌂ Prestige Radium Hot Springs
On the edge of Kootenay National Park and located right next to the Hot Springs, this sophisticated hotel caters to the top end of the market. The rooms are tastefully decorated in warm shades of brown and ochre, and many have their own kitchenette.
7493 Main Street;
Tel (250) 347 23 00.
www.prestigehotelsandresorts.com

TATSHENSHINI-ALSEK PROVINCIAL PARK 34

Out in the extreme north-west of British Columbia, the Tatshenshini and Alsek rivers together form one of the world's greatest river systems. The Tatshenshini, which is up to 1.5 km (1 mile) wide at its broadest point, snakes through a rugged mountain wilderness. Glaciers extend as far as the riverbanks, and icebergs edge into the water. The landscape through which the Alsek wends its way is no less dramatic. Established in 1993, the Tatshenshini-Alsek Provincial Park covers a total area of some 10,000 sq km (3,860 sq miles). It is part of a large park system that includes three national parks – Kluane (in the Yukon Territory), Wrangell-St. Elias, and Glacier Bay (both in Alaska). Together they form the world's largest mainland protected area and the first transnational site to be included on the UNESCO World Heritage List, since conservation organizations in both Canada and the United States were instrumental in its establishment.

Despite their size, grizzly bears (below) are extremely agile, and can reach speeds of up to 60 kmh (37 mph) over short distances. They spend most of their time eating grass, chewing roots, and snacking on berries. The promise of a much bigger feast comes with the arrival of the salmon migration season, when the bears become expert fishermen with no need for rod and line. Grizzly bear cubs generally stay with their mothers for around three years; the same is true of young black bears (right).

BEARS: BLACK, BROWN, AND WHITE

Western Canada's large bears are all brown bears, but the fact that they belong to the *Ursus* species does not mean that they are all brown in appearance. In fact, the grizzly bear, Kodiak bear, black bear, and even the polar bear, which is indisputably white-furred, are all members of this same genus. The most prominent of Western Canada's brown bears is the grizzly. Respected, feared, and even regarded as a god in some First Nations mythology, the grizzly may not be the largest bear of its genus, but it is the strongest. Standing on its hind legs a grizzly can be up to 2.5 m (8 feet) in height, up to 1.5 m (5 feet) at the shoulders when on all fours, and weigh as much as a hefty 680 kg (1,499 lbs) – the males being heavier than the females. It is a formidable creature and therefore best observed from a safe distance. The grizzly feeds on a mostly vegetarian diet, and is – except in the mating season – essentially a loner. Nonetheless, erring on the side of caution is always sensible – make sure you follow the guidelines given to visitors. The same applies to Western Canada's other common large bear, the black bear. Slightly smaller than the grizzly, it has a black coat and lacks the pronounced hump that characterizes the grizzly. Like the grizzly, the black bear's diet is mostly vegetation, supplemented with insects, honey, salmon, and some animals such as deer. Black bears also eat the eggs or chicks from birds' nests.

INFO Atlin Historical Museum

Only when seen from above does the true scale of Atlin Lake really become apparent. The lake is 145 km (90 miles) long and up to 283 m (928 feet) deep. If you want to explore, a kayak is a good option. The lake is home to various fish, including trout and grayling. A permit is required to fish here.

Built in 1902, this former school now houses an exhibition. The objects in the collection really bring the gold-rush era to life. Guided walks around the town and surrounding area are available on request.
3rd Street, Atlin V0W 1A0;
Tel (250) 651 75 22; summer only,
10.00–12.00 and 13.00–16.00 daily.

ATLIN PROVINCIAL PARK AND RECREATION AREA

Covering 3,011 sq km (1,162 sq miles), this protected area on the border with the Yukon Territory was established in 1973. The name Atlin is an anglicization of "Áa Tlein", which means roughly "big body of water" in the language of the local Tlingit First Nations people. That description certainly applies to Atlin Lake, which – spanning an area of 775 sq km (299 sq miles) – is British Columbia's largest natural, freshwater lake. It is famous not only for the water itself, but for its large stocks of fish. There are many other lakes within the park's vast glacial icefields. Two vast glaciers – Llewellyn and Willison – together cover about a third of the park's total surface area, while the Juneau Icefield extends over the border into Alaska. The town of Atlin, to the north, owes its existence to the gold rush that followed the first discoveries of gold in the Klondike River toward the end of the 19th century.

INFO Stikine River tours

The canyon that has been cut into the rock of the Stikine River Provincial Park by the Stikine River (below and right) is often dubbed the "Canadian Grand Canyon". Like the region's other volcanoes, the perfectly shaped Eve Cone, in the middle of a lava field, was formed by a series of small eruptions (below, right).

Dan Pakula's lodge occupies a former post office dating from 1898. He offers river trips through the Coast Mountains, to the Pacific and to Alaska. The shortest takes 1.5 hours, the longest a half or a full day.

Stikine RiverSong, Telegraph Creek, V0J 2W0; Tel (250) 235 31 96.

STIKINE RIVER PROVINCIAL PARK 36
MOUNT EDZIZA PROVINCIAL PARK 37

The Stikine River flows through a long gorge (approximately 80 km/50 miles) in north-west British Columbia. Formed of volcanic rock, its walls are up to 300 m (984 feet) high in places. It was to protect this spectacular river landscape that Stikine River Provincial Park was established at the end of the 1990s – it covers some 2,170 sq km (838 sq miles). Stikine is derived from "Shtax' Héen", which literally means "cloudy river" in the language of the area's Tahltan First Nations people, and the river is indeed cloudy during the salmon-spawning season. Mount Edziza Provincial Park surrounds the summit of Mount Edziza (2,787 m/ 9,144 feet), whose peaks and ridges form one of Canada's highest volcanoes. Bordered to the east by the Spatsizi Plateau Wilderness Provincial Park, it covers an area of over 2,300 sq km (888 sq miles) and protects a truly striking volcanic landscape.

INFO Fish Creek Wildlife Observation

The most spectacular section of the Stewart- Cassiar Highway is the stretch from Dease Lake to the junction with the Alaska Highway, 246 km (153 miles) farther north. There are few if any signs of civilization here. Below: In the shadow of the Cassiar Mountains. Right: The Skeena Mountains.

From the safe vantage point of the viewing platform, watch brown bears, grizzly bears, and wolves fishing for salmon on Salmon River. Armed rangers further ensure onlookers' safety. July to September is the best time to see the action. *Salmon River Road, 3 km (2 miles) north of Hyder; Tel (907) 225 21 48.*

The Stewart-Cassiar Highway (Highway 37) begins south of Kitimat, a coastal town in north-west British Columbia. From a branch of the Yellowhead Highway near Kitwanga, it continues to Watson Lake on the Alaska Highway. The road is suitable for all vehicles, being mostly hard-surfaced with just a couple of short sections in gravel and hardened earth. It leads through some of the most isolated areas of British Colombia, across an unspoilt natural landscape, covered with glaciers, lakes, and wide valleys. It crosses the national watershed at Dease Lake, 65 km (40 miles) north of Iskut. The majestic peaks of the Cassiar and Skeena mountains lie to the north. Work on the highway started in the 1960s. Since its completion in 1972, it has provided a spectacular alternative to the Alaska Highway – the scenery through which it passes is unquestionably some of the most breathtaking in the whole of Canada.

INFO Salmon Glacier Viewpoint

Salmon Glacier (below) forms part of the Boundary Range – the largest and most northerly mountain chain in the Coast Mountains. Stewart (right), a former mining town, is just 3 km (2 miles) from Hyder, the southernmost point in Alaska, on the American side of the USA–Canada border.

You reach **Summit Viewpoint** after driving 37 km (23 miles) down the Salmon Glacier Road. From here you can look down on the glacier itself. Keith Scott has a small mobile store here selling his nature films and books. NB: The road is only maintained from the end of June to the beginning of October.

Branching off the Stewart-Cassiar Highway at Meziadan Junction, Highway 37A winds its way through very beautiful scenery to the west. The landscape is characterized by raging waterfalls and numerous glaciers that flow down from the Cambria range, towering up to 2,700 m (8,858 feet) above.

As darkness falls, the surface of Bear Glacier – which runs more or less parallel to the road – shimmers blue-white in the moonlight. The small, former mining town of Stewart lies about 37 km (23 miles) to the west, on the Portland Canal. Stewart's spectacular mountain scenery has provided a back-

drop for many movies, which is why the town is sometimes dubbed "Hollywood of the North". The border between Canada and the USA's Alaska Panhandle is not far from here. Around 25 km (16 miles) north of Stewart, the enormous Salmon Glacier is like a vast multi-lane highway of ice and snow.

THE HIGHLIGHTS: BRITISH COLUMBIA: NORTHERN DISTRICTS

INFO Gitksan cultural tours

Since it is both easy to work with and durable, the indigenous peoples of Western Canada primarily use cedar wood for their decorative carvings. Totem poles relate the histories of the tribes and families responsible for erecting them. Below and right: The 'Ksan Historical Village and Museum.

Guided tours around the Frog House, Wolf House, and Fireweed House in the 'Ksan Historical Village offer an insight into the traditional culture and sophisticated artistic heritage of the Gitksan people.
Hazelton V0J 1Y0; Tel (250) 842 55 44; Apr–Sept 9.00–15.00 daily, Oct–Mar Mon–Fri 9.30–16.30.

KITWANCOOL 41
'KSAN HISTORICAL VILLAGE AND MUSEUM 42

The historic First Nations village of Kitwancool is in the Kitwanga Valley, not far from the Stewart-Cassiar Highway. Well known for its superb collection of totem poles, the oldest, called Hole in the Ice, was probably erected around 1850. The images carved into it tell the story of a fisherman who, in the midst of a harsh cold spell, prudently hacked a hole in the ice on the frozen river in order to continue fishing and so save the villagers from starvation. Not far from New Hazelton, the 'Ksan Historical Village was built in the 1970s. First Nations women act as guides here, explaining the displays of carvings, clothing, shaman regalia, and ceremonial masks to visitors. The museum has around 600 items on display, while the village consists of a number of replica First Nation longhouses. The area's Gitksan First Nations people are the most easterly aboriginal population in Western Canada.

INFO Muncho Lake Boat Tours

The mountains in Muncho Lake Provincial Park, divided into the Terminal Range and Sentinel Range, are a foretaste of the barren tundra that lies farther north. The park's wildlife includes Dall Sheep (right). The red sky is reflected in the waters of the lake (below), which shimmers deep green in sunlight.

Captain Jack invites you aboard the Sandpiper IV for an entertaining trip around Muncho Lake. You will learn interesting facts about the area's history, landscape, and wildlife – all sprinkled with plenty of anecdotes.

Double C Services are based on the south bank of the lake, on the Alaska Highway; Tel (250) 776 34 11.

Muncho Lake Provincial Park, established in 1957, spans an area of almost 861 sq km (332 sq miles). Muncho Lake ("big water" in the Kaska language) lies in the middle of the park. Framed by the northern peaks of the Rockies, it is 12 km (7 miles) long, up to 6 km (4 miles) wide, and over 200 m (656 feet) deep.

The Alaska Highway, which crosses the park, runs right along the lake's eastern shores. The remarkable jade green of the water is due to the copper oxide washed out of the bedrock. Signs of campsites belonging to the Kaska Athapaskan people have been found in three archeological sites around the lake shore. The first

European trappers are not thought to have discovered the area until around 1800, although it was the construction of the Alaska Highway in 1942 that really opened it up to white settlers. The small community of Muncho Lake caters to the needs of tourists with facilities such as accommodation and restaurants.

Burns Lake

ℹ Burns Lake Chamber of Commerce
On entering the small town of Burns Lake, visitors are greeted by a wooden trout and, below it, the catchy slogan "Three Thousand Miles of Fishing". The focal point of the Lakes District, this town on the Yellowhead Highway really is an angler's paradise.
540 Yellowhead Highway;
Tel (250) 692 37 73.
www.hiway16.com

🛏 Babine Lake Resort
A rustic lodge located on the picturesque shores of Babine Lake, which, at almost 180 km (112 miles) in length, is the longest freshwater lake in British Columbia. You can stay in one of the many cabins, and boat hire is also available. The resort is the perfect place to stay for anglers and game hunters in particular.
532 Comp. 16, R.R.I.;
Tel (250) 692 03 63.
www.babinelakeresort.com

🛏 Burns Lake Motor Inn
This good-value motel has a 24-hour check-in. The rooms are functional, offering basic comforts without the frills.
Highway 16 East;
Tel (250) 692 75 45.

Fort St James

ℹ Fort St James Travel Info Centre
Situated 60 km (37 miles) north of Vanderhoof, this small town has made something of a name for itself – primarily because of its restored fort.
115 Douglas Avenue;
Tel (250) 996 70 23.

🏛 Fort St James National Historic Site
Now faithfully restored, at the height of the fur trade Fort St James was an important commercial trading post. Founded in 1806, it also had the distinction of being the first non-aboriginal settlement in British Columbia. Every July and August, site employees don period costume to recreate scenes from daily life at the fort in days gone by. It is located off the Yellowhead Highway.
Tel (250) 996 71 91;
mid-May–Sept 10.00–17.00 daily. www.pc.gc.ca

🛏 Douglas Lodge
Run by Andy and Ulrike Roessler, this basic lodge on Stuart Lake has five simply furnished cabins. In an isolated location, the lodge is a perfect place to relax, and a great base from which to explore the local area – ideal for anglers and walkers, as well as visitors to the nearby trading post.
5540 Stones Bay Road;
Tel (250) 996 79 17.
www.stuartlodge.ca

Hazelton/Kitwanga

ℹ Hazeltons Travel Information Centre
There are three Hazeltons: modern New Hazelton, the historic Old Town, and South Hazelton. Hazelton Old Town pre-dates the arrival of the railway, while rival investors founded the two newer settlements. West of Hazelton, Kitwanga is the starting point for tours along the picturesque Stewart-Cassiar Highway (Highway 37).
Main Street;
Tel. (250) 842 56 28.

🏛 'Ksan Historical Village
Members of the Gitksan First Nations people exhibit their traditional regalia, carvings, and art in the village's seven restored longhouses, in a natural woodland setting. There are also regular performances of traditional First Nations' dance by the 'Ksan Performing Arts Group.
Highway 62;
Tel (250) 842 55 44;
summer 9.00–18.00 daily, winter 9.30–16.30.
www.ksan.org

🛏 Hotel Inlander
Just a few minutes from 'Ksan Historical Village, this fairly basic hotel and lounge bar is right in the heart of Old Hazelton.
1520 Omineca Street;
Tel (250) 842 52 31.

Houston

ℹ Visitor Information Centre
This small town is primarily dependent upon the timber industry and tourism. The surrounding area, known as Steelhead Country, is popular with the hiking fraternity and with anglers, thanks to its lakes and plentiful stocks of fish in the Morice and Bulkley rivers. The giant fly rod outside the visitor information office is a reminder of the large fish it is possible to catch around here, if you are lucky.
3289 Highway 16;
Tel (250) 845 76 40.
www.houstonchamber.ca

🛏 Houston Motor Inn
This modest motel caters to anglers who just need the basics. The rooms are clean, unfussy, and very reasonably priced. Some have their own kitchenette. There is also a coffee shop, which is open daily.
2940 Highway 16 West;
Tel (250) 845 71 12.

Iskut

🛏 Red Goat Lodge
This lodge is in the wilderness on the edge of the spectacular and rugged Stikine Country, just 3 km (2 miles) south of Iskut. The rooms are comfortable, and some of the wood cabins are right on the banks of Eddontenajon Lake – as is the lodge's own camping ground.
PO Box 119;
Tel (250) 234 32 61.

Prince George

ℹ Visitor information
The "capital of the north" lies at the confluence of the Nechako and Fraser rivers. It is the administrative hub of the Fraser-Fort George Regional District, and an important local transport hub. The city owes its existence to the construction of the Grand Trunk Railroad. Alongside forestry, tourism is now the main industry in Prince George – it offers a range of hotels, motels, bed and breakfasts, campsites, and restaurants.
1198 Victoria Street;
Tel (250) 562 37 00,
www.nbctourism.com

🏛 Prince George Regional Railway & Forest Industry Museum
The locomotives and rolling stock in this small but interesting museum date from between 1899 and 1970. Two particular highlights are locomotive 1520, a steam engine built in 1906, and the luxurious Nechako sleeping car

From left: Boating fun on Burns Lake; the beautiful deciduous woods near Smithers; the endearing pose of these young owls belies the reality of their predatory nature; the university in Prince George.

NORTHERN DISTRICTS

The insider tips listed here refer to the sights described on pages 132–151.

once operated by the Grand Trunk Railway. The special display on the local forestry industry is also worth a look. Timber continues to play an important role in the city's economy today.
850 River Road;
Tel (250) 563 73 51;
summer Wed–Sun
10.00–17.00, winter
Tues–Sat 11.00–16.00.
www.pgrfm.bc.ca

☒ Ric's Grill
This smart restaurant has branches in cities throughout British Columbia and Alberta. It is famous for its superb steaks and salmon. Top dishes to try include the juicy New York Strip, mighty rib eye (for the particularly ravenous), tender prime rib, and wild salmon in lemongrass sauce.
547 George Street;
Tel (250) 614 90 96.
www.ricsgrill.com

☒ Coast Inn of the North
This modern hotel, located in the middle of town, boasts large rooms, a heated pool, and a sauna. The special jacuzzi suites are rather pricey, but all the more comfortable. The hotel also has two very good restaurants.
770 Brunswick Street;
Tel (250) 563 01 21.
www.coasthotels.com

Smithers

ⓘ Visitor Centre
At one time dominated by the timber industry, Smithers has been given an Alpine makeover to boost local tourism – complete with authentic-looking European style timber-framed houses. But, like most of the towns between Prince Rupert and

Prince George, Smithers is best used as a base for fishing trips and hiking into the surrounding countryside. West of Smithers, Moricetown Canyon is popular with First Nations fishermen – equipped with nets and harpoons, they fish for salmon in the turbulent Bulkley River.
1411 Court Street;
Tel (250) 847 33 37.
www.tourismsmithers.com

ⓠ Driftwood Canyon Provincial Park
About 10 km (6 miles) northeast of Smithers, many prehistoric fossils have been found in the park. They have preserved examples of animal and plant life from millions of years ago. Numerous hiking trails lead off into the narrow valley, which was formed by glacial activity thousands of years ago.
www.env.gov.bc.ca/bcparks

☒ Alpenhorn Pub and Bistro
Despite the name, this is no Alpine inn, but a fairly typical Canadian sports bar. It serves pizza, sandwiches, and some particularly juicy burgers.
1261 Main Street;
Tel (250) 847 53 66.

☒ Aspen Motor Inn
If it is good, simple accommodation you are looking for, you could do a lot worse than this very good value motel. Some of the rooms are equipped with their own kitchenette.
4268 Highway 16;
Tel (250) 847 45 51.

☒ Hudson Bay Lodge
Situated right on the highway, the Hudson Bay Lodge has a certain kind of elegance that you would normally only expect of a big city

hotel. The guest rooms in the long timber-framed building are stylishly furnished and extremely comfortable. Internet access and cable television are just two of the many features. The hotel also has its own restaurant, bar, and liquor store.
3251 Highway 16 East;
Tel (250) 847 45 81.

Stewart

ⓠ Stewart and Hyder International Chamber of Commerce
Nestled high up in the mountains, this small mining town at the end of the Portland Canal is surrounded by majestic glacial peaks. Just across the Canada-USA border, Hyder is in Alaska. The area has long been a popular destination among winter sports enthusiasts, hikers, and all lovers of the great outdoors. A little way out of town, the Stewart-Cassiar Highway (Highway 37) passes close by. This famous route crosses some of Canada's most beautiful landscape.
222 5th Avenue;
Tel (250) 636 92 24.
www.stewart-hyder.com

☒ The King Edward Hotel & Motel
Situated on 5th Avenue, Stewart's main street, this hotel has 30 guest rooms and 20 well-equipped motel units. Casey's Pub offers a warm welcome, while the King's Table Dining Room has a menu full of hearty dishes. The many flags flown over the hotel indicate the wide range of visitors to the town.
P. O. Box 86;
Tel (250) 636 22 44.
www.kingedwardhotel.com

Terrace

ⓘ Visitor Centre
The peaks of the Hazelton and Coast mountains surround this small town in the Skeena River valley, which is an ideal starting point for hiking. Terrace is proud of its steamboat heritage and hosts the Riverboat Days Festival each summer.
4511 Keith Avenue;
Tel (250) 635 20 63.
www.terracetourism.ca

ⓠ Nisga'a Memorial Lava Beds Provincial Park
Since a major volcanic eruption in around 1750, life has been slowly returning to the remote lava beds in this conservation area in the Nass River Valley, north-west of Terrace. An exhibition about the ancestors of the local First Nations people can be seen in a traditional longhouse. The park's name echoes the treaty settled between the British Colombian government and the Nisga'a in 1999.
Tel (250) 638 84 90.
www.env.gov.bc.ca/bcparks

☒ Bear Country Inn
A modest and very reasonably priced motel. The basic rooms are clean and functional, while the suites are equipped with jacuzzis.
4702 Lakelse Avenue;
Tel (250) 635 63 02.
www.innbc.com/bearcountry

☒ Coast Inn of the West
An excellent, reliable, mid-range hotel in the middle of Terrace. It has modern rooms and its own restaurant, serving typical Canadian fare. There is also a golf course nearby.
4620 Lakelse Avenue;
Tel (250) 638 81 41.
www.coasthotels.com

ALBERTA

The most westerly of Canada's prairie provinces, Alberta is named after Louise Caroline Alberta, Duchess of Argyll and sixth child of Britain's Queen Victoria. Though Edmonton is the capital, Alberta's largest city is Calgary, whose increasing significance can be attributed to its rich oil reserves. Around a quarter of Alberta is covered by the Great Plains — highly fertile agricultural land where wheat and canola (rapeseed) are grown. To the west, close to the border with British Colombia, the high mountain chains of the Canadian Rockies are a popular tourist destination. The mysterious badlands, where many dinosaur fossils have been found, are in the south-east of the province.

THE HIGHLIGHTS: ALBERTA

44 Calgary

45 Dinosaur Provincial Park

46 Head-Smashed-In
Buffalo Jump

47 Waterton Lakes
National Park

48 **Banff National Park:**
Vermilion Lakes

49 Mount Rundle

50 Ha Ling Peak

51 Johnston Canyon

52 Castle Mountain

53 Valley of the Ten Peaks

54 Moraine Lake

55 Lake Louise

56 **Jasper National Park:**
Athabasca River

57 Sunwapta River

58 Maligne Canyon

59 Medicine Lake

60 Maligne Lake

61 Pyramid Lake

62 Patricia Lake

63 Beauvert Lake

64 Edmonton

65 Elk Island National Park

66 Ukrainian Cultural
Heritage Village

67 Wood Buffalo
National Park

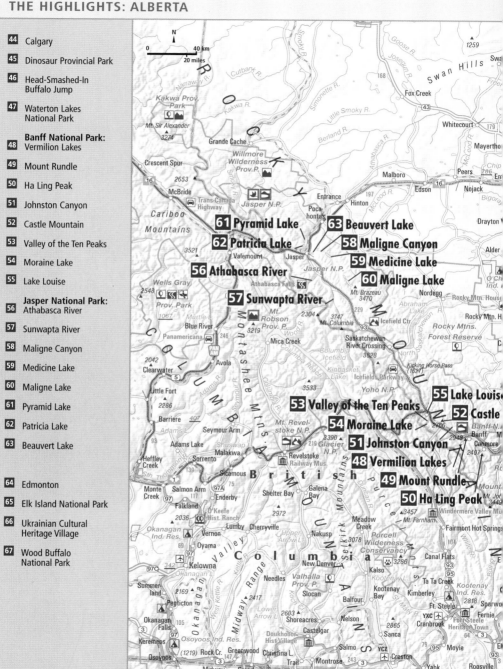

156 **Western Canada**

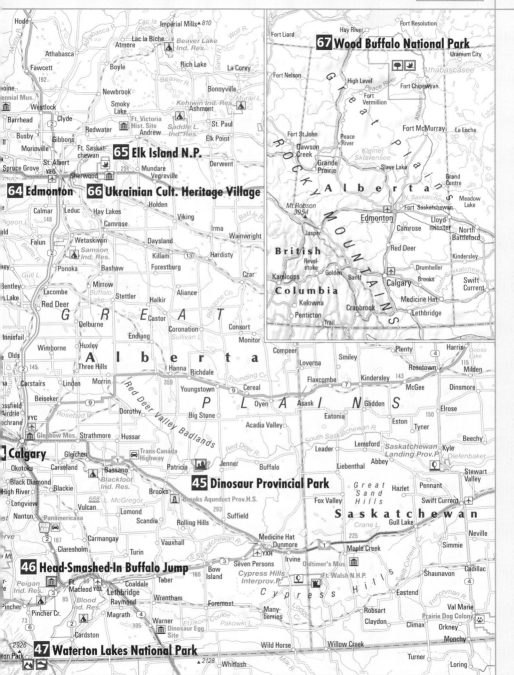

67 Wood Buffalo National Park

65 Elk Island N.P.

64 Edmonton   **66 Ukrainian Cult. Heritage Village**

45 Dinosaur Provincial Park

46 Head-Smashed-In Buffalo Jump

47 Waterton Lakes National Park

THE HIGHLIGHTS: ALBERTA

TIP Calgary Tower

The enormously wealthy city of Calgary is Alberta's main financial hub. Home-grown oil magnates have become rich and powerful on the back of the oil industry, and Downtown Calgary has some of the tallest buildings in Canada – many are connected by a system of elevated pedestrian walkways called +15.

The glass-floored viewing platform of the tower is suspended 190 m (623 feet) above ground. The revolving restaurant is called Sky 360.

101-0 Avenue SW, Calgary, T2P 1J9; restaurant Tel (403) 532 79 66; Mon–Sat 11.00–14.00 and 17.00–22.00, Sun 10.00–14.00 and 17.00–22.00.

Calgary, Alberta's largest city, lies in the south of the province, between the plains of the prairie and the foothills of the Rocky Mountains. The Blackfoot Nation occupied this territory long before the first white settlers arrived here. Named after a picturesque bay on the Scottish island of Mull, Calgary grew up around the North-West Mounted Police post. It was established here in 1875 to combat the unscrupulous white whisky traders who would exchange their "firewater" for the buffalo skins of the Plains First Nations people. Oil was first struck in the Calgary area around 1960. Its dis- covery transformed the sleepy city into a bustling business hub, and palatial office blocks of glass and steel were soon springing up everywhere. Today, almost all the Canadian oil companies have their headquarters in the city (see page 20). Calgary hosted the Winter Olympics in 1988.

The basic objective of participants in the Calgary Stampede is simply to stay on their mount. In the bull riding, cowboys try to maintain their seat on a wild bull that rears and bucks dangerously – risking their lives in a ride that lasts a matter of seconds. The riders must not touch the bull with their free hand. Weighing in at around 1,000 kg (2,205 lbs), the bulls can very quickly unseat their riders (below). Wrestling a steer to the ground is not for greenhorns (below, right). Right: A chuckwagon race takes place every evening.

THE CALGARY STAMPEDE

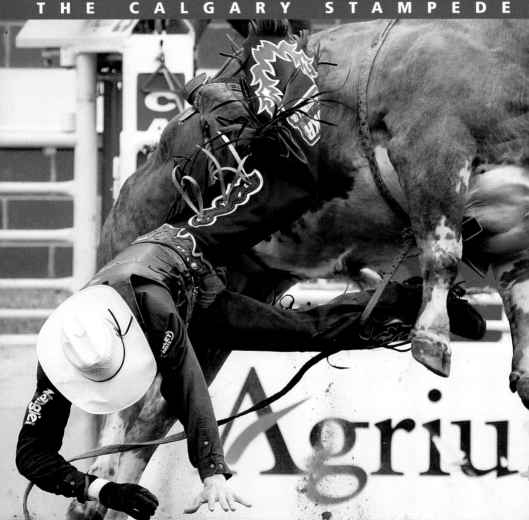

Things get pretty hot in Alberta's biggest city in July – not because of soaring temperatures, but because of the spectacular annual Calgary Stampede. The city really turns up the heat for this ten-day event, when the streets are filled with cowboys and cowgirls. The day traditionally starts with a parade and pancake breakfast. Everyone is in western garb, from corporate managers to drugstore shop assistants, and competition is fierce for a good spot in the Pengrowth Saddledome, the 20,000-seat arena that hosts the action. Shaped appropriately like a saddle, the stadium was opened in 1983, but the history of the Stampede goes back much further. It began in 1886, when Calgary held its first agricultural show. With a population of around just 500 people, Calgary had only been declared a city two years earlier. The original cowboy festival was a modest attempt to make the agricultural show more interesting, but in 1912 the event was marketed as the Frontier Days and Cowboy Championship Contest. By 1919 and the end of World War I, it had become the Victory Stampede – the event from which today's Calgary Stampede developed. Today, along with the rodeo and chuckwagon races, in which teams of horses pull the wagons that were the "mobile kitchens" of the settlers' wagon trains, there are First Nations exhibitions, agricultural competitions, live music concerts, and the Grandstand Show featuring comedians and other entertainers.

THE HIGHLIGHTS: ALBERTA

INFO Royal Tyrrell Museum

Millions of years ago, *Tyrannosaurus rex* and other dinosaurs roamed the Alberta badlands, which looked quite different with lush forests that flourished in a sub-tropical climate. Geologist Joseph Burr Tyrrell discovered the first dinosaur bones here in 1984. Dinosaur Provincial Park is situated in the Red Deer River Valley.

This paleontological museum's collection of 40 complete dinosaur skeletons, discovered in the park, is the largest of its kind, and includes a *Tyrannosaurus rex*.

Highway 838, Drumheller T0J 0Y0;
Tel (403) 823 77 07;
Sept–May Tues–Sun 10.00–17.00,
May–Aug 9.00–21.00 daily.

Dinosaur Provincial Park is named for its wealth of dinosaur fossils – the North American continent was home to a large number of dinosaur species 75 million years ago, during the Cretaceous period. The park was made a UNESCO World Heritage Site in 1979. It is noted for its badland terrain – an arid, barren zone where the rock has been eroded into bizarre, otherworldly formations by wind and water. The interpretive bus tours, guided hikes, talks, and events run by the park authorities are very informative and bring the age of the dinosaurs to life. Book early for the tours and hikes, particularly in July and August, the busiest time. Despite the desert-like climate, significant vegetation can be seen along the riverbanks, which provide an ideal habitat for several species of red deer and also support a large bird population, including bluebirds, eagles, and falcons. You might also see, or more likely hear, coyotes.

INFO Drum & dance

The First Nations used the sandstone rock face of the Porcupine Hills (below) to hunt buffalo. Head-Smashed-In Buffalo Jump is the most famous of the jumps. The Interpretative Centre, built into the sandstone cliff, explains how the area's First Nations people lived. Events and workshops are held throughout the year.

Traditional drumming and Blackfoot dancing is revived in the summer. Performances take place in the Interpretative Centre every Wednesday at 11.00 and 13.30.

Highway 838, Drumheller T0J 0Y0; Tel (403) 823 77 07; Sept–May Tues–Sun 10.00–17.00, May–Aug 9.00–21.00 daily.

The First Nations hunted buffalo on the western prairies, as they did elsewhere, but here they employed hunting tactics with a difference. Using their knowledge of the landscape and the buffalos' habits, they drove the animals over the edge of a cliff. Killed in the fall, the buffalo were then skinned and gutted in the camp below. Buffalo bones can still be found at the base of Head-Smashed-In Buffalo Jump today. Situated near Fort Macleod in south-western Alberta, it was added to the UNESCO World Heritage List in 1981 for its cultural, archeological, and scientific interest. Excavations have revealed that the Blackfoot Plains people were already using this method of hunting thousands of years ago. According to legend, the name "Head-Smashed-In" is a reference to the fate of a warrior who wanted to watch the spectacle from the bottom of the cliff, only to be crushed to death by the falling buffalo.

THE HIGHLIGHTS: ALBERTA

INFO Bear's Hump Trail

The Prince of Wales Hotel, in Waterton Lakes National Park, has fine views of the mountains (below, inset left). The materials for its construction in the 1920s were transported the last 40 km (25 miles) on the backs of mule. Below: A white-tailed deer in front of Cameron Falls. The park is also home to bison (below, right).

One of Canada's best-known hiking trails climbs 240 m (787 feet) over just 1 km (0.6 miles) to reach Bear's Hump. From the top there are tremendous views over Waterton's mountains. The trail departure point is from the Visitor's Centre.

Canada's Waterton Lakes National Park in Alberta and the USA's Glacier National Park in nearby Montana were joined to form the first international Peace Park in 1932, and were designated a UNESCO World Heritage Site in 1995. The union of the two parks was spearheaded by the Rotary Clubs of Alberta and Montana, as a sign of peace and goodwill between Canada, the USA, and the Blackfoot Confederation. Established in 1895, Waterton Lakes National Park is accessible from Fort Macleod via Cardston. It is smaller than Glacier National Park, covering just 525 sq km (203 sq miles) of the two parks' combined 4,500-sq km (1,737-sq mile) area. Given its relatively small size, the diversity of the Canadian park's landscape is all the more impressive. It has also been designated a World Biosphere Reserve for its mountains, lakes, and freshwater wetlands. The park's wildlife includes grizzly and black bears, coyote, and cougars.

THE HIGHLIGHTS: ALBERTA

INFO Fenland Trail

Banff is Canada's oldest national park. The Rocky Mountains are reflected in the Vermilion Lakes. Below: Mount Rundle reaches an altitude of 2,848 m (9,344 feet); Sulphur Mountain (in the foreground) is 400 m (1,312 feet) lower. Ha Ling Peak (below, inset left) lies south of the town of Canmore.

A leisurely trail (2 km/1.2 miles) leading from the Forty Mile Picnic Area near downtown Banff, past Echo and Forty Mile Creek, and on to the Vermilion Lakes. It is closed end May to mid June, when female elk, which are extremely protective of their young, are liable to attack walkers.
Banff Info Centre: Tel (403) 762 84 21.

BANFF NATIONAL PARK: VERMILION LAKES 48
MOUNT RUNDLE 49 HA LING PEAK 50

Established in 1887, Banff National Park covers a total area of 6,641 sq km (2,563 sq miles) along Alberta's western border. It was included within the Canadian Rocky Mountain Parks site on the UNESCO World Heritage list in 1984. The town of Banff, in the valley of the Bow River, is a good base from which to explore the park. Banff is also famous for its hot springs, the warmest of which emerges from Sulphur Mountain, 4 km (2.5 miles) south of the town. The three lakes in the Bow River flood plain west of Banff are collectively known as the Vermilion Lakes. Mount Rundle, which towers above the lakes, is popular for climbing and scrambling – easier than climbing, scrambling is a cross between climbing and hillwalking where you can use your hands to help the ascent. Ha Ling Peak was named after a Chinese cook on the Canadian Pacific Railway. In 1896, he bet that he could climb the mountain in less than ten hours. He won the bet.

INFO Ink Pots Trail

The mountains of Banff National Park (below: the fortress-like Castle Mountain) are superb for climbing in summer, while during the colder months they are a popular winter sports destination. The mountainous terrain of the park includes glaciers and icefields. Right: Stone waypoints at the Lower Falls erected by hikers.

If you have followed the Johnston Canyon Trail to the waterfalls, carrying on to the Ink Pots – only another 3.5 km (2 miles) – is well worth the effort. The six bubbling natural pools are filled by cold springs. Allow 4–5 hours for the round trip.
Banff Info Centre;
Tel (403) 762 84 21.

BANFF NATIONAL PARK: JOHNSTON CANYON 51
CASTLE MOUNTAIN 52

Situated between Banff and Lake Louise on the Bow Valley Parkway, Johnston Canyon is one of the most spectacular in Banff National Park. The trail to the canyon's waterfalls begins at Johnston Canyon Lodge. The Lower Falls cascade 10 m (33 feet) down the rock face, and the Upper Falls 30 m (98 feet). The cat-walks on the Johnston Canyon Trail cling to the rock face. In winter, the trail is particularly popular with ice climbers who like to test their climbing skills and agility when the waterfalls freeze over. The trail continues to the Ink Pots, six clear pools filled with water, two of which are an intense blue-green. Roughly halfway between Banff and Lake Louise, the Bow Valley Parkway winds its way past Castle Mountain, which towers 2,766 m (9,075 feet) above the road and is named for its fort-like shape. An internment camp set up in 1915 for enemy aliens is nearby – though immigrant workers were also held there.

THE HIGHLIGHTS:
ALBERTA

INFO Moraine Lake Lodge

Moraine Lake glistens like a turquoise jewel in the Valley of Ten Peaks (below). With the silhouette of Mount Victoria reflected in the water, and surrounded by the breathtaking grandeur of nature, crossing the lake by canoe is wonderful. Lake Louise (below, inset left) is the name of both the town and the lake.

About 15 minutes from Lake Louise, but located on Lake Moraine, this lodge is an ideal base from which to explore the national park. The well-equipped canoe dock hires out canoes (9.00–20.30 daily).

Tel (403) 522 37 33; Jun–beg Oct.
www.morainelake.com

BANFF NATIONAL PARK: VALLEY OF THE TEN PEAKS 53
MORAINE LAKE 54 LAKE LOUISE 55

The Valley of the Ten Peaks is one of the natural wonders of the Canadian Rockies. These giant mountains – the highest of the Wenkchemna Range – reach altitudes of over 3,000 m (9,843 feet). In the 1970s, they were depicted on the back of the Canadian $20 note. There is a particularly dramatic view of the Ten Peaks from Moraine Lake. Situated at 2,000 m (6,562 feet) above sea level, it turns a deep blue in the summer. Not far away, at an altitude of 1,731 m (5,679 feet), Lake Louise is one of the most popular holiday destinations in the whole of Western Canada, and is often completely overrun during the high season. There are hiking trails around the lake, but people also come here for mountain biking, horseback riding, and canoeing. Approximately 2 km (1 mile) long and up to 600 m (1,969 feet) wide, the lake is nearly 70 m (230 feet) deep. The Stoney First Nation called it the "lake of small fish".

The Icefields Parkway crosses two national parks: Banff (below and below, inset left) and Jasper. The drive along the Icefields Parkway takes about four hours. There is plenty to see along the way, including views of the Athabasca River, which winds along the Columbia Icefield, and the bright, tough Arctic fireweed that blooms around the Athabasca Glacier in summer (right).

THE ICEFIELDS PARKWAY

The Icefields Parkway is an approximately 230-km (143-mile) long stretch of Highway 93 between Lake Louise and Jasper. Running through an impressive landscape of mountains and lakes in the heart of the Rockies, it is one of the world's most scenic highways. Construction was finished in 1939, and the road was opened to the public the following year. It was constructed with the leisure industry and tourism in mind, and there are numerous lay-bys where you can stop and observe the local wildlife. But the route, sometimes known as the "Wonder Trail", had already been used for thousands of years by the First Nations people and later by the fur traders, though they avoided the Bow Valley wetlands and instead followed the Pipestone River Valley to the east. One of the first highlights is the tranquil Bow Lake, which sits beneath two glaciers. The road continues over Bow Pass (Bow Summit) – at 2,088 m (6,850 feet), it is the highest pass in Banff National Park and the watershed between the North and South Saskatchewan river systems. The Athabasca Glacier icefields, part of the Columbia Icefield, lie on the other side of Sunwapta Pass. Columbia Icefield is the largest in the Rocky Mountains, spanning over 325 sq km (125 sq miles) from Mount Columbia (3,747 m/12,293 feet) in the west to Mount Athabasca in the east – some 250 m (820 feet) lower. Tours in specially adapted vehicles offer visitors the chance to explore and walk on the ice.

THE HIGHLIGHTS: ALBERTA

INFO Glacier adventure

At a length of 1,231 km (765 miles), the Athabasca is one of the longest rivers in Western Canada. Its source is in the Columbia Icefield, and it flows into Lake Athabasca. The spectacular Athabasca Falls (below) lie on the upper reaches of the river. Sunwapta River (right) is one of the Athabasca's best-known tributaries.

Brewster's Athabasca glacier tours leave from the Columbia Icefield Centre every 15–30 minutes. Ice Explorer vehicles take you right onto the glacier in just 1.5 hours, where you can get out and stretch your legs on the 400-year-old ice. *Icefield Parkway 103 km; Tel (780) 852 62 88; Apr–Oct.*

Established in 1907, Jasper National Park covers an area of 10,878 sq km (4,199 sq miles). It is the largest and most northerly of the four large national parks that together form the Canadian Rocky Mountain Parks site, which is included in the UNESCO World Heritage list. The park's varied landscape comprises snow-capped mountains rising to heights of over 3,000 m (9,843 feet), hot sulphur springs, over 800 lakes, and – last but by no means least – the Columbia Icefield, the largest single glacial field in the entire Rocky Mountains. The Athabasca Glacier is one of the six glacial tongues of the Columbia Icefield – its meltwater feeds the Athabasca River. Like the Sunwapta River, the Athabasca River is famous for its magnificent waterfalls. Jasper is another of the many Canadian towns that have their origins in a Hudson's Bay Company outpost. Quieter than Banff, it is also the only town in the national park and therefore the park's commercial base.

THE HIGHLIGHTS: ALBERTA

INFO Fishing trips

Hire a canoe from the old boathouse (below) and explore Maligne Lake. The waters of Medicine Lake (right) drain down through layers of limestone into one of the world's largest karst cave networks. In spring, the increased meltwater runoff causes the water level to rise dramatically.

Trout may be the only type of fish anglers can catch in Maligne Lake, but they are plentiful. Fishing tours are available during the angling season (June–end October). Or you can hire equipment (and obtain a fishing permit) from the boathouse on the lake.
Maligne Tours; Tel (780) 852 33 70.

JASPER NATIONAL PARK: MALIGNE CANYON 58
MEDICINE LAKE 59 MALIGNE LAKE 60

The Maligne Road branches off the Yellowhead Highway about 3 km (2 miles) north-east of Jasper. It leads to the wild and spectacular landscape of Maligne Canyon where large waterfalls plunge down sheer limestone walls in three places. Medicine Lake is notable for its fluctuating level, swelling and reducing as if it were tidal, yet it is miles inland with no visible means of drainage. The First Nations people attributed the phenomenon to supernatural forces, but in fact the lake fills and empties through openings in its bedrock. The road continues to Maligne Lake, the largest glacial lake in the Rockies. Overshadowed by the magnificent snow-capped peaks of the surrounding mountains, Maligne Lake is in an enchanting valley at an altitude of 1,673 m (5,489 feet). Tiny Spirit Island can be reached by boat from the lake's southern tip. The lake and the island are one of the most famous sights in Jasper National Park.

THE HIGHLIGHTS:
ALBERTA

TIP Jasper Park Lodge

The mountains of the rugged Miette Range reach altitudes up to 2,563 m (8,409 feet). Below: The Glory Hole – a pool in the Miette Range. The Miette Hot Springs bubble out of the rock at temperatures of up to 54°C (129°F), while small Lake Beauvert (right) is a scenic destination for nature lovers.

This lodge is in an idyllic setting on the edge of Lake Beauvert. It was originally a campsite for construction workers on the Canadian Pacific Railway in 1915. Today, it is a charming complex of chalets and cabins, complete with its own golf course. *Old Lodge Road, Jasper T0E 1E0; Tel (780) 852 33 01.*

JASPER NATIONAL PARK: PYRAMID LAKE **61**
PATRICIA LAKE **62** BEAUVERT LAKE **63**

The English explorer Samuel Hearne (1745–92) was one of the first Europeans to visit Canada. In his diary, Hearne described a land of mountains, cliffs, and lakes dotted with so many clusters of islands that they looked more like untidy networks of small streams and rivers than single bodies of water. He may have been writing over 200 years ago, but little has changed in Jasper National Park today. While Maligne Lake is the park's main attraction, Patricia Lake and Pyramid Lake – both easily accessible from Jasper – are also popular destinations. Patricia Mountain (2,786 m/9,140 feet) towers over the two lakes. The luxurious Jasper Park Lodge is on the shore of Beauvert Lake, which covers just 0.5 sq km (0.2 sq mile). Miette Hot Springs lie farther north-east. The hottest mineral springs in the Rockies, the water cools to around 40°C (104°F) by the time it enters the pools at the hot springs – they are hard to resist after a day's hiking.

THE HIGHLIGHTS: ALBERTA

The Edmonton skyline (right) is a sign of the city's oil wealth. As well as over 800 stores and services, the giant West Edmonton Mall includes amusement parks, an indoor lake with a replica of the *Santa Maria*, sailed by Columbus to the New World in 1492 (below), an ice rink, and cinemas. Below, right: Alberta's parliament building.

INFO Canadian Finals Rodeo

The Canadian rodeo season reaches its traditional climax every November. Over a hundred cowboys from Canada, the USA, and New Zealand test their mettle on bulls and broncos (wild horses).
Rexall Place, 119th Ave Edmonton T5B 4M9; Tel (780) 414 43 00. www.canadianfinalsrodeo.com

Alberta's capital city is on the banks of the North Saskatchewan River. Edmonton is a gateway to the far north, and the perfect starting point for excursions along the Yellowhead Highway. The city became prosperous on the back of the fur trade – the Hudson's Bay Company set up its first trading posts here in the 18th century.

When the increasing importance of the timber industry led to the decline of the fur trade, Edmonton benefited from shipping activity on the North Saskatchewan River. In 1897, the beginning of the gold rush on the Klondike quickly saw Edmonton's population grow sixfold. The most recent boom in the local economy came

with the discovery of oil here in the 20th century, and over 80 percent of Canada's oilrigs are now located in the area around the city. Edmonton's three economic booms in as many centuries are evident in today's high-rise skyline. It is home to what was for many years North America's largest shopping mall.

THE HIGHLIGHTS: ALBERTA

With its scenic aspen forests and lakes (right), Elk Island National Park is home to plains bison, wood bison, and North American elk. The latter – also known as the moose – is the world's largest deer. A male animal can reach 2.3 m (7.5 feet) at the shoulders, and weigh as much as 500 kg (1,102 lbs).

INFO Wildlife viewing

Experienced guide Wayne Millar makes sure visitors see as much of the park's fascinating wildlife as possible. Tours take place in small groups, usually setting off two hours before sunset. They are much in demand, so book early.

Tel (780) 405 48 80.

ELK ISLAND NATIONAL PARK 65
UKRAINIAN CULTURAL HERITAGE VILLAGE 66

Heading east from Edmonton, you can reach the Elk Island National Park in less than an hour. It was originally established as a game sanctuary for the local red deer population in 1906, and declared a national park in 1930. Alongside its deer, the park is now home to a wide range of animals, including large numbers of elk and bison, and over 250 species of bird. The osprey and pelican are two such species, and even the endangered trumpeter swan has returned to hatch its eggs on Elk Island. A trip to the national park can be combined with a visit to the Ukrainian Cultural Heritage Village, which is located just 5 km (3 miles) east of Edmonton. This award-winning open-air museum commemorates the large numbers of Ukrainian pioneers who settled here in the late 19th century. There are over 30 historic buildings to explore, while costumed actor-interpreters portray some of the Ukranian pioneers – they remain in character the whole time.

The Canadian parliament passed the Indian Act in 1876 – it essentially regulates the legal status of the country's First Nations inhabitants. It is still in force today, though some tribes have won special privileges since it first became law. The First Nations regard the preservation of their culture and language as a fundamental objective, something that is vividly demonstrated at events like powwows, where there is ritual dancing in traditional costume and body paint (below and far right). Right: A traditional tipi tent.

THE FIRST NATIONS: THE FIRST AMERICANS

The first aboriginal peoples to inhabit the North American continent are believed to have arrived in Alaska from Siberia in Northern Asia during the last ice age, some 30,000 years ago, when the two continents were joined by a land bridge. The Siberian hunters had followed their prey to the New World, where the culture they developed was influenced by their new environment. They set up villages along the riverbanks in what is now Western Canada, where they hunted caribou, elk, and bear. Salmon and trout were dried and smoked to sustain them through the cold winter months when there was less chance of hunting, although snowshoes helped the hunters negotiate the snow. Their society was organized in clans that were led by the most experienced warriors and hunters. Houses and boats were constructed from birch bark, while tools and clothes were made from bone and animal skins. Potlatch festivals provided an opportunity to impress other members of the clan by making gifts of food and goods. Powwows were traditional meetings attended by members of the related Plains tribes. The term "Indian" dates back to the voyage of Columbus, who in 1492 mistakenly believed he had landed in India, not America. Since the 1970s, "First Nations" has been used as a collective term for all Canada's aboriginal peoples, with the exception of the Inuit and Métis.

THE HIGHLIGHTS: ALBERTA

The powerful bison (below) can grow up to 3 m (10 feet) in length, and weigh up to 1 tonne (2,205 lbs). Right: The extensive Wood Buffalo National Park, designated a UNESCO World Heritage Site in 1983. The descendents of the Chipewyan and Beaver tribes are the only people allowed to hunt within its boundaries.

INFO Sweetgrass Station

Set in the expansive grasslands of the Peace River delta, Sweetgrass Station is a perfect spot from which to observe the bison and wolves. It is a 12-km (7-mile) hike from Sweetgrass Landing.
Visitor Centre, 149 McDougal Road, Fort Smith X0E 0P0; Tel (867) 872 79 60.

Canada's largest nature sanctuary spans nearly 45,000 sq km (17,370 sq miles). Two-thirds of this area fall within Alberta, with the remainder in the Northwest Territories. The sanctuary was set up in 1922 in order to protect what were then the last remaining herds of wood buffalo, a subspecies of the American bison. Today, the wood buffalo population is believed to stand at some 6,000 animals, constituting the world's largest freely roaming bison herd. Plains bison have also been introduced to the park, and the two have sometimes interbred. The protected area can be divided into three distinct natural habitats: the highland prairies cleared by forest fires; a plateau with meandering rivers, salt plains, marshes, and wetlands; and the delta of the Peace and Athabasca rivers, an ideal habitat for over 200 bird species. The culture and ways of life of the Cree, Chipewyan, and Beaver peoples are perfectly adapted to this ecosystem.

Banff

ℹ️ Visitors Centre
Situated at the foot of Cascade Mountain on the Trans-Canada Highway, Banff is the largest town in the national park of the same name. The town offers a mix of upmarket hotels, exclusive restaurants and boutiques, and hot springs, all set in the most idyllic surroundings. The town provides an ideal, although admittedly rather expensive, starting point for excursions to the Rocky Mountains.
224 Banff Avenue;
Tel (403) 762 84 21.
www.banfflakelouise.com

🏛️ Whyte Museum of the Canadian Rockies
Artists Catherine and Peter Whyte run this art gallery and its small adjoining museum dedicated to the Rocky Mountains and its history. The collection features a number of "heritage homes", including two faithfully reconstructed log cabins that evoke the pioneer age, offering a fascinating insight into the past.
111 Bear Street;
Tel (403) 762 22 91;
10.00–17.00 daily.
www.whyte.org

🚡 Banff Gondola
The cable car takes eight minutes to reach the summit of Sulphur Mountain at an altitude of 698 m (2,290 feet). At the top you are rewarded with a breathtaking view of Banff and the surrounding mountains and lakes. Stunning mountain routes lead over the mountain ridges.
Mountain Avenue;
Tel (403) 762 54 38;
summer 7.30–21.00 daily.
www.banffgondola.com.

🚡 Cave and Basin National Historic Site
This site is at the location of the hot pools and underground springs around which the Banff National Park was established in 1885 – it is the oldest national park in the country. The site is currently undergoing extensive renovation, but the boardwalks in the nearby woods and marshes are open, as are the Sundance Day Use area and trail system.
Cave Avenue;
Tel (403) 762 15 66.

🚡 Explore the Rockies
The rugged terrain of the Columbia Icefield leads to the snow-covered mountains above the Icefields Parkway. Athabasca, Dome, and Stutfield, three of the eight glaciers that feed off the Colombia Icefield, can be viewed from the road between Banff and Jasper. Large four-wheel-drive buses with special tyres that allow them to grip on the ice take visitors on tours along the Athabasca Glacier, which is 6 km (3.75 miles) long and 1 km (0.5 mile) wide. Passengers can walk out onto the glacier in places, treading on ice that was formed several hundred years ago. The glacier by the Icefields Parkway is receding gradually, year by year. The new Icefield Centre, opened in 1996, provides a range of information about the glaciers.
100 Gopher Street;
Tel (403) 760 69 34;
summer 9.00–18.00 daily.
www.explorerockies.com

🚡 Hydra River Guides
This operator offers wild water experiences down the rapids of Kicking Horse River with trained guides who know every aspect of this wild river intimately. The classic rafting trips through Upper and Middle Canyon take around four hours. Add another hour for the even wilder journeys through Upper Canyon, Middle Canyon and Lower Canyon.
211 Bear Street;
Tel (403) 762 45 54.
www.raftbanff.com

♨️ Banff Upper Hot Springs
Banff's hot sulphur springs are internationally famous. The minerals in the springs include sulphur, calcium, and magnesium, which are said to have excellent healing properties. You can pamper yourself in the nearby spa and enjoy one of the many different massages on offer. The water temperatures in the pools, both inside and outside, fluctuate between 37 and 40°C (98–104°F). The site, complete with an old 1930s bathhouse, also boasts a restaurant, terrace bar, snack bar, and gift shop.
Mountain Avenue;
Tel (403) 762 15 15;
Mid-May–mid-Oct
9.00–23.00 daily,
mid-Oct to mid-May
Sun–Thu 10.00–22.00,
Fri, Sat 10.00–23.00.
www.hotspring.ca

🎨 Canada House Gallery
This well-known art gallery mainly promotes indigenous and First Nations artists and sells paintings, sculptures, and crafts. Works by Canadian Inuit artists are of particular interest.
201 Bear Street;
Tel. (403) 762 37 57;
Daily 9.00–18.00
www.canadahouse.com

🎨 Nijinska's of Banff
A large souvenir outlet selling Canadian crafts created by First Nations people from the north-west coast and also featuring work by Inuit artists. If you don't want to spend too much, you can also buy more moderately priced souvenirs and clothing.
201 Banff Avenue;
Tel (403) 762 50 06.
www.nijinskasgifts.com

❌ Bison Mountain Bistro & General Store
For a range of tasty sandwiches, delicious cold cuts, and exquisite cheeses, head for the ground floor of this general store. Meat is the order of the day in the restaurant, with numerous bison dishes on the menu. The bison burgers are outstanding but if you fancy trying something you won't find elsewhere, choose the bison pizza. It is certainly something to write home about!
211 Bear Street;
Tel. (403) 762 55 50.
www.thebison.ca

❌ Coyote's Deli & Grill
The folk of Banff love hearty food but this restaurant caters for a different kind of diner. For those watching their weight or counting their calories, it offers a delicious selection of light sandwiches, fresh and tasty salads, and vegetarian fare. And if you fancy a healthy picnic outdoors, all dishes are also available as takeouts.
206 Caribou Street;
Tel (403) 762 39 63.

❌ Grizzly House
Opened in 1967, this rustic restaurant offers both classic and more unusual fondues.

From left: City of skyscrapers – downtown Calgary is a Canadian Manhattan; an advert promotes the delights of pretzels; the Brewster and Buffalo Mountain lodges bring home comforts to the wilderness.

ALBERTA

The insider tips listed here refer to the sights described on pages 154–189.

Traditional versions include Swiss cheese fondue and a very popular meat version. Braver diners might like to try something more unusual, such as the rattlesnake or alligator fondues. But for pudding it's back to normality with a warming and delicious chocolate fondue.
207 Banff Avenue;
Tel (403) 762 40 55.
www.banffgrizzlyhouse.com

☒ St James Gate Olde Irish Pub
Enjoy fish and chips and, of course, Guinness on tap in this atmospheric pub. The woodwork and bar decorations are also authentically Irish.
205 Wolf Street;
Tel (403) 762 93 55.
www.stjamesgatebanff.com

🛏 Brewster Mountain Lodge
Among the top hotels in beautiful Banff, this lodge is one of the more economical options for those on a budget. Centrally located, it has impressively spacious rooms and offers many extras. The Brewsters are one of the wealthiest families in Banff.
521 Banff Avenue;
Tel (403) 762 29 00.
www.brewstermountainlodge.com

🛏 Buffalo Mountain Lodge
Situated in a natural setting on the slopes of Tunnel Mountain, away from the main tourist areas, the hustle and bustle of Banff remains safely at a distance here. This large lodge has spacious rooms and boasts antique furniture and a rustic yet elegant ambience. It is a pleasant place to stay but the enormous lobby is also

worth a look even if you are not staying here. The shuttle bus will have you in Banff in a matter of minutes.
Tunnel Mountain Road;
Tel (403) 762 24 00.
www.buffalomountainlodge.com

🛏 The Fairmont Banff Springs
This luxurious Canadian Pacific château hotel, in an idyllic setting above the city, was established back in 1888. Following extensive renovation, the building, inspired by a Scottish castle, has been restored to its former glory. The Fairmont has huge suites, pools, twelve restaurants, and a shopping arcade. The rambling grounds include a golf course and tennis courts.
405 Spray Avenue;
Tel (403) 762 22 11.
www.fairmont.com

🛏 Rimrock Resort Hotel
Opened in 1993, this resort owes its popularity in part to its tremendous view of the Rocky Mountains. It combines city luxury with a national park ambience. There's a spa offering treatments, an indoor pool, whirlpool, and sauna. Many guests like to spend the early hours of the evening sitting by the open fireplace in the lobby – and who can blame them.
Mountain Avenue;
Tel (403) 762 33 56.
www.rimrockresort.com

Calgary

ℹ Tourist information
In the south of Alberta, Calgary is just an hour's drive from the Rocky Mountains. A well-known winter sports destination, the city hosted the

1988 Winter Olympic Games. It is currently the fastest growing metropolis in Canada.
200 11 Avenue SE;
Tel (403) 263 85 10.
www.tourismcalgary.com

🏛 Ranchman's
This lively Country & Western music club has enjoyed huge popularity in Calgary since 1972 and has often been voted the best country music club in the city. Try dancing the "Two-Step" or "Cotton-Eyed-Joe" – beginners need not worry about their two left feet as free dance lessons are on offer. The saddles of the best rodeo cowboys are on display, and famous country stars perform here regularly – including during the annual Calgary Stampede in July.
9615 Macleod Trail SW;
Tel (403) 253 11 00.
www.ranchmans.com

🏛 Riley & McCormick
Calgary's "cowboy headquarters" has been in existence since 1901 and offers everything a cowboy (or cowgirl) might need: saddles, Stetsons, boots, lassos, dustcoats, and belt buckles. They are all here. And if there's anything you have forgotten, you can stock up on gifts and souvenirs at the small branch at the airport before you leave.
2220 8th Avenue SW;
Tel (403) 262 15 56.
www.realcowboys.com

☒ Buzzards Cowboy Cuisine
This truly authentic cowboy restaurant has been one of the city's most popular dining choices since 1980. The chef cooks to original recipes from the Wild West. Along with juicy, tender steaks, the menu

offers more unusual items, including buffalo tongue, and boasts a choice of over 200 types of beer!
140 10th Avenue SW;
Tel (403) 264 69 59.
www.cowboycuisine.com

☒ La Chaumière
An upmarket gourmet paradise that is renowned for its excellent French cuisine. Top dishes include tournedos of bison with palm hearts stuffed with truffles and Alberta lamb with mustard and mince. The steaks melt on your tongue and the elk tenderloin medallions offer a new culinary experience.
139 17th Avenue SE;
Tel (403) 228 56 90.
www.lachaumiere.ca

🛏 Best Western Suites Downtown
This economical hotel in the heart of the city is a reliable and practical choice with spacious rooms that offer all you need, but no bells, whistles, or costly extras. All rooms include wireless Internet, a coffee maker, and cable TV.
1330 8th Street SW;
Tel (403) 268 69 00.
www.bestwesternalberta.com

🛏 The Fairmont Palliser Hotel
This elegantly appointed hotel has been a Calgary institution ever since 1914. Its nostalgic atmosphere and evident luxury convey the impression of a grand hotel from a bygone era. All rooms and suites are stylishly furnished with antique pieces and comfortable beds. A wealth of extras include cordless telephones, halogen lights, and bathrobes. In addition, unlike in many American hotels, you can actually open

BEST ADDRESSES

the windows. Follow in the footsteps of oil magnates, captains of industry, and rock stars (as they say on their website).
133 9th Avenue SW;
Tel (403) 262 12 34.
www.fairmont.com

Edmonton

ℹ️ Tourist information
Edmonton, the wealthy capital city of the province of Alberta, lies on the bank of the North Saskatchewan River in the heart of the vast wheat-growing regions. The city's origins lie in the forts and outposts of the big fur-trading companies. Edmonton enjoyed a period of prosperity during the Klondike gold rush when it was an important supply base. The construction of the Alaska Highway and the establishment of the petroleum industry led to another boom, and today the city is still a major gateway to the northern wilderness.
9990 Jasper Avenue;
Tel (780) 426 47 15.
www.edmonton.com

🏛️ Royal Alberta Museum
This vast museum celebrates the history of the province of Alberta from its foundation to the present day. Realistic dioramas illustrate the different geographical regions, with much of the exhibition space dedicated to the aboriginal culture of Alberta.
12845 102 Avenue NW;
Tel (780) 453 91 00;
9.00–17.00 daily.
www.royalalbertamuseum.ca

🎡 West Edmonton Mall
This is the world's largest shopping and leisure complex – although not in terms of sales area – and was con-

structed at a cost of over a billion Canadian dollars. Over 800 shops and stores, more than 100 restaurants, and around 20 cinemas are housed under its gigantic roof. There is also the world's largest indoor water park with 22 slides and six wave bays, an amusement park complete with rollercoaster, a shooting range, an indoor lake with sea lions, a music stage ... the list goes on. The mall receives 28 million visitors per year.
1755, 8882 170th Street;
Tel (780) 444 53 21.
www.wem.ca

❌ Hardware Grill
Housed in a historic hardware store, this upmarket restaurant offers Canadian cuisine fused with European and Asian influences. Its highlights include caramelized duck breast with five spices, carrots with ginger, apple compote and creamy polenta, and Alberta beef tenderloin, which is served Bourguignon-style with heavenly mashed potatoes. The quality of the meat is excellent.
9698 Jasper Avenue;
Tel (780) 423 09 69.
www.hardwaregrill.com

❌ Sherlock Holmes
An English pub that has been spiriting its guests away to Victorian London since 1985. You'll find an original telephone box here, as well as a genuine red double-decker bus. Sir Arthur Conan Doyle's legendary master detective is, of course, ever-present. The cuisine is very British too, with beer to accompany the fish and chips.
10012 101A Avenue NW;
Tel (780) 426 77 84.
www.edmontonpubs.com

🛏️ Alberta Place Suite Hotel
The small suites in this hotel, each equipped with its own kitchenette, are perfect for those on a budget. Continental breakfast is included in the price. Jasper Avenue is just a few minutes' walk away.
10049 103rd Street;
Tel (780) 423 15 65.
www.albertaplace.com

🛏️ Fantasyland Hotel
This is Las Vegas in miniature. Hidden away behind austere walls you will find themed rooms, all designed in fabulous if rather kitsch style. Try the Trucker Room (in which you sleep on a pickup truck) or the Igloo Room, which comes complete with a dogsled.
17700 87th Avenue;
Tel (780) 444 30 00.
www.fantasylandhotel.com

Jasper

ℹ️ Tourist information
Smaller and less busy than Banff, Jasper has retained its reputation as a friendly, laid-back provincial settlement. Known for its winter sports, it has interest year round with golfing, rafting, hiking, and horseback-riding facilities. It lies on the border with British Columbia within Canada's largest national park, which is named after the town.
PO Box 98;
Tel (780) 852 38 58. www.jaspercanadianrockies.com

📷 Icefields Parkway
This 230-km (143-mile) stretch of Highway 93 between Lake Louise and Jasper National Park, passing through stunning mountains and lakes, is not to be missed. The Columbia Icefield, visible from

the Parkway, is the largest in the Rockies. One of eight major glaciers that feed off the Columbia Icefield, the Athabasca Glacier is on the far side of Sunwapta Pass, between Jasper and Banff.

📷 Jasper Tramway
Established in 1964, the aerial tramway's valley station is 6 km (3.5 miles) south of Jasper on Whistler Mountain Road. The cable cars travel up Whistler Mountain (2,277 m/ 7,472 feet), from where there is a breathtaking view.
P. O. Box 418;
Tel (780) 852 30 93;
mid-April–Mid-May and end Aug–Mid-Oct 10.00–17.00 daily, mid-May–end Jun 9.30–18.30 daily, end Jun–end Aug 9.00–20.00.
www.jaspertramway.com

❌ Denjiro
Japanese Restaurant
Tokyo Tom's became Denjiro and the new owner introduced a new culinary regime. This excellent eatery now offers sushi, sashimi, tempura, and teriyaki. The food is delicious but the atmosphere lacks a certain something.
410 Connaught Drive;
Tel (780) 852 38 50.

❌ Fiddle River Seafood
A fish restaurant with an informal atmosphere in the historic train station that has made a name for itself with its excellent food. The most popular dishes include those based on salmon and trout. Delicious sauces complement the delicate fish. If you prefer meat, choose one of the tender steaks.
620 Connaught Drive;
Tel (780) 852 30 32.

192 Western Canada

From left: Shop 'til you drop: the West Edmonton Mall has everything under one roof; Jasper National Park is home to many animal species, such as the elk or the bighorn sheep; take a canoe out on Lake Louise.

ALBERTA

The expert tips on these pages supplement the highlights featured on pp.154–189.

☒ Mountain Foods Café
Top dishes at this small café include sandwiches, salads, and soups, making it particularly popular with health-conscious visitors. Two of the small, hearty dishes served for lunch are Hungarian goulash and Thai spinach salad. And the breakfast menu is equally hearty and robust, with options including Mexican Huevos Rancheros.
606 Connaught Drive;
Tel (780) 852 40 50.

☒ Something Else
A restaurant offering a successful mix of Canadian, Greek, and Italian cuisine. The 20 types of pizza alone are worth a visit. It is a popular meeting place for locals and a good lunch spot.
621 Patricia Street;
Tel (780) 852 38 50.

🛏 Athabasca Hotel
This simple but moderately priced hotel was established in 1929 and soon made a name for itself as a popular meeting place for locals. Whereas almost all the rooms boast a magnificent view, not all have their own bathroom. The stuffed animals and open fireplace in the lobby are reminiscent of a trapper's cabin.
510 Patricia Street;
Tel (780) 852 33 86.
www.athabascahotel.com

🛏 Becker's Chalets
The cozy chalets of this romantic lodge are set in an idyllic location on the bank of the Athabasca River. The cabins come in all sizes and are furnished to different levels of comfort, with something for every taste and budget. The Deluxe Log Chalets can sleep six to eight.

PO Box 579;
Tel. (780) 852 37 79.
www.beckerschalets.com

🛏 Château Jasper
After a change of ownership and a costly renovation, this elegant first-class hotel has earned its place in the guidebooks once again. The rooms are luxuriously appointed, and there's a heated indoor pool, a whirlpool spa, and a sundeck. Fairly reasonably priced.
96 Geikie Street;
Tel (780) 852 56 44.
www.visitjasper.com/chateau.htmleern

🛏 Jasper Inn
Alpine Resort
The rooms of this popular hotel, in a very quiet part of town, are spread across three buildings. Some have a kitchenette and open fireplace. Facilities include a small heated pool, a sauna, and a restaurant. Part of the Best Western chain.
98 Geikie Street;
Tel (780) 852 44 61.
www.jasperinn.com

🛏 Lobstick Lodge
This hotel offers visitors good value for money and is particularly popular with families because of its spacious rooms and large kitchenettes. Every suite also has a living room with comfortable armchairs, as well as the bedroom. Additional features include a heated indoor pool and several jacuzzis.
96 Geikie Street;
Tel (780) 852 44 31.
www.lobsticklodge.com

🛏 Overlander
Mountain Lodge
Situated at the edge of Jasper National Park, this historic

lodge has surprisingly comfortable rooms, some with an open fireplace, and boasts a superb restaurant. The rooms have a magnificent view of the Rocky Mountains. Along with the main building there are also some chalets.
Jasper Park East Gate;
Hinton; Tel (780) 866 23 30.
www.overlandermountainlodge.com

Lake Louise

ℹ Visitor Centre
Set in a magnificent mountain landscape, Lake Louise is among the most beautiful lakes in North America, and consequently gets very busy during the summer months. All the key tourist activities are focused around the small village of Lake Louise.
Samson Mall;
Tel (403) 522 27 44.
www.banfflakelouise.com

◉ Lake Louise Ski Area
Take the lift into the alpine world around Lake Louise (Canada's "Diamond in the Wilderness") and enjoy blossoming mountain pastures in the summer or watch winter sports fans at play in one of North America's largest downhill skiing areas. There are slopes to suit all levels of skill.
1 Whitehorn Road;
Tel (403) 522 35 55.
www.skilouise.com

☒ Post Hotel Dining Room
The restaurant of the eponymous luxury hotel has earned several stars, while the hotel is even more popular with visitors. The menu includes classic dishes prepared with the greatest of care. The quality of the meat and fish here is outstanding.

P. O. Box 69;
Tel (403) 522 39 89.
www.posthotel.com

☒ Walliser Stube
Wine Bar
This comfortable Swiss eatery stands out from the many restaurants in the Fairmont Château Lake Louise hotel. Even European visitors from Alpine countries are impressed by the authentic fondue. Raclette is of course also on the menu, and you can choose from a large selection of wines.
Tel (403) 522 18 17.

🛏 The Fairmont
Château Lake Louise
A grand hotel on Lake Louise that looks like a fairy-tale castle and is one of the most impressive buildings in the Rocky Mountains. The rooms offer every conceivable luxury typical of an old-style grand hotel, and the bathrooms are fitted out in marble. Unfortunately it does get very crowded and, needless to say, is not cheap.
Tel (403) 522 35 11.
www.fairmont.com

🛏 Post Hotel
A simple ski lodge back in the 1940s, today it is a grand hotel that meets even the most stringent demands. Almost all rooms have a balcony, open fireplace, and jacuzzi. The beds are extremely comfortable, and the hotel offers countless extras. Each room has a distinct character and the Temple Mountain Spa is renowned for its excellent treatments. A good place to pamper yourself if your budget permits.
PO Box 69;
Tel (403) 522 39 89.
www.posthotel.com

January

Ice Magic
Lake Louise. Professionals and amateurs carve elaborate sculptures out of the ice, including ornate sleighs or even entire fairy-tale castles. When the festival is over, the sculptures are left in place to be enjoyed – until they melt.
www.banfflakelouise.com

Reino Keski-Salmi Loppet
Salmon Arm. This is a cross-country skiing event that is among Canada's most famous sporting fixtures and attracts the best skiers in the country.
www.skilarchhills.ca

Jasper in January
Jasper. The large winter fair in Jasper National Park includes sled races, ski festivals, music events, and a winter beach party. Wrap up warm.
www.jasperinjanuary.com

Banff/Lake Louise Winter Festival
Banff/Lake Louise. Skating parties on the ice and barn dances are among the many events and attractions of this winter carnival.
www.banfflakelouise.com

February

Yukon Quest
The most challenging dog-sled race in the world runs from Whitehorse (Yukon Territory) through Dawson City to Fairbanks (Alaska). It is as important an event in the Yukon as a soccer final is in Europe. With a fully loaded sled pulled by 14 huskies, the mushers (dogsled drivers) battle their way through the cold, wind, and driving snow. The arduous trail, which is 1,600 km (100 miles) in length, takes around 16 days, at temperatures around 40 degrees below zero. The trail leads across the frozen Yukon River, through snow-covered valleys and over steep, craggy mountains. The mushers are in danger from grizzlies, but even more so from elks, which can cross the race track unexpectedly and become entangled with the dogs, or the dreaded overflow, which is warm river water that pushes up through cracks in the ice and combines with the snow. The Yukon Quest has been held every year since 1984 to commemorate the intrepid men and women who first ventured into the seemingly impenetrable wilderness along the Yukon River – the gold prospectors and early settlers. The event also celebrates the legendary Northwest Mounted Police.
www.yukonquest.info

Nokia Snowboard FIS World Cup
Mount Whistler. This World Cup event brings together the best snowboarders in the world. Everything in this chic mountain village is aimed at the overwhelmingly youthful public while the competition is running.
www.fis-ski.com

Yukon Sourdough Rendezvous
Whitehorse. Axe-throwing, dogsled races, fiddle contests: these are just some of the diverse highlights of this winter carnival. It is an entertaining festival with many events and is particularly good fun for children.
www.youryukon.com

March

Pacific Rim Whale Festival
Tofino/Ucluelet. Every spring, more than 20,000 gray whales appear in the waters off Vancouver Island as they head north, and a large festival is held in the coastal towns of Tofino and Ucluelet to celebrate their return. The program of events includes walks, talks, and workshops. Pleasure boats take visitors as close as possible to these extraordinary animals.
Tel (250) 726 46 41.
www.pacificrimwhale festival.org

May

Vancouver International Children's Festival
Vancouver. In addition to many theater performances and circus shows, this festival – staged annually since 1978 – includes storytelling, puppetry, and concerts for children. There are all kinds of snack stands, as well as merry-go-rounds.
www.childrensfestival.ca

July

Calgary Stampede
Calgary. The Calgary Stampede is one of the biggest rodeos in the world. The enormous spectacle transforms the city into a bustling one-horse town, when everyone is kitted out in cowboy gear, regardless of age, sex, or occupation. The event dates back to 1885, when an agricultural exhibition was organized in what was then still a sleepy town. To make the exhibition more attractive, a small cowboy festival was organized, which eventually developed in the greatest wild west show of all time. Stampede fever lasts ten days. Each day, the cowboys ride wild horses, saddled and unsaddled, wrestle steers, and lasso nimble calves. Bull-riding is one of the most eagerly anticipated events. The toughest and bravest cowboys take their chances on the back of a snorting bull, and for the eight-second duration of the ride they risk being crushed by the bull, which can weigh around 1,000 kg (2,205 lb), trampled by its hooves, or impaled on its horns. A gunshot starts the Chuckwagon Races evening. These competitions have been held since 1922, the year the Calgary Stampede became a major event – the drama and tension they provide are somewhat reminiscent of the chariot races in ancient Rome.
Tel (800) 661 17 67
(in USA and Canada).
www.calgarystampede.com

Klondike Days
Edmonton. This large funfair with fairground rides and snack stands is held to commemorate the great Klondike gold rush and the Canadian pioneer age. Along with concerts, the events over the ten days of the festival include covered wagon races and gold-panning competitions.
www.capitalex.ca

Banff Summer Arts Festival
Banff. Well-known orchestras and bands celebrate both classical music and jazz on numerous stages in Banff and its environs.
Tel (800) 413 83 68 (in USA and Canada); July/August.
www.banffcentre.com

From left: The Calgary Stampede: a cowboy competing in the rodeo competition; a member of the First Nations displaying his skills; a skating competition in Vancouver; dogsled races in the famous Yukon Quest.

FESTIVAL CALENDER

The summer months, when most of the open-air events are held, are a busy time for festivals in Western Canada. There's a wide range, often reflecting the country's history, from Pioneer Days, Indian powwows and rodeos, to events celebrating the country's different immigrant groups.

Vancouver Folk Festival

Vancouver. The "Summer of Love" of the hippie era is still celebrated here today. In July, numerous folk bands (including some actually dating from the 1960s) play in Bayside Park, where the ideals of peace and love still rule in a laid-back atmosphere.
Tel (604) 602 97 98.
www.thefestival.bc.ca

Marine Festival

Nanaimo. The most impressive sailing ships, motorboats, and yachts in the country drop anchor in the port of this small city, and delicious seafood dishes are served at numerous stands and in the restaurants. However, the undisputed highlight of the festival is the World Championship Bathtub Race – what else? Bold seafarers set out to negotiate the 58 km (36 miles) from Nanaimo to Vancouver in the oldest tubs they can find – though admittedly converted to race through the water at speed, powered by outboard motors.
www.bathtubbing.com

Billy Barker Days

Quesnel. Each year over four days in July, the legendary gold-prospecting era is celebrated to commemorate the founder of Barkerville (around 80 km/50 miles from Quesnel) with parades, a rodeo, fireworks, and dancing.
3rd weekend in July.
http://billybarkerdays.netbistro.com/

HSBC Celebration of Light

Vancouver. Pyrotechnic experts from around the world compete in this amazing annual musical firework competition, which lasts four days. The night sky over English Bay is lit up in a fantastic spectacle of light to a musical accompaniment.
July/August; www.celebration-of-light.com

August

Big Valley Jamboree

Camrose. This is the big event for all country music fans in Western Canada. For four days, visitors celebrate the world's best and most famous country music bands and artists with noisy enthusiasm. Acts perform on the main stage around the clock. If you fancy a break from the music, other attractions include bull-riding and market stalls.
Beginning August. www.bigvalleyjamboree.com

Peach Festival

Penticton. A peach harvest festival lasting several days is held on the banks of Okanagan Lake in downtown Penticton. In addition to parades, concerts, and dance performances, there are various competitions and a variety of stands, some selling crafts. All kinds of snacks are available to feed the many visitors.
2nd week in August.
www.peachfest.com

Discovery Days Festival

Dawson City. Festive parades, a canoe race, and a cheerful funfair call to mind the first discoveries of gold on the Klondike River, and the world-famous gold rush that followed. For a short time during the festival, Dawson becomes becomes the "capital city of the North" once again. Its numbers are swollen by the tourists who come here every summer, but drop dramatically during the off season.
www.travelyukon.com

First People Festival

Victoria. Many First Nations people native to Vancouver Island and the mainland meet for a large powwow (a gathering of tribal people to celebrate their culture) and potlach (the traditional gift-giving festival). For three days, the focus of the capital city of British Columbia is on its original inhabitants.
www.victoria.worldguides.com

September

Salmon Festival

Port Alberni. In the "Salmon Capital of the World", the salmon rules the roost for three days. The fishing competitions, which offer high-value prizes, are a big draw for both competitors and spectators. Entertainments, a barbecue, and a fireworks display round off this very popular annual festival on Vancouver Island.
1st weekend in Sept;
Tel (250) 724 52 23.
www.salmonfest.ca

October

Okanagan Fall Wine Festival

Okanagan Valley. Wine merchants and producers in the fertile Okanagan Valley liven up the wine-growing villages here with funfairs, food, wine-tasting, and an open house at most wine cellars. More than 165 events take place over ten days.
Beginning October;
Tel (250) 861 66 54.
www.owfs.com

Oktoberfest

Kitchener/Waterloo. This festival, held in the twin cities of Kitchener and Waterloo, is the largest Bavarian Oktoberfest outside Munich. The nine-day beer-based event is impressive with its surprisingly authentic music and somewhat less original Bavarian-style food. The spectacular 5-km (3-mile) parade held every year on Canadian Thanksgiving Day as part of the festival is broadcast on national television.
www.oktoberfest.ca

November

Great Canadian Beer Festival

Victoria. The best beer brewers in the country meet for an animated exchange of ideas and give away free samples of their tasty beer.
www.gcbf.com

Canadian Finals Rodeo

Edmonton. Canada's national rodeo championships and the absolute highlight of the rodeo season takes place in Alberta's provincial capital.
www.canadianfinalsrodeo.ca

December

Canadian Open Dogsled Race

Fort St John/Fort Nelson. Young and old attend this winter carnival, which revolves around a dogsled race but also includes a large funfair.

Christmas Carol Ships Parade

Vancouver. Ships decorated for Christmas sail through the bays and channels of the city.
www.carolships.org

Alberta's southern urban focus, Calgary is also the best departure point for a journey west to the Rocky Mountains. In the inner city all is gleaming towers and skyscrapers, but in the outlying districts, wooden buildings are a reminder of the pioneer days.

KEY

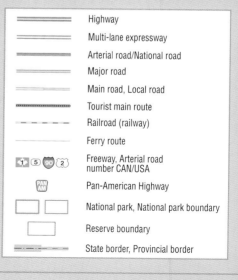

	Highway
	Multi-lane expressway
	Arterial road/National road
	Major road
	Main road, Local road
	Tourist main route
	Railroad (railway)
	Ferry route
1 5 90 2	Freeway, Arterial road number CAN/USA
PAN AM	Pan-American Highway
	National park, National park boundary
	Reserve boundary
	State border, Provincial border

ATLAS

The maps in this section give detailed practical information to help make your stay more enjoyable, including comprehensive road mapping, with symbols that indicate the position and nature of sights and buildings of note, such as national parks, museums, and monuments.

🏛 Museum/Music/Theater	♣ Market/Shopping
♫ Festival	✕ Refreshments/Restaurant
⚽ Sport/Games/Leisure	🛏 Accommodation
🏋 Health and fitness	ℹ Information
■ UNESCO Natural Heritage Site	🐋 Aquarium/ Whale watching
⛰ Glacier	Ⓤ Gorge/Canyon
Lakeland	Waterfall/Rapids
River landscape	Cave
Mountain landscape	Active volcano
Rock landscape	Extinct volcano
Coastal landscape	Fossil site
Nature park	Wildlife reserve
National park (scenery)	Bird sanctuary
National park (plantlife)	Zoo
National park (cultural heritage)	Protected area for sea lions/seals
Beach	Marine reserve
Surfing	Bathing resort
Sailing	Mineral bath/Hot springs
Port	Fishing
Windsurfing	Viewpoint

Camping site	Rock climbing
Cable car	Cycling/Mountain biking
Hiking area	Equestrian sports
Mountain refuge	Canoeing/Rafting
Skiing	
Scenic tourist route	Airport
Scenic shipping route	International airport
Scenic railway	Scenic route
UNESCO World Heritage Site	
First Nations reserve	Olympic city
First Nations cultural site	Open-air museum
Church	Notable lighthouse
Historic town/city area	Notable bridge
Imposing skyline	Dam wall
Palace/Castle	Mine (shut)
Castle/Fortress/Defenses	Industrial monument
Notable building	Monument
Cultivated landscape	Theater
Prehistoric rock paintings	Wine producer/Vineyard

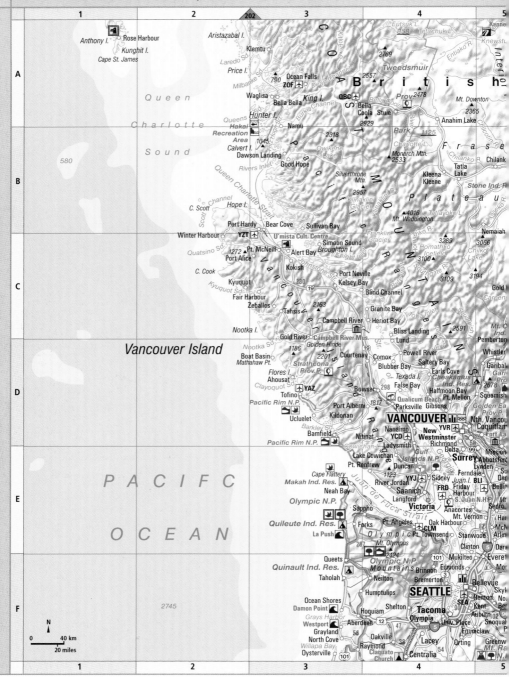

Vancouver Island

PACIFIC

OCEAN

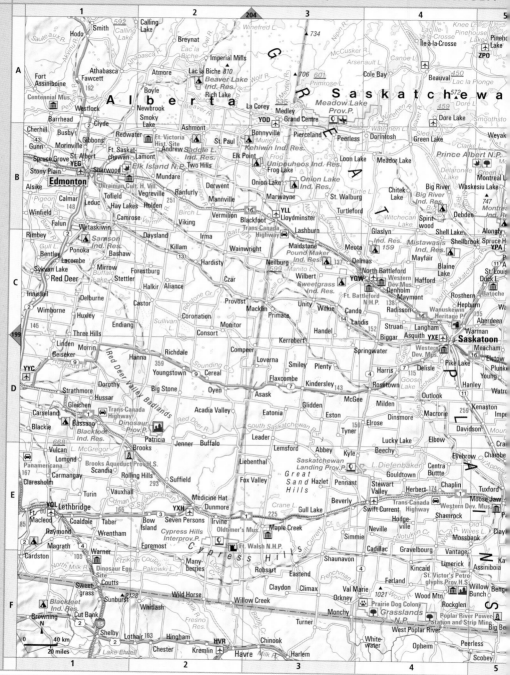

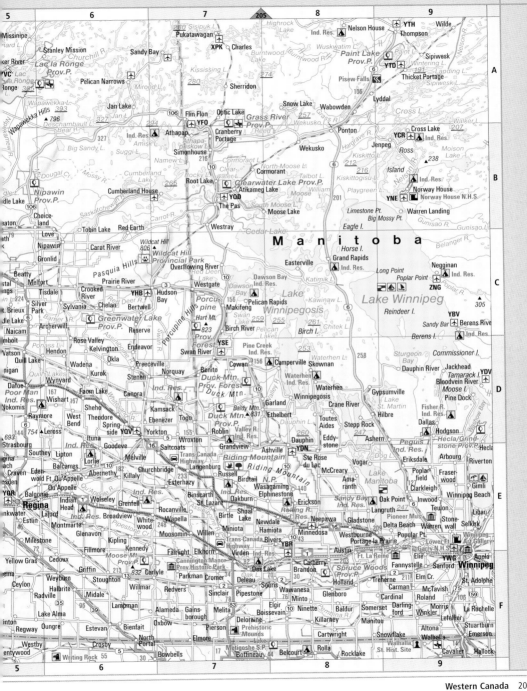

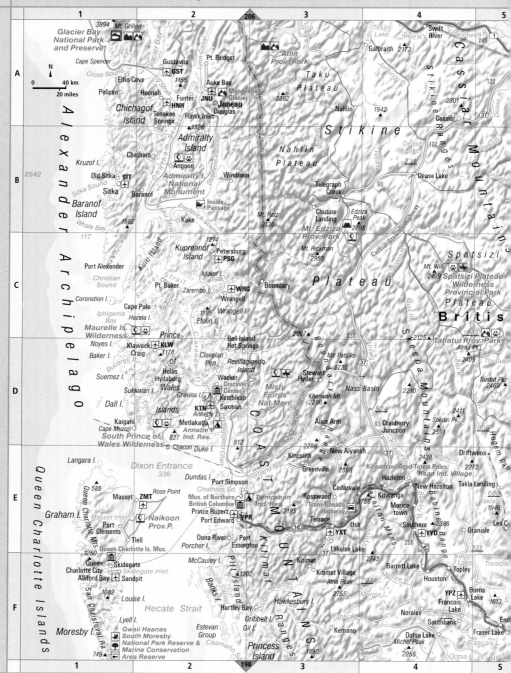

A

3894 ▲ Mt. Grillon

Glacier Bay
National Park
and Preserve

Cape Spencer

Cross Sound

Gustavus
⊕ GST 1155

Pt. Bridget

206

Atlin
Lake

Atlin
Prov. Park

Teslin
Lake

Galbraith 2173

Swift R.

Swift
River

245

1

Cassiar

N
0   40 km
20 miles

Elfin Cove

Pelican

Hoonah

Chichagof
Island

Tenakee
Springs

Funter
JNU
Douglas

Auke Bay

Mendenhall
Glacier

Juneau

Hawk Inlet

Taku
Plateau

Nahlin

2362

1942

Jennings R.

2301

Cassiar

37

122

HNH

▲1326

B

2542

Kruzof I.

Chatham

Old Sitka SIT

Sitka

Baranof

Baranof
Island

Admiralty
Island

Angoon

Admiralty I.
National
Monument

Windham

Inside
Passage

Nahlin
Plateau

Telegraph
Creek

Chutine
Landing

90

Edziza
Peak

Mt. Edziza 2788
Prov. Park

Dease
Lake

Dease Lake

122

731

Stikine Ranges

Cassiar
Stewart
Highway

Stikine

2542

117

Whale Bay

1982

Kake

Mt. Ratz
3136

Mt. Hickman
2956

Skut R.

Spatsizi

Mt. Will
2499 Spatsizi Plateau
Wilderness
Provincial Park

C

Port Alexander

Christian
Sound

Coronation I.

Iphigenia
Bay

Cape Pole

Maurelle Is.
Wilderness

Kupreanof
Island

1214

Petersburg
PSG

Mitkof I.

Zarembo I.

WRG

Wrangell

Wrangell I.

Heceta I.

1195
Etolin I.

Boundary

Plateau

2067

338

Plateau

Britis

2125 ▲ Tallatui Prov. Park

Alma Pk.

2409   Thutade

D

Noyes I.

Baker I.

Suemez I.

Dall I.

Klawock KLW
Craig   ▲1178

Hollis
Hydaburg
Wales

Sukkwan I.

Prince

Clevelan
Pen.

Revillagigedo
Island

Wacker

of

Gravina I.

Discovery
Center

Ketchikan

Saxman

Bell Island
Hot Springs

Mt. Patullo
2730

Stewart
Hyder

Misty
Fjords
Nat. Mon.

Khaswan Mt.
2286

Nass Basin

2210

524

Shedin Pk.
2591

2411

Sustut Pk.
2469

Skeena Mountains

805

Hogem Ra.

E

Langara I.

Graham I.

Masset

Masset Inlet

Port
Clements

Tlell

Queen Charlotte Is. Mus.

Kaigani
Cape Muzon

South Prince of
Wales Wilderness

Dixon Entrance
336

Dundas I.

Chatham Sd.

ZMT

Rose Point

585

Naikoon
Prov. P.

Islands

Annette I.

KTN

Metlakatla

Annette I.
Ind. Res.

827

Duke I.

C. Chacon

812

2286

Kincolith

Greenville 2368

Mus. of Northern
British Columbia

Prince Rupert

Port Edward

Oona River

Porcher I.

Port
Essington

Port Simpson

Tsimpsean
Ind. Res.

YPR

New Aiyansh

Kitwancool Aged Totem Poles
Ksan Ind. Village

Hazelton

Rosswood

Cedarvale

Kitwanga

Trans-Canada
Highway

Terrace

Usk

2195

2438

New Hazelton

Moricetown

Smithers ▲2386

YYD

2272

Driftwoos

Takla Landing

Takla
Lake

689

1946

Leo Cr.

Granisle

F

Queen Charlotte Islands

San Christoval Ra.

1082

749 ▲

Queen
Charlotte City
Alliford Bay

Louise I.

Lyell I.

Moresby I.

Skidegate

Sandpit

Gwaii Haanas
South Moresby
National Park Reserve &
Marine Conservation
Area Reserve

1250

McCauley I.

Banks I.

Hartley Bay

Estevan
Group

Gribbell I.

Gil I.

Princess
Island

1202

Hecate Strait

Hawkesbury I.

Kemano

198

1890

Kitimat

Kitimat Village

Atna Peak
2755

2743

Barrett Lake

Houston

Topley

Burns
Lake

YPZ
Francois
Lake

Noralee

Southbank

Ootsa Lake

Michel Peak

2255

1613

End

Fraser Lake

Francois L.

Tremble

Babine
Lake

771

256

16

797

Morice L.

Morice R.

Coronation I.

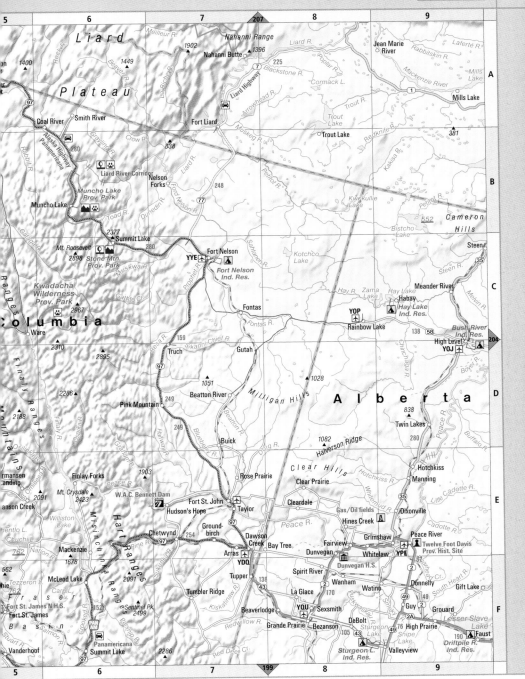

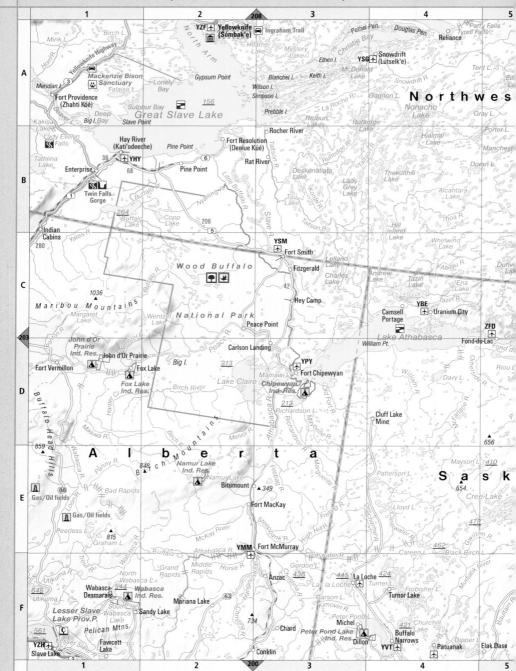

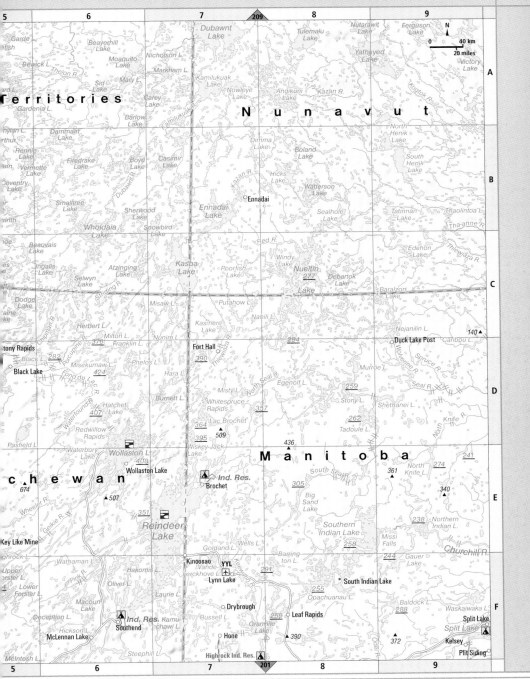

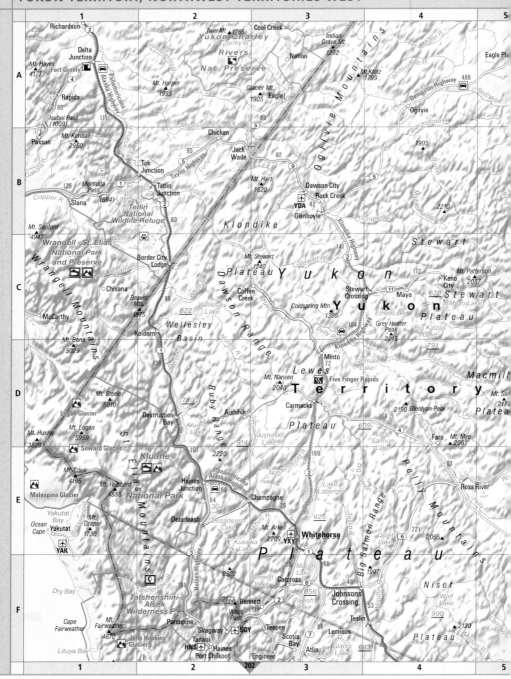

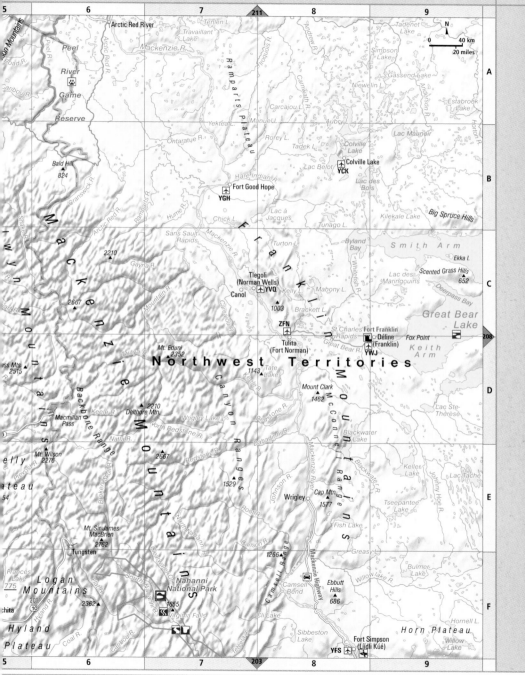

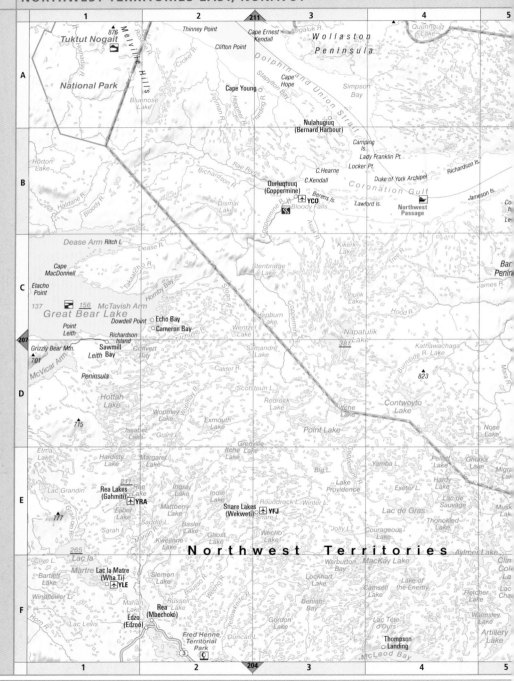

Tuktut Nogait
876
Thinney Point
Cape Ernest Kendall
Kugaluk R.
Wollaston
Peninsula
Quunnguq Lake
National Park
Melville Hills
Rosche R.
Clifton Point
Cape Hope
Dolphin and Union Strait
Stapylton Bay
Bluenose Lake
Croker R.
Cape Young
Simpson Bay
Hornaday R.
Inman R.
Hoppner R.
Harding R.
Nulahugiuq (Bernard Harbour)

Horton Lake
Richardson R.
Rae River
Camping Is.
Lady Franklin Pt.
Locker Pt.
Richardson Is.
Haldane R.
Bloody R.
C.Hearne
C.Kendall
Coronation Gulf
Jameson Is.
Co Is Le
Qurluqtuuq (Coppermine)
YCO
Dismal Lakes
Berens Is.
Bloody Falls
Lawford is.
Duke of York Archipel
Northwest Passage

Dease Arm Ritch I.
Dease R.
Takatchoo R.
Stenbridge Lake
Kikerk Lake
Tree R.
Bar Penin
Cape MacDonnell
Hornby Bay
Inulik Lake
James R.
Etacho Point
137
156
McTavish Arm
Sloan R.
Hepburn Lake
Hood R.
Great Bear Lake
Dowdell Point
Echo Bay
Cameron Bay
Wentzel Lake
Coppermine R.
Napatulik Lake
Point Leith
Richardson Island
Tilchuse R.
Samandre Lake
381
Kathawachaga Lake
Burnside R.
Mara R.
Grizzly Bear Mtn.
701
Sawmill
Leith Bay
Convert Bay
Calder R.
823
McVicar R.
Peninsula
Scotstoun L.
Contwoyto Lake
Hottah Lake
Wopmay R.
Wopmay Lake
Exmouth Lake
Redrock Lake
Itchen R.
Point Lake
Nose Lake
715
Issabel Lake
Grant L.
Grenville
Itchen Lake
Pellatt Lake
Ghurka Lake
Migra Lak
Etma Lake
Hardisty Lake
Margaret Lake
Ingray Lake
Big. L.
Yamba L.
Hardy Lake
Lac Grandin
Grandin R.
211
Rea Lakes (Gahmiti)
YRA
Rea Lake
Indin Lake
Roundrock L.
Winter L.
Lake Providence
Exeter L.
Lac de Sauvage
Musk Lak
777
Faber Lake
Mattberry Lake
Snare Lakes (Wekweti)
YFJ
Snare L.
Thonokied Lake
Saddle L.
Basler Lake
Wecho Lake
Jolly L.
Courageous Lake
Sarah L.
Marian R.
Kwejinne Lake
Ghost Lake
265
Lac la
Northwest Territories
Aylmer Lake
Clive L.
Martre Lac la Matre (Wha Ti)
YLE
Slemon Lake
Warburton Bay
MacKay Lake
Clin Cole La
Bartlett Lake
Bousso R.
Weicho R.
Lockhart Lake
Lake of the Enemy
Camsell Lake
Lac Cha
Windflower L.
Marian Lake
Russell Lake
Beniah Bay
Fletcher Lake
Horn R.
Edzo (Edzoo)
Rea (Mbechokǫ́)
Yellowknife R.
Gordon Lake
Lac Tête d'Ours
Walmsley Lake
Artillery Lake
Lac Levis
Fred Henne Territorial Park
Duncan L.
Thompson Landing
McLeod Bay

207
211
204

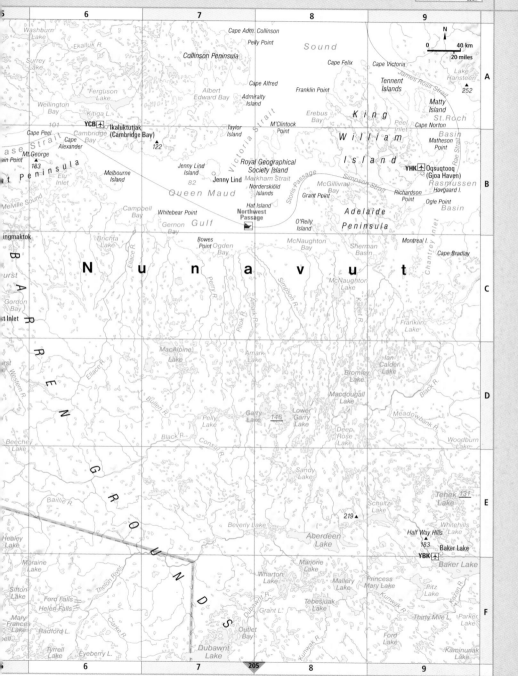

	1	2	3	4	5

A

Tangent Point
Ikiak
Cape Simpson
Smith Bay
Anakruak
Kokruagarok

Cape Halkett

Harrison
Atigaru Point
Bay

B e a u f o r t   S e a

3590

B

Nuiqsut
Oliktok Point
Beechey Point
Jones Is.
Return Is.
Deadhorse
SCC
Prudhoe Bay
11
Kuparuk R.
Sagavanirktok R.

1640

Bullen
Sagwon
Flaxman I.
Brownlow Point
Camden Bay

Shaviovik R.

C

Canning R.

Mt.Salisbury
2152
Kaktovik
Griffin Point

Beaufort

Mt.Chamberlin
2749
Hulahula R.

2365

A r c t i c
2453
Aichilik R.
Lagoon
Icy Reef

2255
Romanzof Mts.
Demarcation Point
Gordon

D

N a t i o n a l

Arctic Village

D a v i d s o n
1601
Mt.Greenough
Kongakut R.
Ivvavik
182
Herschel Island
Herschel

M o u n t a i n s
Bear Mt.
1905
Firth R.
National Park
35

Kay Point

W i l d l i f e   R e f u g e
1601
Babbage R.
Mackenzie

Sheenjek R.

Pelly I.
Hooper I.
Garry I.
Kendal I.
Summer Island

E

Coleen R.
Vuntut
National Park
1143
Ellice Island
Olivier Islands
Richards Island
Kugmallit Bay
Taker Pt.
Warren

O l d   C r o w
Blow R.
Shallow Bay
Langley Island
Tununuk
Kittigazuit
YUB
Tuktoyaktuk
Pingos

F l a t s
Old Crow R.
Mackenzie Delta
Parsons L.

Old Rampart
Old Crow
YOC
P o r c u p i n e   P l a i n
Fish R.
West Channel
Aklavik
Reindeer Station
Noell L.
Urquhart Lake

F

856
Sharp Mt.
1035
Richardson Mountains
Bell R.
Middle Channel
Inuvik
YEV
Sitidgi Lake
Miner R.

Salmon Fork
Grayling Fork
Rock R.
1574
Fort McPherson
54
East Channel
5
130
Caribou L.
Lost Reindeer Lakes
Kugaluk R.

Porcupine R.
207

	1	2	3	4	5

N

0   40 km
20 miles

A

91   Griffiths Point
Bloxsome Bay

Cape Manning   Dyer
Bay

B

Burnett Bay
Bernard Island

Bernard R.   Thomsen R.

C

Storkerson Bay
Meek Point

B a n k s

105

I s l a n d

Aulavik
National Park

34

Big River

Cape Kellett

YSY
Ikaahuk
(Sachs Harbour)

Bernard R.

D

Kellett R.

Northwest Passage

Prince of Wales Strait

Thesiger

Deans
Dundas Bay
104

Bay

Prince Albert

82   Observation Pt.

Durham
Heights
747

Peninsula

Russell
Inlet

Baillie Islands
Cape Dalhousie   Cape Bathurst

Cape Lamberton

Nelson
Head

De Salis Bay

Cape
Cardwell

Berkeley Pt.
Walker Bay

Fort Collinson

Char Pt.

E

Peninsula

Harrowby B.

Cape Richards

Liverpool Bay

Nicholson

A m u n d s e n

214

Cape Wollaston

Minto Inlet

Wood R.

Rufus L.

Mason R.

Kaglik L.

Cape Parry
Booth Is.   Cape Parry

G u l f

Uluksartuuq
(Holman Island)

YHI

Franklin

Parry

Bay

Langton B.

Peninsula

141   Cape
Lyon

Albert Islands

Darnley
Bay

Deas Thompson Point

Anderson River

Horton River

West R.

Paulatuk

YPC

Clinton Point

Cape Baring

sley
s.

Biname Lake

Hornaday River

La Ronciere
Falls

208

F

Abbey CDN   200   E3
Abbotsford CDN   198   E5
Aberdeen USA   198   F4
Aberdeen CDN   200   C5
Abernethy CDN   201   E6
Acadia Valley CDN   200   D2
Adams Lake CDN   199   C7
Ahousat CDN   198   D3
Airdrie CDN   199   D9
Aishihik CDN   206   D2
Aklavik CDN   210   F3
Alameda CDN   201   F6
Alder Flats CDN   199   B9
Alert Bay CDN   198   C3
Alexis Creek CDN   199   B5
Aliance CDN   200   C2
Alice Arm CDN   202   D3
Alliford Bay CDN   202   F1
Alongly CDN   200   C5
Alsike CDN   200   B1
Altona CDN   201   F9
Amaranth CDN   201   E8
Anacortes USA   198   E4
Anahim Lake CDN   198   A4
Anakruak USA   210   A1
Andrew CDN   200   B2
Angoon USA   202   B2
Anola CDN   201   F9
Anzac CDN   204   F3
Arbourg CDN   201   E9
Archerwill CDN   201   C6
Arctic Bay CDN   213   D9
Arctic Red River CDN   207   A6
Arctic Village USA   210   D1
Arlington USA   198   E5
Arras CDN   203   E7
Asask CDN   200   D3
Ashern CDN   201   D9
Ashmont CDN   200   B2
Ashville CDN   201   D8
Aspen Cove CDN   199   D6
Asquith CDN   200   C4
Assiniboia CDN   200   F5
Athabasca CDN   200   A1
Athapap CDN   201   B7
Athol USA   199   F7
Atikameg Lake CDN   201   B7
Atlin CDN   206   F3
Auburn USA   198   F4
Auke Bay USA   202   A2
Austin CDN   201   E8
Avola CDN   199   C7

Babb USA   199   F9
Baker Lake CDN   209   E9
Balcarres CDN   201   E6
Baldur CDN   201   F8
Baldy Hughes CDN   199   A6
Balfour CDN   199   E8
Balgonie CDN   201   E5
Bamfield CDN   198   D3
Banff CDN   199   D9
Baranof USA   202   B2
Barkerville CDN   199   B6
Barrett Lake CDN   202   F4
Barrhead CDN   200   A1
Barriere CDN   199   C6
Bashaw CDN   200   C1
Bassano CDN   200   D1
Bathurst Inlet CDN   209   C5
Bay Tree CDN   203   E7

Bear Cove CDN   198   B3
Beatton River CDN   203   D7
Beatty CDN   201   C5
Beauval CDN   200   A4
Beaverlodge CDN   203   F8
Beechey Point USA   210   B1
Beechy CDN   200   E4
Beiseker CDN   200   D1
Belcourt USA   201   F8
Bell Island Hot Springs USA   202   D2
Bella Bella CDN   198   A3
Bella Coola CDN   198   A3
Bellevue USA   198   F4
Bellingham USA   198   E5
Bengough CDN   200   F5
Benito CDN   201   D7
Bennett CDN   206   F3
Bentley CDN   200   C1
Berens River CDN   201   C9
Bernard Harbour CDN   208   A3
Bertwell CDN   201   C6
Beverly CDN   200   E3
Bezanson CDN   203   F8
Bienfait CDN   201   F6
Big Bear Creek CDN   199   C5
Big Beaver CDN   200   F5
Big Creek CDN   199   B5
Big Lake Ranch CDN   199   B6
Big River CDN   200   B4
Big Stone CDN   200   D2
Bigfork USA   199   F9
Biggar CDN   200   C4
Binscarth CDN   201   E7
Birch Hills CDN   200   C5
Birch River CDN   201   C7
Birdtail CDN   201   E7
Birtle CDN   201   E7
Bitumount CDN   204   E2
Black Diamond CDN   199   D9
Black Lake CDN   205   D5
Blackfoot CDN   200   B3
Blackie CDN   200   D1
Blaine Lake CDN   200   C4
Blairmore CDN   199   E9
Blind Channel CDN   198   C4
Bliss Landing CDN   198   C4
Bloodvein River CDN   201   D9
Blubber Bay CDN   198   D4
Blue River CDN   199   C7
Boat Basin CDN   198   D3
Boissevain CDN   201   F8
Bonners Ferry USA   199   F8
Bonnyville CDN   200   B3
Border City Lodge USA   206   C2
Boston Bar CDN   199   D5
Bottineau USA   201   F7
Boundary CDN   202   C3
Bow Island CDN   200   E2
Bowbells USA   201   F6
Bowser CDN   198   D4
Boyle CDN   200   A2
Brandon CDN   201   F8
Bremerton USA   198   F4
Breynat CDN   200   A2
Bridge Lake CDN   199   C6
Brinnon USA   198   F4
Broadview CDN   201   E6
Brochet CDN   205   E7
Brooks CDN   200   E1
Browning USA   200   F1
Buffalo CDN   200   D2

Buffalo Narrows CDN   204   F4
Buick CDN   203   D7
Bullen USA   210   C2
Burns Lake CDN   202   F4
Busby CDN   200   B1

Cache Creek CDN   199   C6
Cadillac CDN   200   E4
Cadomin CDN   199   B8
Calgary CDN   199   D9
Calling Lake CDN   200   A1
Calmar CDN   200   B1
Cambridge Bay CDN   209   B6
Cameron Bay CDN   208   C2
Campbell River CDN   198   C3
Camperville CDN   201   D8
Camrose CDN   200   B1
Camsell Portage CDN   204   C4
Canal Flats CDN   199   E8
Candle Lake CDN   201   B5
Cando CDN   200   C4
Canim Lake CDN   199   C6
Canmore CDN   199   D9
Canol CDN   207   C7
Canora CDN   201   D6
Cape Parry CDN   211   F7
Cape Pole USA   202   C2
Cape Young CDN   208   A3
Carberry CDN   201   F8
Carcross CDN   206   F3
Cardinal CDN   201   F8
Cardston CDN   200   F1
Carlson Landing CDN   204   D3
Carlyle CDN   201   F6
Carmacks CDN   206   D3
Carman CDN   201   F9
Carmangay CDN   200   E1
Caroline CDN   199   C9
Carot River CDN   201   C6
Carseland CDN   200   D1
Carstairs CDN   199   D9
Cartwright CDN   201   F8
Carway CDN   199   F9
Cassiar CDN   202   A4
Castelgar CDN   199   E7
Castor CDN   200   C2
Cavalier USA   201   F9
Cedarvale CDN   202   E3
Cedoux CDN   201   E6
Centra Buttte CDN   200   E4
Centralia USA   198   F4
Cereal CDN   200   D2
Ceylon CDN   201   F5
Chamberlain CDN   200   E5
Champagne CDN   206   E2
Chaplin CDN   200   E4
Chard CDN   204   F3
Charles CDN   201   A7
Chatham USA   202   B2
Chelan USA   199   F6
Chelan CDN   201   C6
Cherhill CDN   200   B1
Cherryville CDN   199   D7
Chester USA   200   F2
Chetwynd CDN   203   E7
Chewelah USA   199   F7
Chicken USA   206   B2
Chilanko Forks CDN   198   B5
Chinook USA   200   F3
Chisana USA   206   C1

Chitek Lake CDN	200	B4
Choiceland CDN	201	B5
Christina Lake CDN	199	E7
Churchbridge CDN	201	E7
Chutine Landing CDN	202	B3
Claresholm CDN	199	E9
Clarkleigh CDN	201	E9
Claybank CDN	200	E5
Claydon CDN	200	F3
Cle Elum USA	199	F5
Clear Prairie CDN	203	E8
Cleardale CDN	203	E8
Clearwater CDN	199	C6
Climax CDN	200	F3
Clinton USA	198	E4
Clinton CDN	199	C6
Clinton Point CDN	211	F8
Cluff Lake Mine CDN	204	D4
Clyde CDN	200	A1
Coal Creek USA	206	A2
Coal River CDN	203	A6
Coaldale CDN	200	E1
Cochrane CDN	199	D9
Coeur d'Alene USA	199	F7
Coffee Creek CDN	206	C2
Cole Bay CDN	200	A4
Columbia Falls USA	199	F9
Colville USA	199	F7
Colville Lake CDN	207	B8
Comox CDN	198	D4
Compeer CDN	200	D3
Conklin CDN	204	F3
Consort CDN	200	C2
Coppermine CDN	208	B3
Coquitlam CDN	198	D5
Cormorant CDN	201	B7
Coronation CDN	200	C2
Courtenay CDN	198	D4
Coutts CDN	200	F1
Cowan CDN	201	D7
Craig USA	202	D2
Craik CDN	200	D5
Cranberry Portage CDN	201	B7
Cranberry Junction CDN	202	D4
Cranbrook CDN	199	E8
Crane River CDN	201	D8
Craven CDN	201	E5
Cremona CDN	199	D9
Crescent Spur CDN	199	A7
Creston CDN	199	E8
Cromer CDN	201	F7
Crooked River CDN	201	C6
Crosby USA	201	F6
Cross Lake CDN	201	B9
Crossfield CDN	199	D9
Crystal Springs CDN	201	C5
Cumberland House CDN	201	B7
Cut Bank USA	200	F1
Czar CDN	200	C2
Dafoe CDN	201	D5
Dallas CDN	201	D9
Darlingford CDN	201	F9
Darrington USA	198	E5
Dauphin CDN	201	D8
Dauphin River CDN	201	D9
Davenport USA	199	F4
Davidson CDN	200	D5
Dawson City CDN	206	B3
Dawson Creek CDN	203	E7

Dawson Landing CDN	198	B3
Daysland CDN	200	C2
Deadhorse USA	210	B1
Dease Lake CDN	202	B4
Debden CDN	200	B4
DeBolt CDN	203	F8
Delburne CDN	200	C1
Deleau CDN	201	F7
Déline CDN	207	D9
Delisle CDN	200	D4
Delmas CDN	200	C3
Deloraine CDN	201	F7
Delta CDN	198	E4
Delta Beach CDN	201	E9
Delta Junction USA	206	A1
Deming USA	198	E5
Denholm CDN	200	C4
Deniue Kúé CDN	204	B2
Derwent CDN	200	B2
Destruction Bay CDN	206	D2
Dezadeash CDN	206	E2
Dilke CDN	200	E5
Dillon CDN	204	F4
Dinsmore CDN	200	D4
Dixonville CDN	203	E9
Dog Creek CDN	199	C5
Donald CDN	199	C8
Donnelly CDN	203	F9
Dore Lake CDN	200	A4
Dorintosh CDN	200	B4
Dorothy CDN	200	D1
Douglas USA	202	A2
Drayton Valley CDN	199	B9
Driftwoos CDN	202	E5
Drinkwater CDN	201	E5
Drybrough CDN	205	F7
Duck Lake CDN	200	C5
Duck Lake Post CDN	205	D9
Duncan CDN	198	E4
Dundas Harbour CDN	213	C9
Dunmore CDN	200	E2
Dunvegan CDN	203	E8
Dupuyer USA	200	F1
Eagle USA	206	A3
Eagle Plains CDN	206	A5
Earls Cove CDN	198	D4
East Glacier Park USA	199	F9
Eastend CDN	200	F3
Easterville CDN	201	C8
Eatonia CDN	200	D3
Ebenezer CDN	201	D6
Echo Bay USA	208	C2
Eddystone CDN	201	E8
Edenwold CDN	201	E5
Edmonds USA	198	F4
Edmonton CDN	200	B1
Edson CDN	199	B9
Edzo CDN	208	F2
Edzoó CDN	208	F2
Elak Dase CDN	204	F5
Elbow CDN	200	D4
Elfin Cove USA	202	A1
Elgir CDN	201	F8
Elie CDN	201	F9
Elk Point CDN	200	B2
Elkford CDN	199	E9
Elkhorn CDN	201	E7
Elko CDN	199	E9
Elm Creek CDN	201	F9

Elmore CDN	201	F7
Elphinestone CDN	201	E7
Elrose CDN	200	D4
Elstow CDN	200	D5
Emerson CDN	201	F9
Endako CDN	202	F5
Endeavor CDN	201	D6
Enderby CDN	199	D7
Endiang CDN	200	C1
Engineer CDN	206	F3
Ennadai CDN	205	B7
Enterprise CDN	204	B1
Entrance CDN	199	B8
Entwistle CDN	199	B9
Enumclaw USA	198	F5
Ephrata USA	199	F6
Erickson CDN	201	E8
Eriksdale CDN	201	E9
Esterhazy CDN	201	E7
Estevan CDN	201	F6
Estlin CDN	201	E5
Eston CDN	200	D3
Ethelbert CDN	201	D7
Eureka USA	199	F9
Everett USA	198	F5
Evergreen USA	199	F9
Eyebrow CDN	200	E4
Fair Harbour CDN	198	C3
Fairlight CDN	201	F7
Fairmont Hot Springs CDN	199	D8
Fairview CDN	203	E8
Falkland CDN	199	D6
False Bay CDN	198	D4
Falun CDN	200	B1
Fannystelle CDN	201	F9
Faom Lake CDN	201	D6
Farmer USA	199	F6
Faro CDN	206	D4
Faust CDN	203	F9
Fawcett CDN	200	A1
Fawcett Lake CDN	204	F1
Ferland CDN	200	F4
Ferndale USA	198	E5
Fernie CDN	199	E9
Fillmore CDN	201	F6
Finlay Forks CDN	203	E6
Fitzgerald CDN	204	C3
Flaxcombe CDN	200	D3
Flin Flon CDN	201	A7
Fond-du-Lac CDN	204	D5
Fontas CDN	203	C7
Foremost CDN	200	E2
Forestburg CDN	200	C2
Forks USA	198	E3
Fort McPherson CDN	210	F3
Fort Assiniboine CDN	200	A1
Fort Chipewyan CDN	204	D3
Fort Collinson CDN	211	F9
Fort Good Hope CDN	207	B7
Fort Hall CDN	205	D7
Fort Liard CDN	203	A7
Fort MacKay CDN	204	E2
Fort Macleod CDN	200	E1
Fort McMurray CDN	204	E3
Fort Nelson CDN	203	C7
Fort Norman CDN	207	D9
Fort Providence CDN	204	A1
Fort Qu'Appelle CDN	201	E6
Fort Resolution CDN	204	B2

Fort St James CDN	203	F5	Guy CDN	203	F9	**I**kaahuk CDN	211	D7
Fort St John CDN	203	E7	Gypsumville CDN	201	D8	Ikaluktutjak CDN	209	B6
Fort Saskatchewan CDN	200	B1				Ikiak USA	210	A1
Fort Simpson CDN	207	F8				Île-à-la-Crosse CDN	200	A4
Fort Smith CDN	204	C3	**H**abay CDN	203	C9	Imperial CDN	200	D5
Fort Steele CDN	199	E8	Hafford CDN	200	C4	Imperial Mills CDN	200	A2
Fort Vermillon CDN	204	D1	Haines USA	206	F2	Indian Cabins CDN	204	B1
Fox Creek CDN	199	A9	Haines Junction CDN	206	E2	Indian Head CDN	201	E6
Fox Lake CDN	204	D1	Halbrite CDN	201	F6	Innisfail CDN	200	C1
Fox Valley CDN	200	E3	Halbrite CDN	201	F6	Inuvik CDN	210	F4
Francois Lake CDN	202	F4	Halfmoon Bay CDN	198	D4	Inwood CDN	201	E9
Franklin CDN	207	D9	Halkir CDN	200	C2	Irma CDN	200	C2
Fraser Lake CDN	202	F5	Hallock USA	201	F9	Irvine CDN	200	E2
Fraserwood CDN	201	E9	Hamilton USA	198	E5	Ituna CDN	201	D6
Friday Harbour USA	198	E4	Hamiota CDN	201	E7			
Frog Lake CDN	200	B3	Hanceville CDN	199	B5			
Funter USA	202	A2	Handel CDN	200	C3	**J**ack Wade USA	206	B2
			Hanley CDN	200	D4	Jackhead CDN	201	D9
			Hanna CDN	200	D2	Jan Lake CDN	201	A6
Gahmiti CDN	208	E1	Happy's Inn USA	199	F8	Jasper CDN	199	B8
Gainsborough CDN	201	F7	Hardisty CDN	200	C2	Jean Marie River CDN	203	A9
Galbraith CDN	202	A4	Harlem USA	200	F3	Jenner CDN	200	D2
Galena Bay CDN	199	D7	Harrington USA	199	F7	Jenny Lind CDN	209	B7
Garibaldi CDN	198	D5	Harris CDN	200	D4	Jenpeg CDN	201	B9
Garland CDN	201	D7	Harrogate CDN	199	D8	Jesmond CDN	199	C5
Germansen Landing CDN	203	E5	Hartley Bay CDN	202	F3	John d'Or Prairie CDN	204	D1
Gibbons CDN	200	B1	Havre USA	200	F2	Johnsons Crossing CDN	206	F3
Gibsons CDN	198	D4	Hawk Inlet USA	202	A2	Juneau USA	202	A2
Gift Lake CDN	203	F9	Hay Lakes CDN	200	B1			
Gimli CDN	201	E9	Hay River CDN	204	B1			
Gjoa Haven CDN	209	B9	Hazlet CDN	200	E3	**K**aigani USA	202	D1
Gladstone CDN	201	E8	Hazleton CDN	202	E4	Kake USA	202	B2
Glaslyn CDN	200	B4	Hecla CDN	201	D9	Kaktovik USA	210	C2
Gleichen CDN	200	D1	Heffley Creek CDN	199	C6	Kalispell USA	199	F9
Glenavon CDN	201	E6	Hendon CDN	201	D6	Kalso CDN	199	E8
Glenboro CDN	201	F8	Hepburn CDN	200	C4	Kamloops CDN	199	D6
Glenboyle CDN	206	B3	Herbert CDN	200	E4	Kamsack CDN	201	D7
Glidden CDN	200	D3	Heriot Bay CDN	198	C4	Kati'odeeche CDN	204	B1
Gold Bridge CDN	198	C5	Herschel CDN	210	D3	Kayville CDN	200	F5
Gold River CDN	198	C3	Hey Camp CDN	204	C3	Kelowna CDN	199	D6
Golden CDN	199	C8	High Level CDN	203	D9	Kelsey CDN	205	F9
Good Hope CDN	198	B3	High Prairie CDN	203	F9	Kelsey Bay CDN	198	C3
Goodeve CDN	201	E6	High River CDN	199	D9	Kelvington CDN	201	D6
Gordon USA	210	D3	Hilbre CDN	201	D8	Kemano CDN	202	F3
Gouldtown CDN	200	E4	Hines Creek CDN	203	E8	Kenaston CDN	200	D4
Grand Centre CDN	200	A3	Hingham USA	200	F2	Kennedy CDN	201	E6
Grand Coule USA	199	F6	Hinton CDN	199	B8	Keno City CDN	206	C4
Grand Forks CDN	199	E7	Hixon CDN	199	A6	Kent USA	198	F4
Grand Rapids CDN	201	C8	Hodgeville CDN	200	E4	Kent CDN	199	E5
Grande Cache CDN	199	A7	Hodgson CDN	201	D9	Keremeos CDN	199	E6
Grande Prairie CDN	203	F8	Hodo CDN	200	A1	Kerrobert CDN	200	D3
Grandview CDN	201	D7	Holden CDN	200	B2	Kersley CDN	199	B6
Granisle CDN	202	E4	Holland CDN	201	F8	Ketchikan USA	202	D2
Granite Bay CDN	198	C4	Hollis USA	202	D2	Kettle Falls USA	199	F7
Gravelbourg CDN	200	E4	Holman Island CDN	211	F9	Key Like Mine CDN	205	E5
Grayland USA	198	F3	Hone CDN	205	F7	Kildonan CDN	198	D3
Green Lake CDN	200	B4	Hoonah USA	202	A2	Killaly CDN	201	E6
Greenville CDN	202	E3	Hope CDN	199	E5	Killam CDN	200	C2
Greenwater USA	198	F5	Hoquiam USA	198	F3	Killarney CDN	201	F8
Greenwood CDN	199	E7	Horsefly CDN	199	B6	Kimberley CDN	199	E8
Grenfell CDN	201	E6	Hotchkiss CDN	203	E9	Kincaid CDN	200	F4
Griffin CDN	201	F6	Houston USA	202	F4	Kincolith CDN	202	E3
Grimshaw CDN	203	E9	Hudson Bay CDN	201	C7	Kindersley CDN	200	D3
Grise Fiord CDN	213	A8	Hudson's Hope CDN	203	E7	Kinoosao CDN	205	F7
Gronlid CDN	201	C5	Humbolt CDN	201	D5	Kipling CDN	201	E6
Grouard CDN	203	F9	Humptulips USA	198	F4	Kitimat CDN	202	F3
Groundbirch CDN	203	E7	Hunters USA	199	F7	Kitimat Village CDN	202	F3
Gull Lake CDN	200	E3	Hussar CDN	200	D1	Kittigazuit CDN	210	E4
Gunn CDN	200	B1	Huxley CDN	200	C1	Kitwanga CDN	202	E4
Gustavus USA	202	A2	Hydaburg USA	202	D2	Klawock USA	202	D2
Gutah CDN	203	D7	Hyder USA	202	D3	Kleena Kleene CDN	198	B4

Klemtu CDN	198	A3	
Koidern CDN	206	C2	
Kokish CDN	198	C3	
Kokruagarok USA	210	A1	
Kootenay Bay CDN	199	E8	
Kremlin USA	200	F2	
Kurok CDN	201	D6	
Kyle CDN	200	E3	
Kyuquot CDN	198	C2	
La Corey CDN	200	A3	
La Glace CDN	203	F8	
La Loche CDN	204	F3	
La Rochelle CDN	201	F9	
La Ronge CDN	201	A5	
Lac la Biche CDN	200	A2	
Lac la Hache CDN	199	B6	
Lac la Matre CDN	208	F1	
Lacey USA	198	F4	
Lacombe CDN	200	C1	
Ladysmith CDN	198	D4	
Lajord CDN	201	E6	
Lake Alma CDN	201	F5	
Lake Cowichan CDN	198	E4	
Lake Louise CDN	199	C8	
Lakelse Lake CDN	202	E3	
Lamont CDN	200	B1	
Lampman CDN	201	F6	
Landis CDN	200	C3	
Langenburg CDN	201	E7	
Langford CDN	198	E4	
Langham CDN	200	C4	
Langruth CDN	201	E8	
Lanigan CDN	201	D5	
Lashburn CDN	200	C3	
Leader CDN	200	D3	
Leaf Rapids CDN	205	F8	
Leahy USA	199	F6	
Leanchoil CDN	199	D8	
Leavenworth USA	199	F5	
Leduc CDN	200	B1	
Lefellier CDN	201	F9	
Lemieux CDN	206	F3	
Lemsford CDN	200	D3	
Leo Creek CDN	202	E5	
Leross CDN	201	D6	
Lethbridge CDN	200	E1	
Libau CDN	201	E9	
Libby USA	199	F8	
Liebenthal CDN	200	E3	
Líídli Kúé CDN	207	F8	
Likely CDN	199	B6	
Lillooet CDN	199	C5	
Limerick CDN	200	F4	
Linden CDN	200	D1	
Lipton CDN	201	E6	
Little Fort CDN	199	C6	
Lloydminster CDN	200	B3	
Lomond CDN	200	E1	
Lone Butte CDN	199	C6	
Longview CDN	199	D9	
Loon Lake CDN	200	B3	
Loring USA	200	F3	
Lorlie CDN	201	E6	
Lothair USA	200	F2	
Love CDN	201	B6	
Loverna CDN	200	D3	
Lower Post CDN	203	A5	
Lucky Lake CDN	200	D4	
Lumby CDN	199	D7	
Lumsden CDN	201	E5	
Lund CDN	198	D4	
Lútselk'e CDN	204	A4	
Lyddal CDN	201	A8	
Lynden USA	198	E5	
Lynn Lake CDN	205	F7	
Lytton CDN	199	D5	
Mackenzie CDN	203	E6	
Macklin CDN	200	C3	
Macrorie CDN	200	D4	
Magrath CDN	200	E1	
Maidstone CDN	200	C3	
Makifeng CDN	201	C7	
Malakwa CDN	199	D7	
Malboro CDN	199	B8	
Manitou CDN	201	F8	
Manning CDN	203	E9	
Mannville CDN	200	B2	
Manson Creek CDN	203	E5	
Manyberries CDN	200	F2	
Maple Creek CDN	200	E3	
Maple Ridge CDN	198	D5	
Marguerite CDN	199	B6	
Mariana Lake CDN	204	F2	
Marwayne CDN	200	B3	
Masset CDN	202	E1	
Mayerthorpe CDN	199	A9	
Mayfair CDN	200	C4	
Maymont CDN	200	C4	
Mayo CDN	206	C4	
Mazama USA	199	E6	
Mbechokó CDN	208	F2	
McBride CDN	199	A7	
McCarthy USA	206	C1	
McCreary CDN	201	E8	
McGee CDN	200	D3	
McLennan Lake CDN	205	F6	
McLeod Lake CDN	203	F6	
McMurray USA	198	E5	
McTavish CDN	201	F9	
Meacham CDN	200	D5	
Meador Lake CDN	200	B4	
Meadow Creek CDN	199	D8	
Meander River CDN	203	C9	
Meath Park CDN	201	C5	
Medicine Hat CDN	200	E2	
Medley CDN	200	A3	
Melfort CDN	201	C5	
Melita CDN	201	F7	
Melville CDN	201	E6	
Meota CDN	200	C3	
Merritt CDN	199	D6	
Metaline Falls USA	199	E7	
Metlakatla USA	202	D2	
Mica Creek CDN	199	C7	
Michel CDN	204	F3	
Midale CDN	201	F6	
Middle Lake CDN	201	C5	
Milden CDN	200	D4	
Milestone CDN	201	E5	
Mills Lake CDN	203	A9	
Miniota CDN	201	E7	
Minnedosa CDN	201	E8	
Minto CDN	206	D3	
Minto CDN	201	F8	
Minton CDN	201	F5	
Mirrow CDN	200	C1	
Missinipe CDN	201	A5	
Mission CDN	198	E5	
Monchy CDN	200	F3	
Monitor CDN	200	C2	
Monroe USA	198	F5	
Monte Creek CDN	199	D6	
Montmarte CDN	201	E6	
Montreal Lake CDN	200	B5	
Montrose CDN	199	E7	
Moose Jaw CDN	200	E5	
Moose Lake CDN	201	B8	
Moosomin CDN	201	E7	
Moricetown CDN	202	E4	
Morinville CDN	200	B1	
Morley CDN	199	D9	
Morrin CDN	200	D1	
Morris CDN	201	F9	
Mossbank CDN	200	E4	
Mould Bay CDN	212	A1	
Mount Vernon USA	198	E5	
Moyie CDN	199	E8	
Moyie Springs USA	199	F8	
Mukilteo USA	198	F4	
Muncho Lake CDN	203	B6	
Mundare CDN	200	B2	
Nahanni Butte CDN	203	A7	
Nahlin CDN	202	A3	
Naicam CDN	201	C5	
Nakusp CDN	199	D7	
Namu CDN	198	A3	
Nanaimo CDN	198	D4	
Nanton CDN	199	E9	
Nation USA	206	A3	
Nazko CDN	199	A5	
Neah Bay USA	198	E3	
Needles CDN	199	E7	
Neepawa CDN	201	E8	
Negginan CDN	201	C9	
Neilburg CDN	200	C3	
Neilton USA	198	F4	
Nelson CDN	199	E7	
Nelson Forks CDN	203	B7	
Nelson House CDN	201	A8	
Nemaiah Valley CDN	198	B5	
Neville CDN	200	E4	
New Aiyansh CDN	202	E3	
New Denver CDN	199	E7	
New Hazelton CDN	202	E4	
New Westminster CDN	198	D4	
Newbrook CDN	200	A1	
Newdale CDN	201	E8	
Newhalem USA	199	E5	
Newport USA	199	F7	
Nicholson CDN	211	E6	
Ninette CDN	201	F8	
Nipawin CDN	201	C6	
Nitinat CDN	198	D4	
Nojack CDN	199	B9	
Nokomis CDN	201	D5	
Noralee CDN	202	F4	
Nordegg CDN	199	C9	
Nordman USA	199	F8	
Norman Wells CDN	207	C7	
Norquay CDN	201	D7	
North Battleford CDN	200	C4	
North Bend USA	198	F5	
North Cove USA	198	F3	
North Portal CDN	201	F6	
North Vancouver CDN	198	D4	
Northport USA	199	E7	
Norway House CDN	201	B9	

Noxon USA	199	F8	Pincher Creek CDN	199	E9	Rea CDN	208	F2
Nuiqsut USA	210	B1	Pine Dock CDN	201	D9	Rea Lakes CDN	208	E1
Nulahugiuq CDN	208	A3	Pine Point CDN	204	B2	Red Deer CDN	200	C1
			Pinehouse Lake CDN	200	A5	Red Earth CDN	201	B6
Oak Harbour USA	198	E4	Pink Mountain CDN	203	D7	Red Rock CDN	199	A6
Oak Lake CDN	201	F7	Pipestone CDN	201	F7	Redvers CDN	201	F7
Oak Point CDN	201	E9	Plenty CDN	200	D3	Redwater CDN	200	B1
Oakburn CDN	201	E7	Plentywood USA	201	F5	Regina CDN	201	E5
Oakville USA	198	F4	Plit Siding CDN	205	F9	Regina Beach CDN	201	E5
Ocean Falls CDN	198	A3	Plunkett CDN	200	D5	Regway CDN	201	F5
Ocean Shores USA	198	F3	Pocahontas CDN	199	B8	Reindeer Station CDN	210	F4
Ogema CDN	201	F5	Point Angeles USA	198	E4	Reliance CDN	204	A4
Ogilvie CDN	206	A4	Point Baker USA	202	C2	Renton USA	198	F4
Okanagan Falls CDN	199	E6	Point Bridget USA	202	A2	Republic USA	199	E7
Okanogan USA	199	F6	Point McNeill CDN	198	C3	Reserve CDN	201	C6
Okla CDN	201	D6	Point Mellon CDN	198	D4	Resolute CDN	213	C6
Okotoks CDN	199	D9	Point Renfrew CDN	198	E4	Revelstoke CDN	199	D7
Old Crow CDN	210	E2	Point Townsend USA	198	E4	Rich Lake CDN	200	A2
Old Rampart USA	210	E1	Polebridge USA	199	F9	Richardson USA	206	A1
Old Sitka USA	202	B1	Ponoka CDN	200	C1	Richdale CDN	200	D2
Olds CDN	199	C9	Ponton CDN	201	B8	Richmond USA	198	D4
Olympia USA	198	F4	Poplarfield CDN	201	E9	Rimbey CDN	200	C1
Omak USA	199	F6	Popular Point CDN	201	E9	Riske Creek CDN	199	B5
Onion Lake CDN	200	B3	Porcupine USA	206	F2	River Jordan CDN	198	E4
Oona River CDN	202	E2	Port Clements CDN	202	E1	Rivers CDN	201	E8
Ootsa Lake CDN	202	F4	Port Alberni CDN	198	D4	Riverton CDN	201	E9
Opheim USA	200	F4	Port Alexander USA	202	C1	Robb CDN	199	B8
Optic Lake CDN	201	A7	Port Alice CDN	198	C3	Roblin CDN	201	D7
Oqsuqtooq CDN	209	B9	Port Chilkoot USA	206	F2	Robsart CDN	200	F3
Orient USA	199	E7	Port Edward CDN	202	E2	Rocanville CDN	201	E7
Orkney CDN	200	F3	Port Essington CDN	202	E3	Rocher River CDN	204	B3
Orondo USA	199	F6	Port Hardy CDN	198	B3	Rock Creek CDN	206	B3
Oroville USA	199	E6	Port Neville CDN	198	C3	Rock Creek CDN	199	E6
Orting USA	198	F4	Port Simpson CDN	202	E2	Rockglen CDN	200	F4
Osoyoos CDN	199	E6	Portage la Prairie CDN	201	E8	Rockport USA	198	E5
Oungre CDN	201	F6	Porthill USA	199	E8	Rocky Mountain House CDN	199	C9
Outlook CDN	200	D4	Post Falls USA	199	F7	Rogers Pass CDN	199	C8
Overflowing River CDN	201	C7	Powell River CDN	198	D4	Roland CDN	201	F9
Oxbow CDN	201	F7	Prairie River CDN	201	C6	Rolla USA	201	F8
Oyama CDN	199	D6	Preeceville CDN	201	D6	Rolling Hills CDN	200	E1
Oyen CDN	200	D2	Priddis CDN	199	D9	Roosville CDN	199	F9
Oysterville USA	198	F3	Primate CDN	200	C3	Root Lake CDN	201	B7
			Prince Albert CDN	200	C5	Rose Harbour CDN	198	A1
			Prince George CDN	199	A6	Rose Prairie CDN	203	E7
Parkman CDN	201	F7	Prince Rupert CDN	202	E2	Rose Valley CDN	201	C6
Parksville CDN	198	D4	Princeton CDN	199	E6	Rosetown CDN	200	D4
Pasqua CDN	200	E5	Provost CDN	200	C3	Ross River CDN	206	E4
Pateros USA	199	F6	Prudhoe Bay USA	210	B1	Rosswood CDN	202	E3
Patricia CDN	200	D2	Pukatawagan CDN	201	A7	Rosthern CDN	200	C5
Patuanak CDN	204	F4				Ruby USA	199	F7
Paulatuk CDN	211	F7				Russell CDN	201	E7
Pavilion CDN	199	C5	**Q**ausuittuq CDN	213	C6			
Paxson USA	206	B1	Qu'Appelle CDN	201	E6			
Peace Point CDN	204	C2	Queen Charlotte City CDN	202	F1	**S**aanich CDN	198	E4
Peace River CDN	203	E9	Queets USA	198	F3	Sachs Harbour CDN	211	D7
Peerless USA	200	F5	Quesnel CDN	199	A6	Sagwon USA	210	C1
Peerless CDN	200	B3	Quilchend CDN	199	D6	Saint Adolphe CDN	201	F9
Peers CDN	199	B9	Quill Lake CDN	201	D6	Saint Albert CDN	200	B1
Pelican USA	202	A1	Qurluqtuuq CDN	208	B3	Saint Brieux CDN	201	C5
Pelican Narrows CDN	201	A6				Saint Lazare CDN	201	E7
Pelican Rapids CDN	201	C7				Saint Louis CDN	200	C5
Pemberton CDN	198	D5	**R**adisson CDN	200	C4	Saint Mary USA	199	F9
Pennant CDN	200	E3	Radium Hot Springs CDN	199	D8	Saint Paul CDN	200	B2
Penny CDN	199	A6	Radville CDN	201	F5	Saint Walburg CDN	200	B3
Penticton CDN	199	E6	Rainbow Lake CDN	203	C8	Saint-Pierre-Jolys CDN	201	F9
Petersburg USA	202	C2	Ranfurly CDN	200	B2	Salmo CDN	199	E7
Pierceland CDN	200	B3	Rapids USA	206	A1	Salmon Arm CDN	199	D7
Pierson CDN	201	F7	Rat River CDN	204	B3	Saltcoats CDN	201	E7
Pike Lake CDN	200	D4	Raymond USA	198	F3	Saltery Bay CDN	198	D4
Pincher CDN	199	E9	Raymond CDN	200	E1	Sanca CDN	199	E8
			Raymore CDN	201	D5	Sandpit CDN	202	F1

Place		Page	Grid
Sandpoint	USA	199	F8
Sandy Bay	CDN	201	A7
Sandy Lake	CDN	204	F1
Sanford	CDN	201	F9
Sappho	USA	198	E3
Saskatchewan River Crossing	CDN	199	C8
Saskatoon	CDN	200	D4
Savona	CDN	199	C6
Sawmill Bay	CDN	208	D1
Saxman	USA	202	D2
Scandia	CDN	200	E1
Scobey	USA	200	F5
Scotia Bay	CDN	206	F3
Seattle	USA	198	F4
Sedro Wolley	USA	198	E5
Seebe	CDN	199	D9
Selkirk	CDN	201	E9
Seven Persons	CDN	200	E2
Sexsmith	CDN	203	F8
Seymour Arm	CDN	199	C7
Shalath	CDN	199	C5
Shamrock	CDN	200	E4
Shaunavon	CDN	200	F3
Sheho	CDN	201	D6
Shelby	USA	200	F1
Shell Lake	CDN	200	C4
Shellbrook	CDN	200	C5
Shelter Bay	CDN	199	D7
Shelton	USA	198	F4
Sherridon	CDN	201	A7
Sherwood	CDN	200	B1
Shoal Lake	CDN	201	E7
Shoreacres	CDN	199	E7
Sicamous	CDN	199	D7
Sidney	CDN	198	E4
Silver Park	CDN	201	C5
Simmie	CDN	200	E3
Simonhouse	CDN	201	B7
Simoon Sound	CDN	198	C3
Sinclair	CDN	201	F7
Sinclair Mills	CDN	199	A6
Sipiwesk	CDN	201	A9
Sitka	USA	202	B1
Skagway	USA	206	F2
Skidegate	CDN	202	F1
Skownan	CDN	201	D8
Skykomish	USA	199	F5
Slana	USA	206	B1
Slave Lake	CDN	204	F1
Slocan	CDN	199	E7
Smeaton	CDN	201	B5
Smiley	CDN	200	D3
Smith	CDN	200	A1
Smith River	CDN	203	A6
Smithers	CDN	202	E4
Smoky Lake	CDN	200	B2
Snare Lakes	CDN	208	E3
Snoqualmie Pass	USA	198	F5
Snow Lake	CDN	201	A8
Snowdrift	CDN	204	A4
Snowflake	CDN	201	F8
Soap Lake	USA	199	F6
Soda Creek	CDN	199	B6
Sómbak'e	CDN	204	A2
Somerset	CDN	201	F8
Sorrento	CDN	199	D7
Souris	CDN	201	F8
South Indian Lake	CDN	205	F4
Southbank	CDN	202	F4
Southend	CDN	205	F6
Southey	CDN	201	E5
Sparwood	CDN	199	E9
Spences Bridge	CDN	199	D6
Spirit River	CDN	203	F8
Spiritwood	CDN	200	B4
Split Lake	CDN	205	F9
Spokane	USA	199	F7
Springside	CDN	201	D6
Springwater	CDN	200	D3
Spruce Grove	CDN	200	B1
Spruce Home	CDN	200	B5
Squamish	CDN	198	D5
Stanley Mission	CDN	201	A6
Stanwood	USA	198	E5
Ste Rose du Lac	CDN	201	E8
Steen	CDN	203	C9
Steinbach	CDN	201	F9
Stenen	CDN	201	D6
Stepp Rock	CDN	201	D8
Stettler	CDN	200	C1
Stewart	CDN	202	D3
Stewart Crossing	CDN	206	C4
Stewart Valley	CDN	200	E4
Stonewall	CDN	201	E9
Stony Plain	CDN	200	B1
Stony Rapids	CDN	205	D5
Stoughton	CDN	201	F6
Strasbourg	CDN	201	D5
Strathmore	CDN	200	D1
Struan	CDN	200	C4
Stryker	USA	199	F9
Stuartburn	CDN	201	F9
Stuie	CDN	198	A4
Sucker River	CDN	201	A5
Suffield	CDN	200	E2
Sullivan Bay	CDN	198	B3
Sumas	USA	198	E5
Summerland	CDN	199	E6
Summit Lake	CDN	203	C6
Summit Lake	CDN	203	F6
Sunburst	USA	200	F1
Sundre	CDN	199	C9
Swan Hills	CDN	199	A9
Swan River	CDN	201	D7
Sweetgrass	USA	200	F1
Swift Current	CDN	200	E4
Swift River	CDN	202	A4
Sykvan Lake	CDN	200	C1
Sylvania	CDN	201	C6
Ta Ta Creek	CDN	199	E8
Taber	CDN	200	E1
Tachie	CDN	203	F5
Tacoma	USA	198	F4
Taholah	USA	198	F3
Tahsis	CDN	198	C3
Takla Landing	CDN	202	E5
Tanani	USA	206	F2
Tatla Lake	CDN	198	B4
Taylor	CDN	203	E7
Teepee	CDN	206	F3
Telegraph Creek	CDN	202	B3
Tenakee Springs	USA	202	A2
Terrace	CDN	202	E3
Teslin	CDN	206	F4
Tête Jaune Cache	CDN	199	B7
Tetlin Junction	USA	206	B2
Teulon	CDN	201	E9
The Pas	CDN	201	B7
Theodore	CDN	201	D6
Thicket Portage	CDN	201	A9
Thompson	CDN	201	A9
Thompson Landing	CDN	208	F4
Three Hills	CDN	200	C1
Tiger	USA	199	F7
Tisdale	CDN	201	C6
Tlegoli	CDN	207	C7
Tlell	CDN	202	E1
Tobin Lake	CDN	201	B6
Tofield	CDN	200	B1
Tofino	CDN	198	D3
Togo	CDN	201	D7
Tok Junction	USA	206	B1
Tonsaket	USA	199	E6
Topley	CDN	202	F4
Toutes Aides	CDN	201	D8
Trail	CDN	199	E7
Tregor	USA	199	F9
Treherne	CDN	201	F8
Trout Lake	CDN	203	B8
Troy	USA	199	F8
Truch	CDN	203	D7
Tuchita	CDN	207	F5
Tuktoyaktuk	CDN	210	E5
Tulameen	CDN	199	D6
Tulita	CDN	207	D8
Tumbler Ridge	CDN	203	F7
Tungsten	CDN	207	E6
Tununirusiq	CDN	213	D9
Tununuk	CDN	210	E4
Tupper	CDN	203	F7
Turin	CDN	200	E1
Turner	USA	200	F3
Turnor Lake	CDN	204	F4
Turtleford	CDN	200	B3
Tuxford	CDN	200	E5
Twin Lakes	CDN	203	D9
Two Hills	CDN	200	B2
Tyner	CDN	200	D3
Ucluelet	CDN	198	D3
Uluksartuuq	CDN	211	F9
Umingmaktok	CDN	209	C5
Unity	CDN	200	C3
University Place	USA	198	F4
Uranium City	CDN	204	C4
Usk	CDN	202	E3
Val Marie	CDN	200	F4
Valemount	CDN	199	B7
Valier	USA	200	F1
Valleyview	CDN	203	F9
Vancouver	CDN	198	D4
Vanderhoof	CDN	203	F5
Vantage	CDN	200	E5
Vauxhall	CDN	200	E1
Vegreville	CDN	200	B2
Vermilion	CDN	200	B2
Vernon	CDN	199	D7
Victoria	CDN	198	E4
Viking	CDN	200	B2
Virden	CDN	201	F7
Vogar	CDN	201	E8
Vulcan	CDN	200	E1
Wabasca-Desmarais	CDN	204	F1
Wabowden	CDN	201	A8
Wacker	USA	202	D2
Wadena	CDN	201	D6

ATLAS: PLACES INDEX

Waglisa CDN	198	A3	Westray CDN	201	B7	Winkler CDN	201	F9
Wainwright CDN	200	C2	Wetaskiwin CDN	200	B1	Winnipeg CDN	201	F9
Wakaw CDN	200	C5	Weyakwin CDN	200	B5	Winnipeg Beach CDN	201	E9
Walhalla USA	201	F9	Weyburn CDN	201	F6	Winnipegosis CDN	201	D8
Wanham CDN	203	F8	Weyburn CDN	201	F6	Winter Harbour CDN	198	C2
Wapella CDN	201	E7	Wha Ti CDN	208	F1	Winthrop USA	199	E6
Ware CDN	203	C5	Whistler CDN	198	D5	Wishart CDN	201	D6
Warman CDN	200	C4	Whitecourt CDN	199	A9	Wollaston Lake CDN	205	E6
Warner CDN	200	F1	Whitefish USA	199	F9	Wolseley CDN	201	E6
Warren CDN	201	E9	Whitehorse CDN	206	E3	Wood Mountain CDN	200	F4
Warren Landing CDN	201	B9	Whitelaw CDN	203	E8	Wrangell USA	202	C2
Wasagaming CDN	201	E8	Whitewater USA	200	F4	Wrentham CDN	200	E1
Waskesiu Lake CDN	200	B5	Whitewood CDN	201	E6	Wrigley CDN	207	E8
Waterhen CDN	201	D8	Whitlash USA	200	F2	Wroxton CDN	201	D7
Waterton Park CDN	199	F9	Wilbert CDN	200	C3	Wynyard CDN	201	D6
Watino CDN	203	F8	Wilbur USA	199	F6			
Watrous CDN	200	D5	Wild Horse CDN	200	F2			
Watson CDN	201	D5	Wilde CDN	201	A9	Yaak USA	199	F8
Watson Lake CDN	203	A5	Wilkie CDN	200	C3	Yahk CDN	199	E8
Wawanesa CDN	201	F8	Willen CDN	201	E7	Yakutat USA	206	E1
Wekusko CDN	201	B8	Williams Lake CDN	199	B6	Yale CDN	199	D5
Wekweti CDN	208	E3	Willmar CDN	201	F6	Yellow Grass CDN	201	F5
Wenatchee USA	199	F5	Willow Bunch CDN	200	F5	Yellowknife CDN	204	A2
West Bend CDN	201	D6	Willow Creek CDN	200	F2	Yorkton CDN	201	D6
West Glacier USA	199	F9	Willow River CDN	199	A6	Young CDN	200	D5
West Poplar River CDN	200	F4	Wilson Creek USA	199	F6	Youngstown CDN	200	D2
Westbourne CDN	201	E8	Wimborne CDN	200	C1			
Westby USA	201	F5	Windham USA	202	B2			
Westgate CDN	201	C7	Winfield CDN	200	B1	Zeballos CDN	198	C3
Westlock CDN	200	A1	Wingdam CDN	199	A6	Zhahti Kóé CDN	204	A1

GENERAL INDEX

Pages 6–195

A

Abbot Ridge	31
Adams Lake	30, 107
Adams, Bryan	12, 13
Ahousahth First Nation	79
Alaska Highway	151
Alberni Valley	28
Alberta Badlands	162, 163
Alberta	8, 9, 10, 14, 154–193
Alexandra Bridge	102
Allison, Susan	13
Alsek River	136, 137
Angling	57, 152, 178, 179
Animal life	9
Anthony Island	94–95
Armstrong, Jeanette	13
Assiniboine First Nation	129
Athabasca Falls	176
Athabasca Glacier	174, 175, 177, 190, 192
Athabasca River	174, 176–177, 189
Atlin	141
Atlin Historical Museum	140
Atlin Lake	140, 141
Atlin Provincial Park and Recreation Area	140–141
August (events)	195
Avalanche Crest Trails	31

B

B.C. Orchard Industry Museum	118
Babine Lake	152
Bald eagles	74, 96
Bald Mountain	31
Banff	27, 168, 169, 190
Banff National Park	14, 27, 31, 168–173

Banff Summer Arts Festival	194
Banff Upper Hot Springs	190
Banff/Lake Louise Winter Festival	194
Barker, Billy	117
Barkerville	10, 116–117, 118
Barkley Sound	29, 77
Bear Glacier	147
Bear's Hump Trail	166
Bears	9, 82, 113, 138–139, 144, 194
Beauvert Lake	27, 180–181
Beaver First Nation	188
Belaney, Archibald Stansfield Belaney	13
Bella Coola	83
Berg Glacier	114
Berg Lake Trail	114
Bighorn sheep	9, 126, 193
Billy Barker Days	195
Birds of prey	9
Bisons	9, 166, 189
Black bears	9, 138–139
Blackfoot Nation	159, 164, 165
Boughton Archipelago Pacific Marine Park	65
Boundary Ranges	146, 147
Bow Lake	175
Bow Pass	175
Bow River	169
Bow Valley Parkway	171
Bowron Lake	27
Bowron Lake Provincial Park	27
Braddock, Edward	10
Brentwood Bay	73
Bridge of 23 Camels	30
British America Act	11

British Columbia	8, 9, 10, 11, 14, 22, 27, 28, 32–153
British North America Act	10
Broken Group Islands	29, 77
Brown bears	139
Browning Pass	65
Buffalos	164, 165
Bulkley River	26, 152
Bull riding	160–161, 194
Burns Lake	152, 153
Butchart, Jennie	22, 73
Cabot, John	10
Calgary	8, 20, 21, 27, 155, 158–159, 191
Canada Olympic Park	20
Chinatown	20
Devonian Gardens	20
Eau Claire Market	20
Fort Calgary Historic Park	20
Glenbow Museum	20
Heritage Park	20
Saddledome	20
Shaw Millenium Park	20
Stampede Park	20
Telus World of Science	20
Calgary Stampede	21, 160–161, 194
Calgary Tower	20, 27, 27
Cambria Range	147
Cameron Falls	166
Campbell River	29, 84, 85
Camrose	195
Canada geese	9
Canadian Finals Rodeo (Edmonton)	182, 195
Canadian Museum of Rail Travel (Cranbrook)	130
Canadian Open Dogsled Race	195
Canadian Pacific Railway	11, 30
Canadian Rocky Mountains Parks	
(UNESCO World Heritage Site)	169, 177
Canim Falls	112
Capilano Suspension Bridge	36
Cariboo	8, 9, 98–119
Cariboo Country	118
Cariboo Mountains	113
Cariboo Wagon Road	30
Caribou	9
Carr, Emily	13
Cartier, Jacques	10
Cascade Mountain	27
Cassiar Mountains	144
Castle Mountain	170–171
Champlain, Samuel de	10, 12
Charlotte City	96, 97
Chemainus	28, 74
Chemainus murals	28, 74
Chesterman's Beach	78
Chilcotin Country	96, 97
Chilkoot Pass	11
Chilliwack River	102
Chilliwack River Valley	103
Chipewyan First Nation	188, 189
Christmas Carol Ships Parade (Vancouver)	195
Clachnacudainn Icefield	31
Clachnacudainn Range	31
Clayoquot Sound	29, 79
Coast Mountains	8, 55, 82, 83, 146, 147
Coastal Range	67
Cohen, Leonard	12, 13
Colonial battles	10
Columbia Icefield	27, 174, 175, 176, 177, 190, 192
Columbia Mountains	31, 111
Columbia River	8
Cook, James	10, 67, 78, 79
Copperstain Trail	31
Copway, George	13
Cougar Valley	119
Country music	191, 195
Courtenay	29
Cousteau, Jacques	65
Cowboy Junkies	13
Cowboys	160, 161, 194, 195
Cowichan Valley	28, 74, 75, 85
Cowichan First Nation	28
Coyotes	9
Crafts	12
Cranbrook	130
Crane Island	65
Cree First Nation	189
Cretaceous period	163
Dall Sheep	150
Daly Glacier	125
Dawson, George Mercer	129
Dawson City	11, 195
December (events)	195
Deighton, Jack ("Gassy")	11, 18, 39
Dinosaur Provincial Park	162–163
Dinosaurs	162, 163
Dion, Celine	12, 13
Discovery (ship)	22, 71
Discovery Days Festival	195
Dixon, George	87
Dogsled racing	194, 195
Dolphins	29, 64, 67
Dome	190
Dominion of Canada	10
Douglas, James	53
Douglas Channel	66
Driftwood Canyon Provincial Park	153
Duncan	75, 84, 85
Dunsmuir, Robert	22
Eared seals	64
Edmonton	8, 182–183, 192
Edward VII, King of England	10
Elk	9, 113, 184, 194
Elk Island National Park	184–185
Emerald Lake	31
English Bay Beach (Vancouver)	48, 49
Erickson, Arthur	46
Eskimo *see* Inuit	
Father Pandosy Mission	118
February (events)	194
Fenland Trail	168
Fireweed Trail	127
First Nations	10, 11, 12, 13, 14, 15, 26, 28, 29, 56, 65, 67, 70, 71, 74, 79, 84, 85, 89, 90, 91, 94, 95, 105, 141, 143, 148, 149, 152, 159, 164, 165, 179, 186–187, 188, 189, 192, 195
First Nations art	56
First People Festival	195
Fish Creek Wildlife Observation	144
Fjords	8
Fort Langley	52, 53, 59
Fort Nelson	195
Fort St James	152
Fort St John	195

GENERAL INDEX

Fort Steele Heritage Town   130
Fossils   153, 162
Fraser, Simon   10, 27, 103
Fraser Fort George Regional Museum   27
Fraser River   8, 10, 27, 30, 102, 103
Fraser River Canyon   105
Fraser River Valley   103, 104
French and Indian War   10
Friendly Cove   78
Fruit cultivation   30, 107, 118
Furs, animals prized for their   9

Garibaldi Lake   54, 55
Garibaldi Provincial Park   55
Gastown (Vancouver)   11, 18, 38, 39
George III, King of England   27
Giant Cedars Boardwalk Trail   108
Gitksan First Nation   26, 28, 148, 149, 152
Glacier National Park   31, 110–111, 119
Glory Hole   180
God's Pocket Marine Provincial Park   64, 65
Gold diggers   118, 130
Golden   31, 111, 130
Gold rush   10, 11, 30, 183, 195
Goldstream Provincial Park   74–75
Graham Island   90–91, 92, 93
Grand Trunk Railway   152
Granville Island   44, 45
Great Canadian Beer Festival   195
Great Plains   155
Gray owl   13
Gray whales   9, 29, 81, 194
Grizzly bears   9, 82, 113, 138, 139, 194
Grizzly bear safari   82
Group of Seven   12
Gwaii Haanas National Park Reserve   90, 91, 94

Ha Ling Peak   168–169
Hagwilget   26
Haida Gwaii Museum   91
Haida Heritage Site   91, 94
Haida First Nation   12, 67, 70, 84, 85, 89, 90–91, 94, 95
Hazelton   26, 152
Head–Smashed–In Buffalo Jump   164–165
Hearne, Samuel   10, 181
Hell's Gate Air Tram   102
Hell's Gate   103, 105
Helmcken, John Sebastian   22
Helmcken Falls   112
Henday, Anthony   10
Highway 37   144–145, 147, 152, 153
Highway 93   175
Hotels   19, 21, 23, 26, 29, 31, 58, 59, 68, 69, 84, 85, 96, 97, 118, 119, 130, 131, 152, 153
Houston   152
HSBC Celebration of Light   195
Hudson's Bay Company   10, 69, 183
Huron   12

Ice age   187
Ice Magic (Lake Louise)   194
Icefields Parkway   27, 174–175, 192
Illecillewaet Neve   110
Imperial Eagle Channel   77
Indian Act   186
Indianpoint Lake   27

Ink Pots   170, 171
Inside Passage   29, 65, 66–67
Inuit   10, 11, 12, 13, 14, 15
Inuktitut   11
Isaac Lake   27
Isaac River   27
Iskut   152

January (events)   194
Jasper   177, 192, 193
Jasper in January   194
Jasper National Park   14, 27, 115, 176–181
Jasper Park Lodge   180, 181
Jasper Tramway   192
Johnston Canyon   170–171
Johnston Canyon Trail   171
Johnstone Strait   64, 65
July (events)   194

Kaien Island   66
Kamloops   30
Kamloops Lake   30
Kane, Paul   12
Kaska Athapaskan First Nation   151
Kelowna   31, 118
Kibbee Lake   27
Kicking Horse Pass   124, 130
Kicking Horse River   124, 125, 190
Killer whales   9, 64
Kinney Lake   114
Kitwancool   148–149
Kitwanga   152
Kleena Kleene   96
Klondike   11, 195
Klondike Days (Edmonton)   194
Kodiak bears   139
K'omok First Nation   29
Kootenay National Park   126–127
Kootenay River   126, 127
Kootenay Rockies   120–131
Kootenay First Nation   14
Krieghoff, Cornelius   12
'Ksan   26
'Ksan Historical Village   148–149, 152
Kwakiutl First Nation   71
Kwakwaka'wakw First Nation   65, 70

Labrador   10
Lake Athabasca   176
Lake Louise   14, 31, 172–173, 193
Lake Magog   128
Lake O'Hara   124
Lake Okanagan   14
Lakes District   152
Lakelse Provincial Park   26
Lang, KD   13
Langley Centennial Museum   52
Larsen, Henry   47
Lavigne, Avril   12, 13
Lillooet   30
Llewellyn Glacier   141
London, Jack   13
Long Beach   77, 78, 85
Loudoun Channel   77
Louise Caroline Alberta of Great Britain and Ireland, Duchess of Argyll   155
Lower Canyon   190
Lower Fall   170, 171

M

Mabel Lake — 30, 107
MacDonald, John A. — 10
Mackenzie, Alexander — 10
MacKenzie Beach — 78
Maligne Lake — 27, 178–179
Mara Lake — 30, 107
Marble Canyon — 127
March (events) — 194
Marine Festival — 195
Marmots — 9
Masset — 89, 96
May (events) — 194
Medicine Lake — 178–179
Meziadan Junction — 147
Middle Canyon — 190
Miette Hot Springs — 180, 181
Miette Range — 180
Mitchell, Joni — 13
Moodie, Mrs. — 13
Moraine Lake — 172–173
Moresby Island — 90–91, 94
Morice River — 152
Moricetown Canyon — 26, 153
Morissette, Alanis Nadine — 12, 13
Mountain goat — 126
Mount Assiniboine — 128, 129
Mount Assiniboine Provincial Park — 128–129
Mount Athabasca — 175
Mount Blackcomb — 30
Mount Columbia — 175
Mount Edith Cavell — 102
Mount Edziza Provincial Park — 142–143
Mount Garibaldi — 55
Mount Revelstoke — 31, 109
Mount Revelstoke National Park — 31, 108–109
Mount Robson — 8, 114, 115
Mount Robson Provincial Park — 27, 114–115
Mount Rundle — 168–169
Mount Seymour Provincial Park — 59
Mount Victoria — 172, 173
Mount Waddington — 8
Mount Whistler — 30, 194
Mounties (Royal Canadian Mounted Police or North-West Mounted Police) — 10, 47, 57, 159
Muncho Lake — 150, 151
Muncho Lake Provincial Park — 150–151
Mungo Martin — 70
Murtle Plateau — 112
Museums — 70, 71, 84, 85, 91, 116, 117, 130, 152

N

Naikoon Provincial Park — 90, 91, 97
Nakimu Caves — 111
Nanaimo — 28, 84, 85, 195
Naramata — 118
Nass River Valley — 153
Nass Road — 26
Nechako — 27
Nelson — 131
Newfoundland — 10
New Hazelton — 26, 149
Ninstints — 12, 94, 95
Nisga'a Memorial Lava Beds Provincial Park — 153
Nokia Snowboard FIS World Cup — 194
Nootka Sound — 78–79
Northern lights — 8
Northwest Passage — 47
North Saskatchewan River — 183
North West Company — 10
North-West Mounted Police — 10, 159
Northern Districts — 132–153

Northern Lights Wildlife Wolf Centre — 130
Northwest Territories — 189
November (events) — 195
Nunavut — 11
Nuu–Chah–nulth First Nation — 77

O

October (events) — 195
Oil drilling — 159, 183
Objibwe First Nation — 13
Okanagan — 31, 98–119
Okanagan Fall — 195
Okanagan Valley — 14, 30, 106–107, 118, 195
Okanagan Wine Route — 106
Oktoberfest (Kitchener/Waterloo) — 195
Orcas (killer whales) — 65, 80, 81
Osoyoos — 106

P

Pacific Rim National Park — 29, 76–77
Pacific Rim Whale Festival — 194
Patricia Lake — 180–181
Peace River — 188, 189
Peach Festival — 195
Peale, Charles Willson — 10
Pengrowth Saddledome, Calgary — 161
Penticton — 30, 118, 195
Plant life — 9
Polar bears — 9, 139
Porcupine Hills — 164
Port Alberni — 28, 195
Port Hardy — 29, 66
Portland Canal — 147
Potlatch festival — 187
Powwows — 186, 187, 195
Prairie — 9
Prince George — 27, 152, 153
Prince George Regional Railway & Forest Industry Museum — 152
Prince Rupert — 26, 29
Pyramid Lake — 180–181
Pyramid Mountain — 181

Q

Queen Charlotte City — 91, 96, 97
Queen Charlotte Islands/Haida Gwaii — 8, 12, 86–95
Queen Charlotte Strait — 29, 65
Quesnel — 119, 195
Quesnel Museum — 116–117
Quévillon, Louis — 12

R

Radium Hot Springs — 126, 127, 131
Rafting — 136, 190
Rainforest — 8
Rattenbury, Francis M. — 22, 69
Red Deer River — 162
Reid, Bill — 46
Reino Keski–Salmi Loppet — 194
Restaurants — 18, 19, 20, 21, 23, 26, 29, 31, 57, 58, 59, 84, 85, 96, 97, 118, 119, 130, 131, 152, 153, 191, 192, 193
Revelstoke — 119
Revelstoke, Railway Museum — 119
Richards, George Henry — 43
Robson River — 114
Robson, John — 115
Rocky Mountains — 8, 9, 14, 27
Rodeo — 21, 160, 161, 194, 195
Rogers Pass — 31, 110, 111
Royal Academy — 12

GENERAL INDEX

Royal Alberta Museum (Edmonton) 192
Royal Canadian Mounted Police (RCMP) 10, 47
Royal Tyrrell Museum 162

S.S. *Sicamous* (ship) 118
Saanich Peninsula 73
Salish 14
Salish First Nation 13
Salmon 9, 29, 81, 104–105, 112, 138, 144, 195
Salmon Arm 30, 105, 106, 107, 119
Salmon Festival 195
Salmon Glacier 146–147
Salmon Glacier Road 146
Sandspit 97
Saskatchewan River 175
Schulz, Karl 28
Seals 9, 67, 81
Sea lions, Steller 64–65
Selkirk Mountains 31, 109
Sentinel Range 150
September (events) 195
Service, Robert W. 13
Seven Years' War 10
Seymour, Frederick 59
SGang Gwaay 94–95
Shopping 19, 21, 23, 38, 44, 56, 57, 72, 85, 96, 97, 119, 130, 131, 152, 153, 190, 191, 192, 193
Shuswap Lake 14, 30, 105
Shuswap Lake Area 106–107, 108, 119
Shuswap First Nation 105
Sicamous 107, 119
Skeena Mountains 8, 144
Skidgate 91
Skiing 30, 131, 193, 194
Sleeping Beauty Mountain 26
Smithers 27, 153
Sockeye salmon 104
Spatsizi Plateau Wilderness Provincial Park 143
Spiral Tunnels 130
Spirit Island 179
Squamish 55
St Eugene Mission Resort 130
Stanley Glacier 127
Stanley, Frederick Arthur, 16th Earl of Derby 51
Steelhead Country 152
Steller sea lions 64–65
Stewart 146–147, 153
Stewart-Cassiar Highway 144–145, 147, 152, 153
Stikine River 142, 143
Stikine River Park 142–143
Stoney First Nation 173
Strait of Georgia 48, 49
Strathcona Provincial Park 75
Stuart Lake 152
Stutfield 190
Sulphur Mountain 168, 169, 190
Summit Viewpoint 146
Sun Peaks Resort 30
Sun Yat–sen, Dr. 41
Sunwapta Pass 175
Sunwapta River 176–177
Sweetgrass Landing 188

Tahltan First Nation 143
Takakkaw Falls 31, 125
Tatshenshini River 136–137
Tatshenshini–Alsek Provincial Park 136–137

Telegraph Cove 29
Terminal Range 150
Terrace 26, 153
Thompson, David 10
Thompson River 30
Thompson River Gold 103
Thompson Plateau 98–119
Thomson, Tom 12
Three Valley Gap (western town) 119
Timber industry 183
Tipis 186
Tla–o–qui–aht First Nation 79
Tlingit First Nation 67, 141
Tofino 28, 29, 78, 79, 84, 85, 194
Tofino Sound 78–79
Totem animals 12
Totem poles 12, 18, 28, 46, 50, 70, 71, 75, 85, 90, 91, 92, 93, 94, 95
Trans-Canada Highway 8, 11, 30, 31, 111
Tundra 8, 150, 151
Turner Lake 82
Twain, Shania 13
Tweedsmuir, John Buchan 83
Tweedsmuir Park Lodge 82
Tweedsmuir Provincial Park 82–83, 96, 97
Twin Falls 124
Tyrrell, Joseph Burr 162

Ucluelet 85, 194
Ukrainian Cultural Heritage Village 184–185
Upper Canyon 190
Upper Falls 171

Valley of a Thousand Waterfalls 114
Valley of Ten Peaks 172–173
Vancouver, George 11, 22, 67, 71
Vancouver 8, 14, 18, 19, 30, 32–51, 56, 57, 58, 59
  Art Gallery 37
  Burrard Peninsula 43
  Canada Place 18, 37
  Capilano Suspension Bridge 36
  Chinatown 18, 40–41
  Christmas Carol Ships Parade 195
  Commodore Ballroom 56
  Downtown 36–37
  Dr. Sun Yat–sen Classical Chinese Garden 56
  English Bay 48–49, 56
  False Creek 42–43
  False Creek Ferries 42
  Garden of Dr. Sun Yat–sen 40, 41
  Gastown 18, 38–39
  Granville Bridge 42
  Granville Island 18, 44–45
  Grouse Mountain 18
  H.R. MacMillan Space Centre 47
  Harbour Centres 36
  HSBC Celebration of Light 48, 49, 195
  Kitsilano 48
  Maple Tree Square 39
  Maritime Museum 47
  Museum of Anthropology 18, 46, 47
  Pacific Centre 37
  Robson Square 37
  Robson Street 18, 37
  Science World 18
  Stanley Park 18, 30, 50, 51
  Steam Clock 38, 39
  Sunset Cruises 42

Telus World of Science	20, 42
Vanier Park	18, 47
University of British Columbia (UBC)	46, 47
Vancouver Aquarium Marine Science Centre	50, 51, 56
Vancouver Coast	60–85
Vancouver Folk Festival	195
Vancouver International Children's Festival	194
Vancouver Island	8, 12, 28, 195
Vancouver Lookout	36
Vancouver Museum	46, 47
Vancouver Opera	56
Vermilion Pass	127
Vermilion River	127
Vermillion Lakes	168–169
Vernon	119
Victoria, Queen of Great Britain and Ireland	155
Victoria	14, 22, 23, 28, 68–73, 85, 195
Art Gallery of Greater Victoria	22
British Columbia Aviation Museum	22
Butchart Gardens	22, 28, 72–73
Craigdarroch Castle	22
Crystal Garden	22
Empress Hotel	69
First People Festival	195
Great Canadian Beer Festival	195
Helmcken House	22
Inner Harbour	68, 69
Old Town	68
Parliament Buildings	22, 68, 69
Royal British Columbia Museum	22, 70, 71
Thunderbird Park	70, 71
Wapitis	9, 193
Wapta Falls	31
Washington, George	10

Waterton Lakes National Park	166–167
Wedge Mountain	55
Wedgemount Lake Trail	54
Wellbeing	56, 131
Wells Gray Provincial Parks	112–113
Wells Gray–Clearwater Volcanic Field	113
Wenkchemna Range	173
West Coast Trail	29, 77
West Edmonton Mall (Edmonton)	182, 192
Whales	9, 29, 50, 51, 56, 64, 65, 67, 79, 80, 81, 194
Whale watching	29, 64, 79
Whistler Mountain	27, 192
Whistler Blackcomb	30
White Pass Trail	11
Whitehorse	194
Whyte Museum of the Canadian Rockies (Banff)	190
Wildlife viewing	184
Willison Glacier	141
Wine	8, 30, 118, 195
Wine Festival (Okanagan Valley)	195
Wolves	9, 130
Wonder Trail (Icefields Parkway)	174–175
Wood Buffalo National Park	9, 188–189
Wood buffalo (wood bison)	9, 189
Yellowhead Highway	152, 183
Yellowhead region	26
Yoho National Park	31, 124–125
Young, Neil	12, 13
Yuh–hai–has–hun	115
Yukon	11
Yukon Quest	194
Yukon River	194
Yukon Sourdough Rendezvous	194
Yukon Territory	8, 10, 14, 15

MONACO BOOKS is an imprint of Verlag Wolfgang Kunth

© Verlag Wolfgang Kunth GmbH & Co.KG, Munich, 2010
Concept: Wolfgang Kunth
Editing and design: Verlag Wolfgang Kunth GmbH & Co.KG
English translation: JMS Books LLP, cographics

For distribution please contact:

Monaco Books
c/o Verlag Wolfgang Kunth, Königinstr.11
80539 München, Germany
Tel: +49 / 89/45 80 20 23
Fax: +49 / 89/45 80 20 21
info@kunth-verlag.de

www.monacobooks.com
www.kunth-verlag.de

ISBN 978-3-89944-590-9

Printed in Slovakia

All facts have been researched with the greatest possible care to the best of our knowledge and belief. However, the editors and publishers can accept no responsibility for any inaccuracies or incompleteness of the details provided. The publishers are pleased to receive any information or suggestions for improvement.